The New
Professional Image

SECOND EDITION

SUSAN BIXLER,

CEO OF THE PROFESSIONAL IMAGE, INC.,

AND NANCY NIX-RICE

Adams Media

Avon, Massachusetts

*This book is dedicated first and foremost to Lisa Scherrer Dugan—
an extraordinary professional, partner, and the best kind of friend.*

*To all our clients who support our work in corporate image,
leadership, and professional presence.*

And to Christopher, always to Christopher.

❧

Published by
Adams Media, an F+W Publications Company
57 Littlefield Street, Avon, MA 02322. U.S.A.
www.adamsmedia.com

ISBN: 1-59337-297-3

Printed in the United States of America.

J   I   H   G   F   E   D   C   B   A

Library of Congress Cataloging-in-Publication Data
Bixler, Susan.
The new professional image / Susan Bixler and Nancy Nix-Rice.— 2nd ed.
p.   cm.
ISBN 1-59337-297-3
1. Clothing and dress. 2. Fashion. I. Nix-Rice, Nancy. II. Title.
TT507.B547 2005
646'.3—dc22
2004030417

This publication is designed to provide accurate and authoritative information with regard to the subject matter covered. It is sold with the understanding that the publisher is not engaged in rendering legal, accounting, or other professional advice. If legal advice or other expert assistance is required, the services of a competent professional person should be sought.

—From a *Declaration of Principles* jointly adopted by a Committee of the
American Bar Association and a Committee of Publishers and Associations

Many of the designations used by manufacturers and sellers to distinguish their products are claimed as trademarks. Where those designations appear in this book and Adams Media was aware of a trademark claim, the designations have been printed with initial capital letters.

Photos courtesy of Susan Bixler.

*This book is available at quantity discounts for bulk purchases.
For information, please call 1-800-872-5627.*

contents

acknowledgments

i am grateful to so many wonderful people . . .

Larissa Bixler—My amazing niece. I couldn't have finished this book without you!

Mama B.—Much love and appreciation for a lifetime of encouragement

Lynn Seligman—My talented literary agent who has stayed with me for twenty years and guided me through six books

Tracy Penticuff and Allison Reid—My colleagues at The Professional Image who worked diligently and with grace to meet each editorial deadline

To all the Adventure Women—Claire Bowen, Mary Yates, Lynne Marks, Rebecca Bernson, Margarita Porto, Joey Bixler, and Peggy Hart

Aric C. Cosmetics—Many thanks to Aric and Roger, two wonderful professionals with talent and style galore

Mary Jane Starke—For her keen eye, gracious Southern style, and photographic excellence, there is no one like her

Mark Shale Men's Store—For their exceptional men's wear contribution, and especially to Mark Hunter

Nordstrom—For their beautiful women's apparel contribution and outstanding customer service

Merrideth Colwell, President of Merci Woman, Inc.—For her expertise on the plus-size woman

TEC 388—All my colleagues and buddies who have taught me so much—especially Alan Lowe, Steve Yungerburg, David Geller, Ramie Tritt, Russ Umphenour, and that lovable bear, Darren Margolias

part one

the new professional image

chapter one

appearances count

> Long before I am near enough to talk to you on the street, in a meeting or at a party, you announce your sex, age, and class to me through what you are wearing—and very possibly give me important information (or misinformation) as to your occupation, origin, personality, opinions, tastes, sexual desires, and current mood. By the time we meet and converse, we have already spoken to each other in an older and more universal tongue.
>
> Alison Lurie, author of *The Language of Clothes*

if something on the cover of this book enticed you to pick it up, you are one of the millions of individuals who make decisions based on appearance. Books are judged by their covers, houses are appraised by their curb appeal, and people are initially evaluated on how they choose to dress and behave. In a perfect world this is not fair, moral, or just. What's inside should count a great deal more. Eventually it usually does, but not right away. In the meantime, a great many opportunities are lost.

In our lives, hundreds of important decisions have already been made for us that impact every aspect of our lives. Our gender, skin color, height, the number of hair follicles on our head, the shape and size of our hands and feet, as well as who our parents are, our siblings, our early-childhood circumstances, and the country of our birth are factors that we do not control or influence.

However, we can control how we portray ourselves to the outer world. In transformational coaching, the idea is to start at a place that is most visible and that allows for immediately recognized results. Wardrobe, grooming, and nonverbal communication are aspects that are apparent on the outside to the outside world. Combined, these factors can frame us as competent, knowledgeable, elegant, gracious, powerful, or anything else we choose to communicate.

You Have Just Thirty Seconds

Social psychologists studying the impact of image have determined that's how long it takes for someone meeting you to form a whole laundry list of impressions about your character and abilities. The list of impressions encompasses:

- Educational level
- Career competence and success
- Personality
- Level of sophistication
- Trustworthiness
- Sense of humor
- Social heritage

Now, thirty seconds doesn't give you time to pull out your college transcript, showcase your resume, or present character references. It doesn't allow any time to explain that you have talent, skills, training, and a substantial list of truly satisfied employers and customers.

In thirty seconds, people form all those different impressions based almost entirely on what they see—your clothes, hairstyle, carriage, smile, and the rest of your nonverbal communications. Appearances do count.

These quick impressions can be lasting ones. Psychologists call it the halo effect. When your visual message is positive, the person you've just met will tend to assume that other aspects about you are equally positive. But unfortunately, if your visual message is negative, that new customer, client, coworker, or prospective employer may not spend the time and effort to discover the talented person inside, even with a terrific grade point average.

"College is something you complete. Life is something you experience. In life people will no longer be grading you. Your success will be defined in myriad ways so get competent and credible in what you love to do."

Jon Stewart, host of *The Daily Show*, Comedy Central

Appearances count in today's world—as much or even more than in earlier decades. Rigid "success dressing" rules have yielded to new, more flexible guidelines that encompass casual business looks as well as traditional power suits. But as the speed of the business world accelerates, the importance of making a positive first impression increases, too. Technology has made face-to-face meetings more rare, and thus even more critical and influential.

Appearances count, not only in first impressions, but also in ongoing interactions. In his comprehensive research on communication, socio-linguist Albert Mehrabian found that in a face-to-face encounter, 7 percent of a verbal message comes from the words used; 38 percent comes from the vocal tone, pacing, and inflection; 55 percent of the message is transmitted by the speaker's appearance and body language.

Appearances count, especially in the business world. When one college's career planning and placement center surveyed 150 employers, they discovered that the number one reason for rejecting an applicant after the first interview was poor personal appearance.

Interestingly, those employers ranked poor appearance as even more significant than being a "hostile, overbearing know-it-all" (reason number nine) or "late for the interview without good reason" (reason number twenty-eight). Hostility or tardiness isn't encouraged either, but the findings certainly support the importance of appearance.

Courses that help managers become better interviewers stress learning to bypass those first impressions and go deeper. They train the interviewer to suspend judgment in the first thirty seconds and even the first five minutes. Why? Because those immediate instinctual reactions are so ingrained.

Thousands of years ago a human's survival often depended on how shrewdly and quickly he or she could size up a situation. Only those who could "read" others accurately lived to fight another day.

Amazingly, appearances count even when nobody else sees you! One study says that Americans have the opportunity to see their own reflection (in mirrors, windows, elevator doors, etc.) up to fifty-five times every day. That means fifty-five opportunities to feel instantaneously good, indifferent, or even negative about your physical self.

Appearances count—often in cold, hard cash. Dr. Judith Walters of Fairleigh Dickinson University researched the impact of an effective business appearance on a starting salary. She sent out a group of identical resumes to more than a thousand companies. Some resumes were accompanied by a "before" photo of the applicant, others by an "after" photo. Each company was asked to determine a starting salary.

The results were amazing. Starting salaries ranged 8 to 20 percent higher as the result of upgrading a mediocre business appearance to one that is polished and effective. Employers are willing to pay for people who look the part. If the employee already projects an image of professionalism, that's one less thing—one potentially unpleasant thing—that the firm has to worry about.

First Impressions, Lasting Impressions

Your image transmits a message about you all day every day. There is no erase button. Business casual has become a way of life in corporate America. Some companies even place signs in their reception areas that say: "We are a Business Casual Environment." They want to ensure that clients know what to expect in dress standards and that clients won't be negatively swayed by what could be perceived as unprofessional.

Appearances count for career advancement, too. John Trinta, who heads the partner development and selection committee for Deloitte, puts it this way: "The decision on whether or not to promote a senior manager to full partner depends almost entirely on the professionalism of the candidate's appearance and demeanor . . . his or her professional image."

Does that mean that a junior accountant can buy a couple of terrific power suits and coast straight to the top? Of course not. But it does mean that at the upper levels of business, where stellar job performance is the norm, the differentiating factors often can be image, polish, and presence.

"That's not fair," you say? "I know my job inside out. I come in early and stay late. I'm the hardest worker in the office. Why should it matter how I look?" We're not saying it should matter, only that it does. Business life is fast-paced and impatient. Time is money. Classifying people visually is such an efficient shortcut that we often use it unconsciously. For some firsthand experience with this concept, record your first impressions about the individuals pictured on pages 8 and 9, based on these five criteria:

1. Education
2. Job or career
3. Level of competence
4. Ability to interact with people
5. Respect in his or her industry

Did you readily develop a distinct "success profile" for each photo? Nearly everyone does, but the before profile and the after profile that you created are probably remarkably different.

In *Travels with Charlie,* John Steinbeck tells about a local boy he once hired to repaint his house. When he asked the boy to go to the store for more paint, the boy looked down at his paint-spattered clothes and said he'd have to go home and clean up first.

"Nuts," Steinbeck replied. "Go as you are."

"I can't do it," the boy replied. "You've got to be awfully rich to dress as bad as you do."

The Exception Proves the Rule

Each of us can come up with a short list of high-profile individuals who have succeeded in spite of a poor image: the computer genius who looks like a pile of dirty laundry; the movie mogul who sports extreme makeup, outrageous hair, and skin-tight clothes; the multimillionaire entrepreneur who is significantly overweight, wears worn-out jeans, and drives an old, beat-up, pickup truck.

This minor group seems to have succeeded in spite of appearances. Or perhaps their appearance is a calculated effort intended to communicate their defiant indifference to superficial concerns. Their talents may be so formidable that they outshine their exterior. Most of us, though, are not so gifted; we need every advantage we can get—especially one as easy to attain as visual presence.

before&now

But if image is so important to business success, why do many aspiring executives fail to maintain a polished professional presence? Our corporate clients consistently tell us about four barriers:

1. Some feel self-conscious, afraid that looking good will create the impression that they are lightweights in their area of technical expertise. Certainly, different styles are appropriate for different job categories. An engineer or chemist would probably look foolish in the same attire that would spell success for an investment broker. But Chicago career consultant Marilyn Moats Kennedy sums up the situation perfectly when she states, "I have yet to discover the job where it pays to look less than your best."

2. Cost, of course, is another deterrent to a professional appearance. But wise planning can overcome most budget obstacles, as many of us waste more of our wardrobe dollars than we ever invest. The average American wears less than 50 percent of what is in his or her closet. Instead

before A light-colored suit can be a good choice, but paired with a bow tie, it looks almost comical. Bow ties are best left to professors wearing cardigans or worn with a tuxedo. **now** Elegance personified in a dark suit, crisp white shirt, and contrasting tie, this look is clean, corporate, and powerful. The combination of fabrics and colors commands respect and adds stature and credibility.

of buying quality clothing, we often buy sale garments that don't enhance our appearance. Or we buy two cheaper versions of an item, instead of investing in only one of better quality. Our closets are often loaded with clothes, but we have nothing to wear. Eliminating the waste and dressing well does not cost more. In the long run, it actually costs less. Garments of quality are made with exceptional fabric. They last longer, are more attractive because they drape better, and can be amortized over the years to pennies per wearing. Rather than saying, "I can't afford to pay a lot of money for my clothes," the smart businessperson says, "I can't afford to dress badly by buying poorly fitting, inexpensive clothes."

3. Few businesspeople have time for a high-maintenance high-fashion look. Unless you are in the fashion business or located in New York City, where trends and new styles dominate, the better choice is always attractive, updated classics. Maintaining a classic business look, one that is extremely flattering to all figure types and changes more slowly, is far less time-consuming. After the initial development effort, a well-designed image system is nearly self-sustaining, avoids confusion, and saves significant time. High-profile corporate leaders choose a designer, craft a look, and stay with it every day. They are consistently camera-ready because they simplify and keep with the classics.

4. Lack of basic fashion knowledge is a problem for some professionals. College courses and most corporate-training programs stress "hard skills"—the nuts and bolts of doing the job. So many professionals have never acquired the fashion awareness needed for

before&now

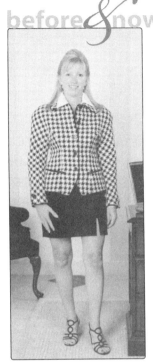

before A skirted suit requires that both pieces work together. The houndstooth jacket makes a rather classic statement, but the skirt is so short and the slit is so high that the overall look is cheapened. Paired with strappy, fashion sandals, the overall impact is lessened. Hair pulled back in a claw barrette and no makeup on pale skin washes her out. **now** The well-shaped haircut flatters her face, and the natural makeup polishes and refines her look. This three-piece knit suit is flattering, versatile, and travels well. Closed-toe pumps complete a well-put-together look.

today's more individualized business dressing. The wider range of options, from business casual to boardroom, creates more opportunities for confusion and error.

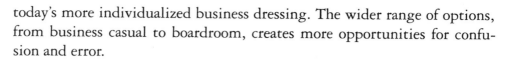

"True fashion is a deep current that changes only every four or five years and is the inspiration of some particular creator, while passing fashions are ripples of no great importance, which are carried off by the winds of a single season and are invented by a number of different designers."

Geneviève Antoine Dariaux,
former directrice of Nina Ricci in Paris and author of *Elegance*

This book is designed to contribute to your existing knowledge of image, presence, and your personal brand. It is written to provide you with hundreds of ideas to enhance the exterior so that the interior can be discovered, both personally and professionally.

Wardrobe and nonverbal communication, taken together, are your most visible credentials. The encouraging truth is that you can control and change how these visual credentials are displayed and perceived, and therefore manage them so they contribute to your success.

First impressions are 67 percent accurate.

chapter two

the straight "A" image

We need a balance between basics and luxuries, and we need enough range in our wardrobe to accommodate a body that expands in the heat, dries up in the cold, and shrinks when we fall in love.

Anna Johnson, fashion journalist

whether you consider yourself a salesperson, every businessperson sells—because the first thing that ever gets sold is you. Product and company becomes secondary. Most of us come in contact with well over 100 people every day—on the elevator, on the transit system, in meetings, or in the hallway. We don't want to be just one of the crowd. Most of us want to be unique and valued for our own individual contributions. Image is a way to define that. It is the way we show how comfortable and confident we are in our own skin.

"Eighty-two percent of people will eventually buy your product or idea when their style and behaviors are matched and mirrored."

Cargill Consulting Group

In today's multifaceted, global business world, everyone from new hires to chief executive officers faces the challenge of developing or maintaining this personal, versatile, flexible professional image. "The Straight A Formula" is a way to understand the most important components of image, in both traditional and casual business environments.

Assuming that an individual already possesses the all-important *A*, ability, his or her opportunities will be enhanced by an image that incorporates these additional *As*:

1. *Appropriate*—fitting the industry and job category, the geographic area, and the occasion
2. *Attractive*—enhancing one's features, coloring, and body build
3. *Affordable*—not exceeding one's budget and time resources; money first, then things
4. *Assured*—conveying, both visually and behaviorally, a sense of competence and confidence

1. Appropriate

The answer to the question, "What should I wear for business?" is a clear, concise "It all depends." There no longer is a single rigid standard for correctness. Instead, an appropriate choice depends on the industry or job profile, the area of the country, the specific business occasion, and the message you want your image to transmit.

The financial industry generally adheres to a more conservative dress code. When money is involved, customers and clients like to see tradition and stability. The advertising industry and businesses that need to show creativity and out-of-the-box thinking favor a more fashion-forward look. Again, the idea is that internal creativity needs to be displayed on the outside so that it becomes tangible. Residential real estate salespeople usually adopt an approachable, friendly business style, but with great attention to details and accessories. But the human factor also is part of the equation.

Ann McQueen of Image Development, Inc., states that "appropriate" is important even for businesspeople who have no face-to-face contact with their clients. "I worked with a telemarketing company to develop a dress code that required minimal attention to the employees' appearance," says Ms. McQueen. "Our dress code only restricted wearing of sweatsuits, jeans with T-shirt, and tennis shoes. Clean, well-groomed hair was required.

With these minimal standards in dress and grooming, sales increased by approximately 20 percent over a period of four to six months."

Carol Weisman, a consultant to nonprofit agencies, recalls interviewing a very qualified candidate for a position as a pediatric oncology social worker. She wore a navy wool suit with a starched blouse, tiny gold ball earrings, and rather severe-looking navy pumps. Before passing this well-qualified woman along to the next interview phase, Weisman offered her some off-the-record advice.

"I asked if she had read one of those rigid, possibly dated success dressing books," Weisman recalls, "and she proudly answered that she had. I told her pointedly that she should lose the navy blue suit . . . fast. The job involved counseling parents whose children had just been diagnosed with cancer. Those parents needed to have faith in her professionalism—it's true—but they also needed to relate to her compassionate, caring side. Pairing the same navy skirt with a soft sweater would create a much better 'success' look for her second interview, and for the job she eventually won."

Within a single large company, each department may have its individual style. Most employees can predict in the lobby which floor their fellow elevator passengers will exit, based simply on their departmental "look."

Geographic differences can be equally dramatic. A style that looks right at home in Los Angeles might seem too risqué in Boston. A high-fashion, black-leather look that works in New York City will be out of place in colorful Miami. We advise our clients, many of whom travel extensively in this country and around the world, to adapt to varying geography. A red-wool crepe suit could work well for a professional woman in Los Angeles, Atlanta, Dallas, and Chicago, but it might seem too flashy in Milwaukee.

The cowboy boots that are normal business wear in parts of Texas and Wyoming would certainly attract attention—not necessarily favorable—in most other parts of the country.

A style that's more casual may work in some parts of the country, but when the same businessperson travels to corporate headquarters, he or she will need to adopt a more polished, sophisticated presence.

Various situations demand different looks. Delivering a presentation to an important client may require the all-out power look. Leading the group planning session for that same presentation calls for more relaxed dress. Even your private life can have a dress code dictated by your corporate culture. One brewery executive, for example, was called to task by higher-ups for mowing his lawn bare-chested. They explained that his appearance reflected on the company's image, even on Saturday morning in his own neighborhood.

Attorneys routinely plan their appearance—and that of their client—for the specifics of the day's court appearances. Many admitted dressing more sedately for a lower-income jury and more elegantly for trials in affluent suburbs. One female attorney revealed that she chooses softer colors and styles when she intends to deliver a particularly aggressive cross-examination. A defense lawyer who readily wears her red suit early in a trial sticks to something fairly conservative for closing arguments. A sportcoat and trousers will give way to a well-cut suit when a plaintiff's attorney feels a loss of power and respect in the courtroom.

Martha Stewart wore luxurious fur wraps and carried very expensive handbags during her trial for insider trading. These wardrobe items may have served to create a distinct socioeconomic difference between her and the jury.

Professional speaker Steve Epner uses appearance to "lessen the intimidation factor" of his presentations on computer and technology issues. "On the platform, I need to look like a consummate professional—the expert the group is paying good money for," Steve explains. "But I make sure the suit-and-tie-guy isn't the first impression the group gets of me.

"I make a point to arrive at the conference the night before. I mix and mingle in the halls and at the cocktail party. For those events, I dress just like the participants, even if that means jeans and a plaid shirt. They begin to see me as a regular guy, someone who can make complex topics understandable and usable and someone who relates to them easily."

"Comfortable" and "respectful" are the messages most attorneys want a client's appearance to convey. Very wealthy clients are sometimes advised to "dress down" to minimize envy and resentment from jurors. One specific client, suing the company that had allegedly fired him because of his weight, made a point to arrive in court each day meticulously groomed and wearing perfectly fitted suits.

One way to test the appropriateness of a particular business look is to ask, "What message does this look convey? Looking through the eyes of my client, audience, or a potential employer, what would I want to see to make me want to do business?" For example, a financial planner usually wants to communicate a message of conservative competence through high-quality, traditional styling, subdued colors, and classic accessories; a salesperson can build rapport with clients who wear business casual by choosing clothing with a more relaxed styling and softer colors to convey a friendly impression that mirrors and matches the client's dress; an advertising executive's bold styles, bright colors, and high-fashion accessories clearly say, "I have creativity and flair that I can bring to your ad campaign."

Narrow your range of wardrobe choices by designing a three-word description of the personal brand message you want your business look to communicate.

professional	*organized*	*powerful*
cutting-edge	*high energy*	*scholarly*
solid	*analytical*	*friendly*
competent	*wealthy*	*aggressive*
attractive	*warm*	*expressive*
calm	*astute*	*successful*
artistic	*creative*	*easygoing*
elegant	*intelligent*	_____
dependable	*original*	_____
fun-loving	*meticulous*	_____

It may take several tries to select the right words that satisfy you and fit with your work. Use this as a standard to evaluate every single business wardrobe purchase you make to determine whether or not it matches your personal brand. Consider whether your personal brand is being accurately communicated every time you leave your home.

2. Attractive

Attractive wardrobe choices complement your personal coloring, flatter your body shape, and enhance your features. Some people mistakenly believe that attractiveness is somehow a "lightweight" concern that is not relevant in business. But the truth is, attractive sells, whether attaining it requires little work or more time and attention.

The television program *20/20* investigated the impact of attractiveness in both social and business situations. Well-groomed men and women were placed in identical situations with poorly groomed participants. Every single time, the more highly groomed individual got not only the date or the help with a flat tire, but also the job offer and the higher salary.

The University of Pittsburgh studied this "attractiveness" phenomenon. The surveyors had photos of 700 MBA graduates ranked by a panel of business executives on a scale from one (least attractive) to five (most attractive). The study was based less on natural, physical attributes than on a concerted effort to enhance features and pay attention to grooming details. Ten years later the graduates' careers were surveyed again and a direct correlation was found between the "attractiveness" scores and every measure of career success: number of job offers after graduation, starting salary, number of raises and promotions, increments of raises, current total salary.

Rather than taking offense at these findings, take action. Unlike aspects that we can't control, attractiveness is not an unchangeable characteristic. We impact it every single morning as we prepare for our day. It takes a fair and honest evaluation and a base of knowledge coupled with specific action to develop the most visible of all our credentials.

Color

Color is a powerful element of attractiveness, often the first thing noticed. It either immediately establishes presence and substance, or it mitigates against them. This important element of wardrobe is absolutely free. It costs no more to buy a suit in an attractive color than in a draining,

unflattering one. It costs no more to buy a polo shirt or casual top styled in your most flattering color than one in your worst color. In the morning, it takes no longer to put on well-coordinated colors, either.

Color has a significant impact on how we perceive things. In consumer testing, 1,200 people who taste-tested chocolate-colored vanilla pudding indicated that it was their favorite chocolate pudding choice. It looked chocolate, so it tasted chocolate.

Each of us has certain colors that give us energy and make us sparkle—and others that make us look as if we belong six feet underground. A professional color analysis can create a personalized report of your best colors. Or you can start with a simple self-analysis.

Look at yourself in the mirror, using natural daylight instead of artificial lighting. Hold pieces of both gold and silver metallic fabric under your chin. Which enhances your personal coloring more, gold or silver?

If gold looks more flattering, you have undertones in your skin, hair, and eyes that are classified as warm—a golden, peachy look—and look healthier and more attractive in colors with more yellow pigment. If silver looks more flattering, you have cool undertones in your skin, hair, and eyes—a blue-pink or ash coloring—and look your best in colors with less yellow and more blue pigment.

Select wardrobe colors from those listed for your undertone group. The colors within each group blend well with one another, creating more mix-and-match opportunities within a wardrobe.

Warm	*Cool*
Brown/black*	Black*
Camel	Gray
Cream	White
Teal	Navy/royal
Plum	Royal purple
Olive	Hunter green
Deep rust	Burgundy
Coral	Pink
Tomato red	Ruby red

* Black is a wardrobe classic for everyone, but it works best on a person with warm coloring only when combined with accents of warmer colors near the face.

Certain colors are always more appropriate than others for career wear. Deep colors and classic neutrals—navy and gray for men, red and black for women—are right for business. They are the best choices for bottom garments, jackets, and basic accessories. Brighter fashion colors and pastels can also work in both less formal environments and the business casual category. Use them confidently for shirts, blouses, ties, and fashion accessories. Garish shades such as neon brights and metallics are inappropriate for any business situation.

One of our favorite fashion journalists who covers European fashion made this observation about color: "The color story was 'neon' one season, 'key lime' the next, and then it would veer off into earth tones six months later. I began to notice that there were three types of women attending these fashion shows . . . the ones who spent a small fortune to be fashionable in today's colors, the ones who wore black all the time, and the third group that consisted of the real women of distinction who dressed in classic colors that flattered them."

Body Type

Very few business offices are staffed with perfect Barbie or Blaine (the new Ken) bodies. Professionals with more real-life shapes can minimize figure challenges and emphasize assets to create the illusion of a more perfectly proportioned silhouette.

One recent workshop participant was unhappy about a twenty-pound weight gain and was reluctant to improve her wardrobe until she shed the unwanted pounds. But as we tried on more flattering styles, she commented again and again, "I just can't believe how much thinner I look immediately, just by changing to the right style."

It's an issue of simple optical illusions.

before A woman with a pear-shaped figure needs to pay special attention to fit and proportion. Light colors enlarge, so these trousers are not flattering. Tucking in a top, rather than leaving it out, shortens the distance between her shoulders and waistline. She needs to lengthen her torso with jackets or longer tops. Hair styling and a blended makeup application will enhance her eyes and smile. **now** A well-fitting black suit works well for this figure type. The knit sweater worn untucked and belted balances her top and bottom. The fuller trousers are more flattering and the hair and makeup add polish. Her confidence and impact have increased.

before Large or tall men need to pay special attention to fit, proportion, and fabric. The fabric of the jacket is a more formal, hard finished wool and the trousers are soft, 100 percent cotton. The trousers are also too short and the haircut is too young. **now** This suit fits well and emphasizes his stature and build. The trousers drape nicely over the well-polished shoes. His hair is more professionally cut. His opportunity to make a successful first impression has changed significantly.

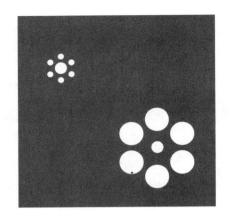

◀ *Which inner circle looks larger? Smaller?*

Even though our brain may realize that both circles are the same size, our eyes "see" the top one as larger. When bracketed with smaller circles, the inner circle appears larger. Bracketed in larger circles, the inner circle appears smaller. This is a clear metaphor for dressing to flatter our various shapes and body types. Proportion dressing is simply bracketing our bodies with the most attractive lines and styles.

◀ *Which square looks larger?*

Lighter, brighter colors appear to advance toward the viewer, making the area they cover appear larger. Darker, duller colors recede from the viewer making those areas appear smaller. Pairing a black skirt with a red blouse to balance wide hips, or a dark trouser with a light shirt, will create this effect.

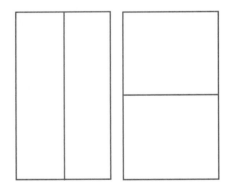

◀ *Which rectangle looks taller? Shorter? Wider? Narrower?*

Vertical (up and down) design lines make a body appear taller and trimmer, whereas horizontal design lines make the identical body look shorter and heavier. For example:

- Large, horizontal stripes in a sweater would unattractively enlarge a heavy man, but make a thin man appear more filled out.
- The vertical-design details of trousers slim and elongate the silhouette.
- The horizontal-design details of jeans add fullness to the body.
- Wearing one color value head-to-toe creates a slimming vertical effect.
- Breaking up a color scheme (dark pants, light shirt) creates a widening horizontal line.

- Wearing a light jacket unbuttoned over dark pants and a dark shirt is slimming.
- Shoulder pads create a strong horizontal look that visually widens shoulders. For women it balances wide hips. For men it balances a large stomach.

A few looks are unflattering on virtually any body type:

- Anything too tight looks cheap and skimpy.
- Stiff or bulky fabrics add to round bodies and emphasize too-thin ones.
- Clingy fabrics reveal even slight figure imperfections.

Issues of attractiveness are very individualized. We offer a variety of ideas and suggestions in future chapters, but you may still want to go further and seek the trained eye of a qualified image consultant. Be discerning of free advice that is tied to product purchases. Sometimes the advice is excellent. At other times, it is based on simply selling product.

A consultant with an independent perspective will charge for his or her professional opinion. But considering the thousands of dollars invested in the typical business wardrobe, a "free" mistake in color or style advice could be very costly indeed.

3. Affordable

The world's greatest wardrobe plan isn't worth much if it substantially exceeds your budget. Most people would love to drive a Lamborghini, Porsche, or Ferrari—but at what cost? No furniture? Living in an unsafe neighborhood? No tuition money, vacations, or gifts? If your clothing expenditures significantly cramp your ability to live where and how you want, they are out of balance. However, keep in mind, that your most portable asset is your image. Most people won't see your home, car, motorcycle, vacation destinations, or stock portfolio. But they will certainly see the quality of your garments and the care with which you put yourself together.

Fortunately, the solution has less to do with dollars than with sense. A moderate budget doesn't preclude looking good any more than a generous budget guarantees it. The secret is using your resources wisely, however limited or abundant they are.

In individual wardrobe consultations, we repeatedly see closets packed with inappropriate, unwearable, and often expensive items. Instead of selecting classic, flattering, coordinated pieces, most people waste more than half their clothing budget on mistakes such as:

- A famous-name item that doesn't fit into an existing wardrobe
- An unusual color that coordinates with nothing or makes the wearer look drab or tired
- Fabric that is stiff, shiny, itchy, see-through, or cheap
- A style so trendy that, next season, it will be clearly labeled "last year"
- That irresistible markdown item that doesn't quite fit . . . but is rationalized by "I'll lose a few pounds"
- A discount store purchase that faded, shrunk, or just never hung right
- A style that looked great on a mannequin whose body type bore no resemblance to that of a real human being

"You're a better shopper before noon than after noon. You bring more processing skills, judgment, and perspective to the task earlier in the day. Also, the store is restocked in the morning and less picked over."

Paco Underhill, founder of Envirosell,
a marketing research firm specializing in shopping behaviors

When you learn to eliminate the senseless 50 percent waste and buy only wearable, flattering, quality items, it's as if every store you enter has a sign on the door:

> FOR YOU ONLY
>
> VERY SPECIAL SALE
>
> EVERYTHING
>
> 50% OFF

Don't use that savings to buy twice as many items. Instead, develop an eye for better garments that are twice as good-looking. Quality is the real bargain. Better garments are made from more beautiful fabrics, are cut more precisely, and are constructed more painstakingly. They are more flattering, keep their good looks longer, and stay in fashion year after year.

The True Cost per Wearing

If you have an attack of sticker shock as you begin to shop for a higher level of clothing, use the cost-per-wearing formula to evaluate the true cost of any item:

initial cost ÷ the number of lifetime wearings = cost per wearing

For example, a pair of $90 wool gabardine trousers in either black or charcoal could be worn at least once a week for nine months of the year, or thirty-six times yearly. If they last for three years, each of the 108 wearings costs 83 cents. By contrast, $20 bargain trousers made from cheap synthetic fabric will lose shape and develop fiber "pills" in stress areas in only six wearings. The cost per wearing is a whopping $3.25. Which item is the true bargain?

The (Space) Capsule

The cost-per-wearing concept operates most efficiently when you plan your wardrobe in "capsule" groupings. A capsule simply is a group of six to twelve garments selected to work together in multiple ways. This could be a collection of suits, shirts, and ties for men. For women, it might be a group of coordinated skirts, jackets, pants, tops, and sweaters. Fitting each individual garment into several attractive combinations ensures that you'll wear it frequently enough to get your money's worth.

No single formula defines every wardrobe capsule, but here are some helpful guidelines:

- Select six to ten pieces that work together.
- Choose pieces that work with at least three others items in the capsule (it isn't realistic to expect everything to work with everything else).

- Stick to classic styles, selected to flatter your body type.
- Look for season-spanning colors and fabrics such as lightweight wools for maximum wear.
- Begin with solids in your most enhancing colors and add patterns sparingly except in ties.

If you're feeling overwhelmed, discouraged, and ready to torch the current contents of your closet . . . wait. Nobody builds a professional wardrobe in a weekend. The process requires careful planning, and it begins with the pieces you already own.

Take a critical look at your clothes. Try on each item, and have someone photograph you from the front and back. Carefully evaluate the photos; then divide your clothes into three groups:

1. Winners—good-quality, flattering classics that you love to wear. These are the foundation for your future wardrobe.
2. Losers—cheap, unflattering, worn, or ill-fitting. These items need to find a new home. Rotate them out of your closet immediately. Don't hang them back up just to fill space. Chances are you'll never wear them.
3. Potential winners—items with potential, but in need of some attention and assistance. A good alteration specialist may be able to turn these garments into winners by shortening the hemline, letting out the waistband, or simply replacing a button or zipper.

Since few of us can afford to replace everything at once, start by considering the options for upgrading the potential winners to full-fledged winners:

- Have a tailor alter the garment to improve fit and flatter your figure, but changing any garment more than two sizes will ruin the proportion.
- Add a quality leather belt.
- Remove or replace poor-quality trims or unattractive buttons.
- Consider restyling—shorten the hemline, change the buttons, or remove shoulder pads—if the garment's quality warrants the investment.

You can learn valuable lessons from your wardrobe "losers," too. Ask yourself why each discard item didn't work. Did you choose it for the designer label, the marked-down price, the hot new color? Was it just too small to begin with? Were you pressured into buying it? Vow to avoid those same mistakes in the future.

On the other hand, if you wore a garment until it needed to be replaced, evaluate what made it such a favorite. Color? Style? Fit? Comfort? Did it travel well? Was it a particularly good designer or manufacturer? Plan to buy more new pieces with those characteristics.

Before you actually dispose of the "losers," calculate an approximate total of their cost. It may be depressing, but that total carries a powerful lesson. Next time you hear yourself saying, "I can't afford it," remember that avoiding just two or three of those "losers" can easily fund the purchase of one exquisite item of professional clothing. The less you have left after your closet clean-out, the better.

Most people own far too much clothing and still have nothing to wear because they've never developed a wardrobe plan. Starting with fewer carry-over pieces will allow you to shape your wardrobe toward your personal plan more quickly and with fewer compromises. Upcoming chapters will describe in detail how to create a professional look in each category of business dress.

"One of the striking differences between a well-dressed American woman and a well-dressed Parisienne is in the size of their respective wardrobes. The American would probably be astonished by the very limited number of garments hanging in the French woman's closet . . . she wears her beautiful clothes over and over again, discarding them only when they are worn or dated."

Sterling Nelson, American expatriate living in Paris

List your activities every waking hour for a full week. Next to each entry, note which wardrobe category would be most appropriate for that activity. Graph the results on a pie chart to get a visual picture of your personal wardrobe needs. Build on the winners from your current wardrobe to develop capsule groupings in each category that fit your lifestyle, your career style, and your aspirations.

4. Assured

Even the most elegant wardrobe by itself can't create a successful image. People aren't paper dolls who can immediately assume a new identity with an external layer of paper clothing. Appearances and actions need to be congruent to complete the picture of an assured professional, and that takes time and reinforcement. Often, when dramatic visual changes are made for clients, initially they feel as if they are not "in their own skin." Although they are almost always amazed at the improvements, it takes time for them to feel authentic with a new haircut, clothing, accessories, and—for women—a big makeup change. It takes time for the nonverbal communications to catch up with a dramatic new image.

We confirm or contradict our powerful visual image by using behavioral tools such as confident posture, engaging eye contact, a strong handshake, and a ready smile. Nonverbal cues such as stance, head movements, facial expressions, and gestures clarify our spoken messages. Later chapters explain how to maintain an effective presence in business dealings, face-to-face, on the telephone, or in writing.

Looking good is not a matter of being beautiful or handsome, it is about being alive.

part two

traditional business dress

chapter three

traditional business attire

> Excess either way shocks, and every wise man should attend to this in his dress as well as language; never be affected in anything, but follow, without being in too great haste, the changes of fashion.
>
> Molière

it seems that early reports stating that the traditional business look was dead were, as Mark Twain said of his own premature death notices, "highly exaggerated." Most businesspeople find themselves, at least part of the time, dressing for situations or occasions that require a traditional approach to attire, even if they work in a more casual industry or workplace on a daily basis. Regardless of the rules of your workplace, you still need to know how to prepare yourself, and build your wardrobe, for these situations.

Traditional Business Dress for Men

The suit remains a man's most reliable business attire, and his most significant wardrobe investment. There are always occasions when a well-cut suit in a beautiful fabric, and a deep, powerful color is appropriate. For some positions, it is a daily necessity. For others, twice a month fits the bill.

Suits

The cut and styling of men's business suits change very slowly, and the variables are subtle. You could get by with a closetful of navy worsted suits and white broadcloth shirts, but with just a bit of added know-how you can develop a much more interesting and fashionable wardrobe.

It pays to buy the very best suits you can afford, as each one will last five to eight years and will make a visual statement about you each time you wear it. Presumably, your career will advance during those years, so the concept of "dressing for the job you want, not the job you have" will prevent early obsolescence and ensure the long-term value of your investment.

After many of our seminars, managers who have already spent twenty years in the corporate world say, "If I had been in this course earlier, if I had purchased only a few quality garments instead of the closetful of cheap suits that I now own, I would have saved so much money and looked so much better."

Selection

Choosing a wardrobe of suits wisely requires an understanding of the indicators of quality, the choices available, and how those choices interact with your body build and coloring. Suit coats are manufactured in three distinctly different shapes:

1. **The Ivy League cut**—also called Brooks Brothers, natural-shoulder, or "sack" suit—has minimally padded shoulders, a natural, comfortable tapering at the waistline, a higher button stance, and a center back vent. This styling provides the easiest fit for men with fuller figures or a desire for comfort. Men who wear their suits twelve to fourteen hours a day often prefer a more generous, unrestricted fit.
2. **The Updated British/American** is another traditional choice for a business wardrobe. Its cut features lightly padded shoulders, moderate waistline tapering, lower button stance, and a longer lapel. It is available in single- and double-breasted versions, with or without the center back vents. This shape can adapt to the widest range of men's bodies.
3. **The European suit** has squared, padded shoulders and greater waistline suppression. Its angularity is often emphasized with double-

breasted styling and slightly exaggerated or peaked lapels. This style offers the easiest fit for men with dominant shoulders and narrow hips, but may be too fashion-forward for some conservative industries.

The button arrangement also affects a jacket's figure flattery:

A well-cut lighter-colored 100 percent wool suit is extraordinarily attractive in a three-button, traditional styling. His grooming is impeccable.

- A two-button single-breasted style is the most universally flattering because of the sleek line created by its long lapel. It elongates the torso.
- A three-button model, with its higher button stance, shortens the roll line and makes the lapel appear proportionally wider, creating a boxier silhouette. It also shows less shirt, chest, and tie.
- A six-to-one double-breasted (a six-button jacket that fastens only the bottom button) also creates a flattering, longer lapel line.
- Six-to-two double-breasted (a six-button jacket that fastens only the two bottom buttons) and the four-to-two double-breasted (a four-button jacket that fastens only the two bottom buttons) require a taller, trimmer physique. Double-breasted styles are generally worn buttoned, unless they are cut with less fabric in front and don't flap open when walking.

Variations in pocket styling contribute to the dressy or casual flavor of the overall garment:

- A besom pocket (welts with no flap) is the sleekest, dressiest option. It is slimming and elegant. It was formally found mainly in double-breasted suits. Today, both double-breasted and single-breasted suits feature the besom pocket.
- A horizontal flap pocket is the most traditional and conservative. It works well for daytime wear but not dressy evening attire. It also adds extra attention to the hips and stomach. Some designers have

created a pocket flap that can be worn outside for a traditional look or inside (the besom pocket) for a slimmer look. Most men who like the slimmer look have the pockets permanently stitched down.

- Patch pockets are only for very casual sportcoats and overcoats. They give a suit a more relaxed, casual look, and in an overcoat, they offer a place to put your gloves.

Outside jacket pockets today are strictly a design feature, not a functional feature. Trouser pockets allow for the utility aspect of carrying one or two keys, change, and other light items.

The choice of back vents has both practical and fashion considerations:

- A ventless jacket creates a smooth, unbroken look in the back but bunches unattractively when you put your hands in the trouser pockets. It needs to be well fitted so it doesn't look too tight from the back. The ventless jacket is a widely used design feature.
- A single vent is classic and conservative, but it can spread apart, exposing the seat of the pants when you stand with your hands in the trouser pockets. Its center position does create a narrower silhouette for a broad-hipped man.
- Double vents flow into and out of fashion favor. When they are in fashion, they actually are more functional. When you put your hands in the trouser pockets, the side vent opens, leaving the center back panel gracefully in place.

Even the most expensive jacket can look awkward and cheap unless it fits the body perfectly. Some fit issues can be altered; others require changing to a larger or smaller size or to a different brand. The shoulders are the first place to check for fit. If the jacket doesn't fit there, no amount of alteration will ever make it work.

A soft pastel shirt with a complementary patterned tie and subtly patterned suit is a winning combination. Whether he is interviewing for a job or targeted as a high-potential employee, his confident image and presence will enhance his success.

- The jacket should button comfortably, without pulling in front, spreading the vents, or forming horizontal wrinkles above the seat in back. Nothing accentuates extra girth more than a jacket that fits too snugly. Move up to a larger size if necessary. No one ever knows by looking what size someone is wearing unless the tags are still on.
- The jacket shoulder should be wide enough so that the sleeve falls straight and perpendicular to the ground. If not, try a larger jacket.
- The armhole should fit as snugly under the arm as comfort allows. Although this sounds confining, a fitted armhole actually allows greater freedom of motion as well as a more elegant appearance.
- The sleeve should just barely cover the wrist bone. Lengthening or shortening a sleeve is a fairly simple alteration. Be sure to have each sleeve measured separately, as many men have one arm longer than the other.
- The jacket should be long enough to cover the curvature of your seat. A jacket cannot be effectively lengthened and can be shortened only an inch or two without distorting the pocket position. Fortunately, most manufacturers offer their jackets in a variety of lengths.

The shorter the jacket, the longer the man's legs appear to be. A very tall man with long legs might wear his jacket slightly longer to avoid looking gangly, whereas a short man could keep his jacket just barely on the shorter side to expose more leg length.

The jacket hem should hang parallel to the floor. If one side hangs lower, you may have one shoulder lower than the other. Have the tailor add a bit of shoulder padding to the suit on your low side for a more balanced appearance. The back of the jacket collar should hug the wearer's neck, exposing about ½" of the shirt collar underneath.

- If the jacket collar sits too low, too much shirt collar shows. This problem can be altered by reattaching the jacket collar higher onto the jacket back.
- If the jacket collar sits too high, little or no shirt collar is exposed. Horizontal wrinkles may form on the jacket back, just below the collar. This can be corrected by sewing the jacket collar farther down onto the jacket neckline.

- If the jacket collar stands away from the neckline, the jacket can be altered where the collar meets the lapel, making the distance around the back of the neck smaller.

If you are having a jacket altered by the store from which it was purchased, keep a critical eye on the fitting process. Some store employees see it as their responsibility to do as few alterations—at as little cost to the store—as possible. Politely but firmly insist on any alterations you feel are necessary, and try on the suit again after the changes have been made.

Fabric

Fabric is a key determinant of quality, comfort, and durability in a suit. For decades the best advice has been to choose all-wool suits. Fine, light-weight wools are comfortable year-round because they allow air to circulate freely between the body and the garment. They can be worn continuously throughout the seasons. Heavy wool fabrics such as flannel are warm in winter but hang in the closet seven to nine months of the year even in colder climates.

The continued improvement of synthetic microfibers is some of the biggest news in fabric. Microfiber suiting is expensive and beautiful, and has an almost three-dimensional appearance. For an investment piece that has durability, elegance, comfort, and maintains its appearance for hours, men are selecting microfiber suits.

Color Choices

Color choice has a great impact on the message a suit communicates:

- Navy and gray are the traditional business colors for men. The darker the shade is, the more authoritative the suit's image.
- Solid black is too dressy for a business suit, except on a man with exceptional fashion savvy. The average man is safer wearing black only for formal wear or as a blazer mixed with contrasting trousers or shirt color. Black background stripes and subtle plaids can work well in a business wardrobe. Also, black-and-white herringbone or houndstooth can be extremely handsome.

- Earth tones—olive, taupe, brown, and tan—convey a more relaxed or fashion-conscious message. Olive has become a wardrobe staple. It has a wide variety of intensity and can have undertones of gray or yellow. The easiest olive for most men's complexions is an intense, deep shade. Taupe, brown, and tan are great secondary colors to add only after a solid wardrobe of business basics in navy, gray, and olive has been established.

Each of the appropriate colors can be found in an assortment of patterns for added interest. Some appropriate business patterns include the following:

- Pinstripe is a very narrow line of light color, evenly spaced at about ¼" intervals against a dark background. A pinstripe conveys a high-authority image.
- A chalk stripe is a slightly wider band of light color, spaced farther apart on a dark background. The light stripe is faint and slightly irregular, resembling a chalk line on a blackboard.
- Multicolor stripes feature unevenly spaced bands of several colors against a dark background. Narrow stripes and subtle colors create the richest, most authoritative look. Wearing any lengthwise striped pattern creates the impression of a longer, leaner body.
- Muted plaids use both horizontal and vertical bars of color to form an overall rectangular pattern. Subtle colors on a dark background are classic.
- A glen plaid is a rectangular design formed by rows of various size checks. Usually done in a light and dark color combination accented with fine lines of a brighter color, only subtle glen plaids work in business suits. Bolder or coarser plaids belong in the sport-coat category.
- Miniature all-over patterns such as a tiny herringbone, ¹⁄₁₆" houndstooth, or a nailhead design look almost solid from a distance but add an element of elegance to a suit. Blends of a dark color with white are most traditional, but other color mixes can be equally acceptable. As always, the darker the overall color, the more conservative and authoritative the look becomes.

The manufacturing quality of a suit can sometimes be hard to gauge because the lining covers much of the inner construction. But these items can be key indicators:

- Look at the interfacing. In finer suits, the canvas interfacing used to add body to the jacket front and lapels is hand-stitched in place rather than fused. Technological advances have created new fusible canvas that closely mimics the hand-stitched feel. Rub the jacket front between your fingers, and test for any telltale stiffness that would indicate a lesser-quality fused interfacing. Too much glue and stiff interfacing will bubble after dry cleaning.

- Look at the underside of the collar. The best jackets have the collars attached with hand-stitching rather than by machine.

- Good-quality suits can be fully lined or partially lined. A partial lining leaves the garment more visible, so factors such as firm stitching and finished seam edges can be evaluated. Sleeves should always be lined so the arm slips in easily. Evaluate a fully lined jacket by checking the quality of the lining fabric. It should feel both durable and slippery enough to let the garment slide on easily. Run your fingernail across the fabric or tug lightly crosswise at a seam; then look to be sure the threads of the fabric have not shifted under the pressure. If a manufacturer skimps on a visible item like the lining fabric, you might wonder what shortcuts were taken in the jacket's inner or outer construction.

- Buttons and buttonholes also are a quality indicator. Suit buttons should be made of genuine horn or an excellent synthetic imitation. Avoid any suit with cheap, obviously plastic buttons. Buttons should be sewn on firmly, with a thread shank creating a small space between the fabric and the button. The best buttonholes are handmade, recognizable by their slightly heavier thread and the distinctive right and wrong sides. Top-quality, machine-made buttonholes are also acceptable if the stitching is dense and covers any loose threads of the fabric. Even the best ready-made jackets do not have working buttons on the sleeves. That is usually a feature found only on custom-made suits. The sleeve of the ready-made jacket should have four nonfunctioning buttons, spaced very close to one another.

Three-piece suits cycle in and out of fashion; however, a coordinated, but not matching, vest adds elegance and formality to a suit and maintains a more finished look when the jacket is removed. Today it is generally found in a softer or contrasting fabric, not a matching one. This adds dimension and interest. So don't bother keeping old vests and hoping the look will return. Vests, like other fashion items, return to fashion with a different twist each time. A vest should generally follow the lines of the body, but not pull at the buttons. A vest should be long enough to cover the trouser waistband, without showing any shirt fabric between. The bottom vest button remains open. The vest neckline should show slightly within the neckline of the buttoned jacket.

Most men select a suit for the styling and fit of the jacket, but the trousers also must be considered. Trousers can be traditional or follow fashion trends. Flat fronts and pleated designs are both appropriate. The two options ebb and flow in fashion's favor, but a few issues of figure flattery are ongoing:

- Double-pleated styles are traditional and generally camouflage tummy or thigh fullness.
- Triple-pleated styles and the inverted-plus-one design (two pleats pressed to face each other, plus a third pressed toward the side seam) are other pleated fronts. They allow plenty of fabric for camouflage and comfort, but the leg can be too full for a short man or one whose fuller waistline demands a larger size.
- Flat-front pants provide a trimmer look but are less forgiving of body bulges. Leaner, more fashion-conscious men wear these pants.

The leg shape of a well-designed trouser tapers slightly from thigh to hem in order to appear straight on the body. A true straight leg cut will actually appear flared. Fold the pant's hem edge up to the knee area and compare the width. The hem edge should be ½" to ¾" narrower (1" to 1½" smaller total circumference).

The bottom width of the trousers should be approximately three-fourths of the wearer's foot length. A wider hem looks baggy and sloppy; a narrower bottom edge creates an off-balance appearance. Cuffs are optional, but they create a more finished look. The added weight at the hemline causes the pants to fall more gracefully.

The typical suit is cut with a 6" drop; that is, the difference between the chest measurement of the jacket and the waist measurement of the trousers is

6". For men with less standard body builds, manufacturers offer "portly" suits cut with a 2" drop and "athletic" models with an 8" or even 10" drop. Choose the cut for jacket fit at the shoulders and adjust the trousers for the waistline.

The waistline should fit comfortably at the natural waist, not be slung below a protruding stomach. A trouser waistline can be altered to add or subtract up to 2" without distorting the lines of the garment. Look for adequate, but not excessive room through the thighs, allowing any pleats to lie flat. Side pockets should not pull open, even when you are seated. Have trousers hemmed to create a slight break over the shoe. A cuff, though optional, adds a distinctive touch and enhances the drape of the pant leg.

Recent improvements in fabric dyeing technology also make it possible for high-quality suit makers to address this fit dilemma in another way—separates. Several fine-quality lines offer suit coats and matching trousers that are sold as individual pieces, guaranteeing the customer an exact color match and a fit for both his upper and lower body with far fewer alterations.

Shirts

The choice of shirts can upgrade or diminish the look of any suit. The best shirts are made of long-staple pima, Sea Island, or Egyptian cottons, grown from plants specially bred to produce longer, thinner fibers. Lustrous long-staple broadcloth is a fine choice for business shirts. Pinpoint oxford is a more refined version of traditional oxford, which has a more textured, casual appearance. Made from finer threads, as many as eighty per inch of fabric, pinpoint has a finer surface texture and more lustrous look.

Some men like the wrinkle-resistance of polyester-cotton-blend shirts, but the synthetic fiber can make the shirt feel clammy next to the skin, pill around the neckline, and stubbornly hold stains and body odor through washings. A 100 percent cotton shirt is always a better choice.

To maintain a crisp, fresh look, shirts must be professionally laundered. Even in the most skilled hands, home pressing equipment cannot possibly duplicate that crisp edge. Opt for the least amount of starch that still gives a crisp look. Surprisingly, lightly starched shirts are actually more comfortable than shirts with no starch at all. They hold their shape better, rather than clinging to the body and soaking up perspiration.

One of the best indicators of a quality shirt is the term "single-needle tailoring" on the package. That means that each step of the construction has been stitched individually. Lesser-quality shirts are sewn with special two-needle machines that make the construction process faster, but less exact, with more puckering, and the shirt is less durable.

Color choices, in order from most authoritative to most relaxed, include:

- White—classic, traditional, always correct
- Pale blue—behind white, ahead of everything else
- Ecru or cream—adds elegance to textured fabric suits and muted ties
- Yellow, pink, and other pastels—acceptance varies by region and industry
- Pinstripes—a single color, narrow stripe on white—gray, blue, red, or burgundy convey a powerful look

The design of business shirts is fairly standardized—front button placket, long sleeves, yoked back, collar mounted on a band. The collar styling is the major variable:

- A button-down collar is the least formal option. Its more casual feel is out of step with a very authoritative suit and absolutely incorrect with the formality of a double-breasted style. Still, many businessmen, especially in some geographic areas, enjoy wearing button-downs with more casual business suits. This style is always made in oxford cloth, never dressier broadcloth.
- A straight collar is the most versatile, correct with virtually any suit style. This style needs collar-stays to maintain its crisp appearance. Points should be moderate in length (2½" to 3") to balance with moderate lapel widths and moderate-size ties. The typical spread (distance from point to point) is 2" to 2½". A slightly narrower spread makes a thick neck look trimmer.
- A tab collar, with fabric tabs that snap together behind the tie knot, adds elegance and flair to an outfit. This look is not flattering to a short or thick neck.
- A rounded collar is a youthful fashion look, slightly more casual in image. Men with full, round faces or severely angular features do not look their best in a rounded collar.
- A contrasting white collar on a colored or striped shirt is elegant and attractive.

Regardless of its style, the collar edges should lay flat against the shirt, not lift away like a bird taking flight. The collar ends should nearly touch at the upper edge, creating an inverted V around the knot of the tie.

Cuff options include a barrel (lap over and button) style or the dressier French cuff. With a French cuff, select top-quality, conservatively styled cuff links. For the best look, avoid the style with a clip back, and opt for links that look attractive from both sides.

Proper shirt fit is essential for both comfort and style. The most common mistake is in neckline fit. Many men continue to buy the same size year after year, even though their shirts feel increasingly tight. You should be able to turn your head from side to side without rubbing against the neckline fabric. The neck should be snug enough to keep it from drooping at the center front or from gathering in when you add a necktie.

Most retailers offer shirts in three distinct body styles:

- Tapered shirts fit a man with broad shoulders and a torso that tapers to a trim waist. The fairly high armhole and narrower sleeve and cuff create a slim silhouette. This style is also called "European."
- Regular shirts also narrow somewhat from the shoulder to the hem, eliminating excess fabric at the waistline for a man with an average physique.
- Full-cut shirts (also called "traditional") have little or no shaping to the waistline. This is the best fit for a more full-figured man.

Select the appropriate shirt cut to eliminate the bulk of excess fabric tucked into the waistband. A quality shirt should extend at least 6" below the waist so the shirttails stay neatly tucked in. Sleeves should be ½" longer than the break of the wrist, and show slightly beyond the jacket sleeve.

Ties

The right necktie can add personality and panache to even a fairly ordinary suit. The most versatile, year-round fabric for business ties is pure silk. Wool and silk blends and wool challis make more casual ties for cool-weather months. Synthetic fibers just won't work in a tie; they will never knot as well as natural fibers. Evaluate the quality of a tie in two additional ways:

- The quality of the interfacing (the inside layer of woven fabric that gives the tie its body) should be soft and substantial. Gently unfold the end of the tie and feel the inner fabric. Looking at the woven stripes at the fabric's edge is not a reliable indicator; markings vary by brand.
- The tie should be cut on a true bias grainline—diagonally of the fabric's lengthwise and crosswise threads. Cut correctly, the tie will mold to your neckline, knot gracefully, and fall smoothly. Cut slightly askew, the tie will never perform properly. Hold the tie from its midpoint, ends dangling freely. If the tie tends to twist on itself, leave it in the store.

Red is the traditional power color for ties, but the "red" category includes a wide range of mauves, burgundies, true reds, and rusts to complement any man's coloring. Navy, black, yellow, gold, teal blue, gray, and taupe are other suitable background colors for neckwear.

The best patterns for basic business ties include the following:

- Woven pin-dot, usually a light or bright dot on a dark background
- Foulards—small, evenly spaced geometric motifs
- Diagonal stripes and paisleys

Solid ties are versatile for coordinating with patterned suits and shirts. Combining a solid tie with a solid shirt and solid suit, however, is dull and uninteresting. Avoid large dots that create a clownish appearance. Conversational prints (pictures of objects or characters) may be fine for the company Christmas party, but don't wear them for important business occasions.

We know one accountant executive who lived to regret his cavalier wearing of a Three Stooges tie to a meeting with visiting senior management. His subsequent nickname, Curly Moe, stayed with him for years.

A tie should be knotted so that a dimple forms just below the knot and the tie's tip reaches your belt buckle. Ideally, the tie should arch slightly away from the shirtfront rather than lying flat and lifeless. The size of the knot should fill up the spread of the shirt collar.

The four-in-hand is the smallest knot (your mirror reflection):

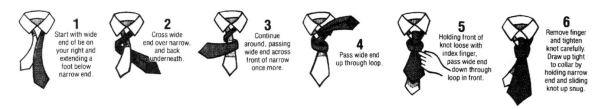

The half-Windsor is a somewhat larger knot (your mirror reflection):

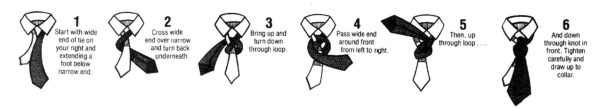

The bow tie is generally reserved for the tuxedo (your mirror reflection):

(Used with permission of Robert Talbott)

Bow ties are not considered conservative businesswear. We do know a few professionals—trial lawyers, entrepreneurs, and men in creative fields—who have made a bow tie their personal trademark. The choice conveys a clear message of individualism. The look also has a kind of professorial character, especially coordinated with a soft cardigan sweater.

A bow tie looks best on a shorter man; on a taller figure, it leaves too great an expanse of uncovered shirtfront. The bow tie's softer shape is compatible with even, rounded facial features but easily looks "geeky" on a more angular man. Any bow tie (tuxedo ties included) worn by an adult male must be hand-tied. The right to wear a clip-on tie ends promptly at kindergarten graduation.

Coordination

Assembling the correct pieces is just part one of being well dressed for business. Mixing them into well-coordinated ensembles is part two. In general, a combination with a high degree of color contrast creates the most authoritative image. Develop contrast in one of several ways:

- The dark suit, white or light shirt, and bright tie make up the traditional "power look." Because the human eye sees colors in relationship to their surroundings, a man with paler personal coloring could wear a mid-dark suit, and it would appear very dark without overpowering him.
- A medium suit combined with a light shirt and darker necktie still creates a suitable amount of contrast.
- Even a lighter-colored summer suit can form a contrasting color scheme when worn with a light shirt and dark tie. Pairing a light suit with a dark shirt creates contrast but is not a traditional business look.

Combining colors and patterns into tasteful outfits may seem like a remote art form, but a few basic guidelines should get you started:

- Use a maximum of two patterns in an outfit. It takes an expert eye to combine a patterned suit, patterned shirt, and patterned tie without looking like a clown.
- Very small suiting patterns—nailhead or miniature check or herringbone—count as a solid for coordination purposes.
- One pattern should be dominant. If the plaid of the suit is fairly bold, mix it with a subdued tie pattern. If the pattern in the suit is a subtle check, a stronger tie pattern becomes the focal point.
- Avoid using two patterns of the same scale. A tie with aspirin-sized dots would be monotonous with a ¼" striped shirt. Substitute a pin-dot tie instead.
- Two striped patterns generally don't combine well. With a striped shirt, choose a unique geometric tie rather than a rep stripe.
- Use color variety rather than repeating one color throughout the ensemble. With a navy suit and light blue shirt, a navy tie would be less exciting than a red or yellow one with navy accents.

- Use the accent color in the dominant pattern to suggest colors for the coordinating pieces. If a navy suit has a narrow burgundy stripe, then burgundy would be an ideal background color for the tie.

Of course, fashion trends at any given moment may contradict the long-term dress concepts in this chapter. But few businessmen have the time or interest to update their fashion statement each season, so these conservative, perennially correct guidelines should serve you for years.

"

"A gentleman in his forties was constantly being turned down for promotions. He had the expertise and people skills, but the wrong image for interaction with upper management and the board of directors. The last time he had worn a suit was when he was in college working part-time for a men's clothier store. His overall business manner was also a concern. As long as he had the expertise and experience, he could not understand why the way he dressed and presented himself should be an issue. A personal shopping trip introduced him to clothing of excellent fabrication and good fit. He upgraded his business casual wardrobe by replacing khakis with microfiber trousers and added a traditional business suit with dress shirts and striking ties. The result was an increased presence that commanded immediate respect. He carried himself with a more confident walk and posture. His visual perception took on a more credible aura. Management was impressed with his improved appearance and attitude and has taken his advancement in the company more seriously."

Gloria Petersen, Gloria Petersen and Associates, corporate image and protocol consultant

Suggested Traditional Business Wardrobe for Men

A man who dresses primarily in business basic needs to develop the following wardrobe. Those who dress less formally for some of their business activities can adjust these guidelines proportionally.

- Suits (suggested number: 6 to 8)
  - *Solids and Pinstripes*
    - Medium shade of navy
    - Navy pinstripe or chalk stripe
    - Medium shade of gray
    - Gray multicolor stripe
    - Medium shade of olive
    - Medium shade of taupe or tan
  - *Plaids*
    - Black or navy subtle plaid
    - Black or white nailhead
  - *Houndstooth*
    - Black and white
- Shirts (suggested number: 10). You will need ten long-sleeved business shirts: seven white, two blue, one burgundy stripe.
- Shoes (suggested number: 3 pairs). You will need one pair of each: black cap-toe, black tassel loafers, and cordovan slip-ons. Each pair will need a pair of cedar shoetrees.
- Socks (suggested number: 10 pairs). Select only dark-color socks.
- Belts and/or braces (suggested number: 2). Black or brown belt; braces complement the tie.
- Ties (suggested number: 12 to 18). Choose assorted colors to coordinate with suits.

Traditional Business Attire for Women

As the American designer Bob Mackie said, "When a woman enters the world of business, she is merely extending herself naturally. She should dress the same way. Her clothes should be a natural extension of her own personality." When women first came into the more significant ranks of selling, marketing, management, and executive positions, those who were serious about their careers practically had to sneak into the workplace disguised as men—wearing navy blue "clone" suits, starched white shirts, and red floppy ties and hoping nobody would notice the difference. A great deal has changed since then. Women have unquestionably earned their place in every field of work. Their unique characteristics are not only accepted but also greatly valued.

The look of women's traditional business wardrobe has changed accordingly. The safe navy formula suit that once seemed like the ticket to the executive suite is now marked as outdated and uninspired. Business suit options today include more color choices, more silhouette variations, and more ways for a career woman to express her individuality in her clothing. Separates, pantsuits, shorter skirts, opaque stockings, sweaters, and interesting shoes are only a few of the many updated options.

One of our clients, updating her wardrobe for a new corporate position after a five-year sabbatical, was almost giddy over the changes she saw at her workplace. "I can't believe how much more flexibility I have now," she exclaimed. "Women look so much more stylish and attractive than I remembered. Of course," she added, "a few carry the flexibility to extremes and look downright ridiculous, but for the rest of us, what a breath of fresh air!"

On the downside, more options inevitably mean more opportunities to make poor choices. Many women are ill prepared for making wardrobe decisions. Style savvy is not necessarily connected to the X-chromosome. Contrary to the popular shop-a-holic stereotype, most career women are far too busy juggling work and personal responsibilities to read fashion magazines or cruise the shopping malls. In fact, the majority of busy career women avoid shopping or place it low on their priority list. Yet these same women place their image and presence on the top of their list.

Working with our "Straight A Formula," this chapter outlines ways to look both appropriate and attractive easily, and at an affordable price. Five distinct clothing categories fit into traditional business attire. They are listed in order from the most conservative and powerful to the most fashionable and updated:

- Matched skirted suit—skirt and jacket in same color and fabric is traditional and the most formal choice.
- Unmatched suit—skirt and jacket in coordinating colors and fabrics is only slightly less formal than a matched one.

- Business dress—worn with or without a coordinated jacket creates a more relaxed, friendly message.
- Matched pantsuit—trousers and jacket in same color and fabric is a popular choice these days.
- Ensemble—fitted dress with long or short matching jacket is an elegant way to simplify business dressing.

This broader definition of "appropriate" can mean more mix-and-match possibilities, more outfits from fewer pieces. For instance, two skirted suits with traditional jackets could be cross-matched, pairing each jacket with the opposite skirt to create four different suit looks for the price of two.

But don't get so carried away with all this wonderful flexibility that you lose sight of your individualized standards for appropriateness. Think of clothing options as a continuum from the most conservative to the most fashion-forward.

Chart your clothing on Continuum A and calculate an average point score for your outfit: A matched pantsuit (10) with a short zip-front jacket (10) done in a rich purple color (8) would have an average score of 9.3. Results: a fashion-forward outfit.

Likewise, you can chart your industry, your company, your department, and/or your clients on Continuum B. For example:

Continuum A

CONSERVATIVE   FLEXIBLE

Category

1	2	3	4	5	6	7	8	9	10
Skirted suit		Contrast suit and shirt		Dress		Knit dress with jacket		Matched pantsuit	

Styling

1	2	3	4	5	6	7	8	9	10
Jacket with lapels		Jacket without lapels				Belted cardigan		Zip-front jacket	

Color

1	2	3	4	5	6	7	8	9	10
Navy	Black	Cobalt Blue	Burgundy	Hunter Green	Crème	Jade Green	Red	Purple	Fuchsia

Continuum B

By Industry

1	2	3	4	5	6	7	8	9	10
Banking/Finance		Insurance		Sales		Real Estate		Advertising	

By Title or Department

1	2	3	4	5	6	7	8	9	10
Executive Officer		Finance		Sales & Marketing		Human Resources		Design Group	

By Clients

1	2	3	4	5	6	7	8	9	10
CEOs		VPs		Product Managers		Support Staff		Retail Owner	

Average your job's individual scores for an overall "CQ," or "conservatism quotient." A bank CEO might have an average score of 1 (very conservative), whereas the CEO of an ad agency might average a more flexible 5. This isn't an exact science, but it is usually safe to keep your wardrobe score no more than about two points above or below your job's CQ.

Jackets

A wide range of jacket styles fit into the suits, pantsuits, and ensembles of a basic business wardrobe.

- A tailored lapel jacket or blazer is classically correct in any of its three versions. The jacket can be thigh, hip, or waist length. Details such as a contrasting collar and/or pocket flaps in suede, leather, or a complementary color make the style more sporty or fashion-forward.
- Single-breasted is the most traditional and universally flattering. Gentle waistline shaping is more classic than very straight or very fitted shaping.
- Shawl-collared blazers have a spare, sophisticated look, implying elegance and femininity.
- Double-breasted styles convey an elegant, yet authoritative feel.

- The sleek, uncluttered lines of a no-lapel jacket are both dressier and more feminine, blending readily with a softer skirt or a slim tailored one. This style works well over a blouse with a draped front or collar interest.
- A straight-cut cardigan with a banded front sends a comfortable, relaxed message. Whether the bands overlap and button or simply meet at center front, this jacket can often be belted for a distinctive style variation.
- A waist-length jacket is a great answer for the slightly bottom-heavy figure. Pairing a bright-color short jacket with a dark neutral bottom places all the focus on the wearer's upper body and away from lower-body challenges. This styling also sidesteps the fitting issues associated with being a larger size in the hips than in the shoulders.
- Fuller, longer smock and duster-style jackets, though slightly less formal, provide welcome camouflage for a figure with a heavier torso. Their easy fit makes them a fine answer for plus-size women as well, especially when worn open and over a bright contrasting blouse for vertical emphasis.

Any jacket style looks dressier and shows its design details best in a solid color, but subtle stripes and muted plaids also are appropriate. A bold, red tartan plaid probably makes even the most tailored jacket silhouette more suited for casual day than for traditional business.

A career jacket is a significant wardrobe investment. Be demanding about fit, but realize that it's impossible for standardized off-the-rack clothing to fit the wide range of female bodies without some fine-tuning and customization. The following explains what to look for and which problems can be altered:

- The jacket should button comfortably, without straining. If not, look for a larger size. If the larger size is too roomy, consider repositioning the buttons for an improved fit.
- The lapel or front neckline should lie flat against your chest, not bow apart. Bowing, usually caused by a full bust line, is nearly impossible to alter.
- The collar or back neckline should hug your neck, not stand away. A problem here can be corrected with a shoulder alteration.

- The fabric should not form a horizontal ridge below the neckline. A shoulder/neckline alteration also can correct this problem.
- Long sleeves should reach the middle of the wrist bone. Sleeve length is relatively easy to shorten or to lengthen up to 1".
- Buttons should be spaced to avoid gapping at the bust line.
- Surprisingly, a slightly higher cut in the armhole usually gives more comfort and freedom of movement. If a lower, fuller armhole is a design detail of your jacket, test for easy movement before you purchase, since this feature can't be modified.
- The jacket hem should fall parallel to the floor. Adjusting this correctly requires an alteration at the shoulder.
- The jacket shoulder should be slightly wider than your body. A greater difference must be supported by appropriate shoulder padding. Narrowing is very difficult.

Skirts

Pair the jacket with a matching skirt for the dressiest look or with a coordinating skirt for less formality. Several skirt styles are appropriate:

- The slim skirt is the usual companion for a suit jacket. Some women prefer fuller styles to cover wide hips, but a slim skirt may actually be their most flattering choice. A skirt that falls straight from the hips makes the wearer look as wide as her hips from top to bottom. Ask a dressmaker to taper the side seams gradually from hip to hem and the entire silhouette looks remarkably trimmer. Slim skirts coordinate well with any of the traditional business jackets.
- Mock-wrap styles, with a subtle diagonal drape of fabric in front, also can slim the body by diverting attention from lower-body figure challenges. Pair a mock-wrap skirt with a shorter jacket, cardigan style, or one with no lapel. More-detailed jackets may compete with the draped skirt front.
- Slightly fuller skirts with soft or stitched-to-the-hip pleats are a good alternative with short jackets, but may look too bulky with longer ones. A fuller skirt needs a longer hem length to maintain a graceful proportion.

Poor fit can make even the most expensive skirt look cheap and unflattering. Check these points carefully:

- The waistline should be loose enough for comfort, but snug enough to stay in place. If you tend to gain and lose weight regularly, look for short sections of elastic in the waistband at the side seams. A waistband can readily be made smaller; larger is more difficult.
- The hip area should fit smoothly, without pulling, even when you sit. Side seam pockets shouldn't pull open. In fact, sewing the pockets closed creates a smooth line and avoids bunching. Any pleats should lie flat. Correct problems in this area by trying on a larger size. If the size that fits your waist is too full through the hips, a dressmaker can easily stitch out the excess.
- The skirt should fall straight from your tummy and fanny. If it cups in below your body bulges, you will look and feel fat. Try a larger size.
- The hemline must be parallel to the floor. A hem that pulls up in front is usually caused by a protruding tummy. Have your dressmaker remove the waistband, raise the back of the skirt until the hem is even, and reattach the band at the new position.
- Skirt length should be conservative and flattering. Most skirts can easily be shortened, unless a pleat or button detail interferes, but a change of more than 4" may disrupt the garment's style lines. Lengthening is limited by the depth of the existing hem.

When it comes to skirt lengths, career wardrobes should not fall into extremes. Follow these guidelines:

- Skirt style influences length. Slimmer styles look fine shorter, but a fuller style requires a longer length to balance the proportion.
- Your body will look taller and trimmer in a skirt that looks longer than it is wide.
- The shape of your leg affects your choice of hem length. A hemline that cuts across a fuller area will make your legs look thick. Identify the narrower places on your leg, usually just below the knee, above the knee, or just below the bulge of the calf.

When the jacket and skirt coordinate rather than match, it generally looks more balanced to have a darker or more subdued color on the bottom and a lighter or brighter color on top. Brightly patterned skirts tend to draw attention away from the wearer's face, but a subtle stripe or muted plaid can work well. Beware of creating an attention-getting color break (light-to-dark transition) at a figure trouble spot such as the fullest point of your hip line.

Be careful to avoid a fifty-fifty color proportion in an unmatched suit. A long jacket over a contrasting long skirt showing equal amounts of each color looks awkward. Instead, when pairing contrasting items, select a longer jacket with a shorter skirt, or a waist-length jacket with a longer skirt.

left This perfect classic suit shapes the waistline as it follows the natural curves of the body without being tight. Her hair, makeup, and jewelry are simple and sophisticated.

right Hemlines that reach above the knee work well for shapely legs. Sheer black hosiery creates a leaner, longer line. The jacket adds a confident, updated look to the outfit. A fresh haircut and makeup complete a very successful presence.

Pantsuits

Matched pantsuits have gained acceptance as traditional business wear in even the more conservative fields. In 1990 when Congresswoman Susan Molinari (R–NY) gave her first speech to Congress, she received hundreds of phone calls. The overwhelming response wasn't for her speech, though. She had unknowingly become the first woman to wear pants on the House floor.

A pantsuit for a businesswoman is definitely not an imitation of a man's business suit; it has a clearly feminine flavor. The most popular styles feature impeccably fitted trousers and a matching longer jacket, gently fitted to the wearer's body curves. Pantsuits look most formal worn buttoned. Accessories are key to keeping a pantsuit dressy enough for business. Choose slightly heavier pumps with at least a 1" heel. Your hose or very fine-gauge, dark socks, belt, jewelry, and blouse should be the same high quality you would wear with a skirted suit.

Because the jacket accounts for about two-thirds of the pantsuit's cost, it makes sense to purchase a matching skirt to maximize your investment. Finding an exact match later is usually impossible, so when you have the option to buy the three coordinated pieces, do it.

Blouses

Tailored shirts and fine-gauge sweaters work well with traditional business suits and pantsuits. This category also adds a range of beautifully feminine blouses in soft silk crêpe de Chine and high-quality man-made fabrics.

- A sleeveless jewel-neck or mock-turtle knit shell is a wardrobe staple. Its plain neckline doesn't conflict with any jacket lapel or collar and is an ideal backdrop for jewelry. Knit shells are extremely comfortable, and they pack and travel well.
- A crisp, white, long-sleeve cuffed blouse is another must-have. Trim torsos are especially flattered with a dart-fitted bodice. Look for a firm knit that holds its shape well and doesn't cling to the body.
- Softly draped blouses add graceful softness to a structured suit look. Variations include cowl necklines and draped front panels that wrap across or meet at center front. Their soft fullness enhances a small bust line and fits easily over a fuller one. The play of light off the folds creates subtle design interest, even in solid-color fabrics.
- Although lace and eyelet appear too juvenile for the office, limited amounts of sophisticated openwork embroidery can add style and femininity to the collar, cuffs, or front placket of a basic blouse. White-on-white embroidery is the subtlest choice, but a dark color on white makes a sophisticated contrast. Identify quality embroidery by its dense stitching, with no fabric showing between threads, and by the absence of any raveling edges where the base fabric is cut away. The stitching should have a right and wrong side, with smoother stitching on the surface and all thread knots on the back. Top-quality rayon embroidery thread has a subtle sheen, neither glittery nor matte.
- Solid-colored shirts and blouses create the most businesslike impression, mix readily with other wardrobe pieces, and form an effective backdrop for beautiful accessories. Prints, however, can be an accessory themselves, adding visual interest and linking a solid jacket

and contrasting skirt into a coordinated ensemble. Best prints for business are small and tailored. Choose a small dot or stripe, controlled geometric or abstract look. Splashy oversized or bright-colored prints capture attention, overpowering the wearer.

Dresses

An assortment of dress styles fit the traditional business category. Though somewhat less authoritative than a suit, a dress offers the convenience of one-stop shopping in your closet—no need to coordinate several separate pieces. Here are some styles to consider:

- A sheath is a very basic, body-skimming silhouette that works especially well with a matching jacket for an ensemble. Because of its plain styling, a sheath worn alone quickly assumes the personality of accompanying accessories and moves easily from daytime to evening business occasions.
- A wrinkle-resistant, two-piece knit dress can be a lifesaver on an especially hectic day or one that includes travel. Dresses in cotton T-shirt fabric are too casual for the office, but the same style in a fine-gauge sweater knit has a refined look that is very comfortable. An easy-fitting tunic or a matching shell paired with a slim skirt is a winning combination. Add a matching cardigan and the impact can be nearly as strong as an unmatched suit.
- A two-piece dress is the ultimate wardrobe extra. The blouse and skirt are constructed separates. Each piece can be worn with other bottoms, other tops, and other suits.
- A coatdress is defined by soft body shaping, front button closure, and lapel and sleeve detailing reminiscent of a jacket. Many coatdresses have contrasting collars or band trim, piping, or decorative buttons that function as accessories. Shoes and earrings are the only extras needed to finish the look.

Certain details are too frilly, sporty, or sexy for the office, such as:

- Necklines that show cleavage
- Semi-sheer fabrics

- Full-gathered, tiered, or handkerchief-hem skirts
- Puffy sleeves
- Overdone ruffles
- Oversized floral prints or wallpaper stripes

Colors

Color choices offer great personal flexibility:

- Classic neutrals are versatile. Although beige can look expensive, it can also look washed out on pale coloring.
- Jewel tones, such as sapphire, emeralds, reds, and amethyst, imply energy and confidence.
- Dusty midtones, such as mauve, cadet blue, and sage green, blend well with blond coloring.
- Even pastels, used sparingly, can soften black, navy, and brown.

High-contrast combinations convey the highest authority, but high contrast doesn't have to mean navy and white. A wardrobe combination with contrast stronger than your personal coloring will create the appearance that the clothes are wearing you rather than the other way around. Tone on tone (i.e., gray with gray) is understated and sophisticated.

A business wardrobe built mostly in solid colors has a more elegant feeling and offers more mix-and-match opportunities. Solid colors also make an easier transition from daytime to after-hours business events. Avoid boredom by combining your solid-colored pieces in new ways. Try your basic navy suit with a knit shell in fuchsia, gold, or jade green instead of traditional white; or mix espresso brown with pale pink or turquoise. Belts and great shoes complete the look.

Suggested Traditional Business Wardrobe for Women

Women who dress primarily in business traditional attire should acquire and maintain the following essentials. A less formal look can be achieved by further developing the separates category.

- Separates that can combine into suits (suggested number: 5 to 8)
  - *Primary Solids*
    - Black jacket
    - Navy jacket
    - Cobalt blue jacket
    - Red jacket
  - *Secondary Solids*
    - Hunter green
    - Cream
    - Red
    - Purple/eggplant

- Separates (suggested number: 5)
  - *Primary*
    - Brightly colored jacket
    - Black or navy jacket
    - Black skirt—above the knee
    - Black skirt—below the knee
  - *Secondary*
    - Houndstooth, herringbone, or glen plaid jacket
    - Patterned skirt: houndstooth or subtle plaid

- Tops (suggested number: 5 to 10)
  - *1 Black mock-turtleneck sleeveless knit shell*
    - same but with long sleeves
  - *1 cream/ivory jewel neckline sleeveless shell*
  - *1 white cotton shirt, darted and fitted*
  - *1 pinstriped blouse with long sleeves*
  - *1 soft pink, yellow, or gold shell*
  - *1 bright red, purple, or emerald green shell*

- Shoes (suggested number: 5 to 10 pairs)
  - *Black pumps and slingbacks*
  - *Navy pumps*
  - *Taupe or chocolate brown pumps or sling-backs*

- Dresses (suggested number: 2)
  - *1 tailored business dress*
  - *1 two-piece knit dress*

- Hosiery (suggested number: 9 pairs)
  - *6 pairs of neutral or taupe hosiery*
  - *2 pairs of sheer black hosiery*
  - *1 pair sheer navy hosiery*

- Handbag (suggested number: 1 each)
  - *Black leather handbag*
  - *Navy leather handbag*
  - *Black leather briefcase*

- Leather or skin belts (suggested number: 2)

- Quality watch (suggested number: 1)

- Earrings (suggested number: 7 pairs)
  - *1 pair pearl earrings*
  - *1 pair 14-karat gold or quality sterling silver earrings*
  - *5 pairs costume earrings*

- Necklaces (suggested number: 2)
  - *1 strand pearls*
  - *1 gold or silver choker necklace (with complementing earrings)*

- Coats (suggested number: 1)
  - *All-weather coat/winter coat*

"Don't occasion shop. Last-minute purchases are almost always misses. If you come across a special dress that fits, buy it. Go for dark colors if you are on a budget. Bright shades can look cheap in less expensive pieces, but dark colors cover up gaps in quality."

Laura Mannix, director of Studio Services at Barneys New York

chapter four

boardroom attire

Elegance is something more than ease—more than a freedom from awkwardness and restraint. It implies a precision, a polish, and a sparkling which is spirited.

William Hazlitt

those at the upper echelons of business dress to communicate the subtle, but clear, message, "I made it." From exquisite fabric to exceptional fit to investment-quality accessories, the boardroom look is noticeable. Following the familiar advice to "dress for the job you aspire to," many second-tier executives also adopt this boardroom style of dress. They want to be visually established even before they are established in a position.

Interestingly, men's wardrobe choices become more strictly defined at this level, whereas women's choices tend to become more flexible. Both genders, though, incorporate the very finest fabrics, fit, and tailoring into a look that clearly displays professional status.

 "It's a funny thing about life; if you refuse to accept anything but the best, you very often get it."

Somerset Maugham

58

Boardroom Dress for Men

"One shouldn't spend all one's time dressing. All one needs are two or three suits, as long as they, and everything to go with them, are perfect" were important words stated by Coco Chanel. She probably had women's wardrobes in mind when she said them, but they apply as well to men's boardroom dressing.

Many businessmen dress for boardroom occasions in a uniform nearly as rigidly prescribed as that of a military officer. The traditional look is an exceptionally fine-quality gray or navy suit, white straight-collar shirt, with optional French cuffs, worn with dark socks and expensive, thin-soled leather shoes. The distinctive signature is usually the tie—100 percent silk from a designer like Hermes, Chanel, or Brioni. The formula is simple; it's the "perfection" part that can be challenging.

One component of perfection is to select the styling and details to balance an individual man's physique, creating an appearance that is as attractive as it is appropriate:

- Thin men should avoid lengthwise stripes. Width and stature can be added with textured fabrics, moderate shoulder padding, pockets with flaps, trousers with cuffs, slightly spread shirt collars, and horizontal patterns in neckties.
- A diminutive man can look taller by choosing a pinstripe or narrow chalk stripe suit with single-breasted, two-button styling. Details such as besom pockets and a single back vent elongate the look. Choose not-too-full trousers, and keep cuffs about 1½" wide, or omit them entirely. Slightly elongated collar points and a bright tie with a small knot are the best choices. Jacket length, sleeve length, and trouser length must be precise to avoid accentuating a small stature.
- For heavy men, two-button single-breasted jackets are flattering, especially if the jacket has a slightly enhanced shoulder line. Be sure the jacket is roomy enough to button and wear it closed for photo opportunities and presentations. Dark colors, smooth fabric surfaces, and pinstripes all create the illusion of a narrower figure. Braces keep a large man's trousers in place effectively and comfortably, and they repeat the slimming vertical of the necktie when the jacket is removed.

Exquisite suiting fabrics are another component of the "perfect" look. One noteworthy development in all-wool fabrics is a group of lightweight suits termed "Super 100s." Yarn spun from the fleece of Merino sheep, raised in Tasmania and Australia, is so fine that one pound can yield a thread thirty-one miles long. Fabric woven from this yarn weighs only eight ounces per yard. Capable of absorbing a third of its weight in water, the fabric draws moisture away from the body and releases it into the air. Super 100 suits are crease resistant and extremely strong, elegant, and comfortable year-round in most climates.

left This dark worsted wool suit creates a very credible first impression. Extremely well styled with perfect tailoring, this is an impressive look. The tie is the focal point of a suit. In a high-quality 100 percent silk, it literally billows beneath the knot.

right Boardroom attire at the highest level of impact includes pinstripes. There is a sense of wealth and financial acumen conveyed by this suit pattern. A clean, elegant hairstyle, immaculate collar and cuffs, and a high-quality silk tie finish a boardroom look. The contrast of high-quality 100 percent silk on 100 percent cotton on 100 percent wool conveys elegance and power.

Custom

Men in boardroom-level positions often appreciate the advantages of custom clothing—selection, convenience, and fit. A custom suit line may offer as many as 500 fabric choices, often of a quality not available in ready-made suits. The option of having a suit made exactly to one's body measurements is of special value to men with fitting challenges. Other extremely discerning men simply appreciate the nuances of appearance and comfort that exact fit contributes.

Three distinctly different versions of "custom" clothing are available:

- A true custom suit is individually made by a man's personal tailor, who drafts a pattern, bastes (temporarily stitches) the garment, and tries it on the customer repeatedly to ensure an exact fit. Fewer tailors are doing this highly skilled work these days, and the cost of a suit can range from $2,000 upward.

- What most men consider a custom suit is technically "made to measure." A trained company representative meets with the customer to decide on fabrics and measure the body. Over twenty measurements are taken, not just with a tape measure, but also with special patented tools that determine the degree of shoulder slope, curvature of the spine and shoulder blades, and other particulars. In a made-to-measure suit the client can customize the design, adding to the basic suit silhouette details (such a full lining of trousers and jacket or unpleated trousers) that suit his personal taste, even when they are less prevalent in current ready-mades. In three to six weeks the completed, well-fitting suit arrives. The measurements are retained on computer, so for future purchases the customer can spend as little as fifteen minutes selecting the suit style and fabric he prefers. Many custom clothiers bring their service right to the client's office for even greater convenience. Given the value of many executives' time, that convenience can justify the cost of the suit. Made-to-measure suits range in price from $700 to $3,000 and up, depending on the fabric.

- Several popular suit manufacturers offer a third option, so-called personalized service. The selection includes a range of traditional and contemporary styles, optional details, and fairly high-end fabrics. The manufacturer doesn't stock the suits but sews each one as a customer orders it. Only standard sizes are available, not made-to-measure fit. This option is helpful for men with portly or athletic builds who have limited selection in off-the-rack suits. It allows a client to order a matching vest or a second pair of trousers. "Personalized" suits generally cost $700 to $1,000 and take three to six weeks to deliver. Though not widely promoted, the service is available on request through most fine department stores and men's specialty stores.

One of our clients who loves his custom suits insists that you have to wear one to appreciate its value. "It's exactly like the Mercedes you never thought you wanted until you test-drove one," he says, "or the vintage wine you thought was overpriced until you tasted it."

Business shirts also are available on a made-to-measure basis. Available options include making the collar band wider to camouflage a long or unattractively wrinkled neck, or narrower to visually elongate a short, thick neck. An initial order for custom shirts is usually four of the same style, and they are usually reordered in pairs.

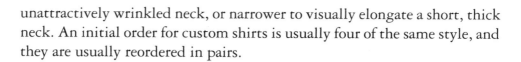

"Despite the commonly held myth that stylish men are born, not made, dressing well is an acquired skill. Becoming proficient in matters of self-attire is much like honing the talents needed to become a great golfer. While playing frequently can improve your game, until you start practicing the correct technique, your potential will always remain unfulfilled."

Alan Flusser, author of *Style and the Man*

Formalwear for Men

Owning a tuxedo is an investment in your career. For formal occasions, you will certainly want a level of style, quality, and fit unavailable in rental clothing.

An interesting survey by Around Your Neck—a men's clothing company—discovered that men who own a tuxedo actually attend more formal events (five to eight per year) than men in similar positions who rent their formalwear (two each year). Considering the mix-and-mingle opportunities such events offer, along with the caliber of the crowd, a tux is a wise investment. Renting a tuxedo can easily cost $100, so purchasing one will quickly pay for itself.

Ignore the array of pastel-colored suits, ruffled shirts, and paisley cummerbunds the rental outlets provide for prom-goers, groomsmen, and ushers. Executive formalwear is crisp, classic black and white. A dinner jacket is black with horizontal welt (besom) pockets and lapels in satin or grosgrain (a woven fabric with a light rib in one direction). A shawl collar, in single-breasted or double-breasted styling, is the most popular look. Single-breasted jackets with notched collars and double-breasted styles with peaked lapels also are correct.

Pair the jacket with trousers in the same fabric, trimmed with a satin or grosgrain band at the outside of each leg. Formal trousers often have an adjustable waistline to help ensure that you can wear them for years despite minor weight fluctuations.

If the event is nontraditional, consider having an immaculate white T-shirt that stars wear with their tuxes on opening night. But traditional evenings will require a shirt with a pleated bodice and a vertical front band closed with small, elegant studs, French cuffs, and matching cuff links. A turned-down or wing collar is worn with the black bow tie, from which the look derives its name. The higher-fashion banded collar is worn without a tie.

Braces (suspenders) hold the trousers in place on the body. The traditional black pleated cummerbund and black bow tie should ideally be the same fabric as the jacket lapel. The bow tie should be hand-tied.

For a statement of individuality, some men select a tuxedo in deep midnight blue or dark gray. An alternative way to personalize a formal-wear look is by adding a cummerbund or formal vest in a rich, interesting printed or brocade fabric, but not paisley. Forgo the matching print tie in favor of traditional black. Slip on lightweight cashmere, over-the-calf socks and black patent leather formal shoes to complete the look.

In the winter, temperatures may require an overcoat with your tuxedo. A tweed coat or khaki trench coat is too casual, but a solid dark wool or cashmere coat will do nicely.

For formal events in the summer months, pair a white dinner jacket with the same formal trousers. For dressy events that are not designated "black tie," select your darkest suit (solid or very subtle pattern), and wear it with a straight-collar white shirt and elegant tie.

White tie and tails are the correct costume for the most formal occasions—state dinners and the like. The suit is worn with a stiff-front shirt with detachable wing collar, white vest, and can be topped with a black silk top hat. Unless you are a diplomat or a concert musician, occasions for finished "white tie" are extremely limited.

Boardroom Dress for Women

Women's boardroom dressing takes two distinct interpretations, depending on the profile of the company, and the personality and the rank of the individual woman. We call the two categories: Classic Chic and Fashion Finesse. Both categories incorporate jacket, skirt, and dress styles similar to those in the traditional business realm.

■ Classic Chic is the choice of top-level women in more conservative companies and industries. Second-tier women in very conservative and rather traditional companies also dress this way, at least for their highest-visibility occasions. Classic Chic creates a look of impeccable elegance with streamlined styles and sophisticated colorations. Rich neutrals predominate with designers like Armani. Women with strong personal coloring may also choose sophisticated brights in exceptional fabrics and knits with designers like Escada, Chanel, and St. John Knits. Women with silver hair create a distinctive look with boardroom styles in winter white or dusty pastels. Silhouettes are usually body-skimming, hinting at, but not overemphasizing, the shape of the woman inside. Colors are largely solids, with texture rather than pattern for added visual interest. Both trouser suits and skirted suits predominate, and hemlines are above, at, or slightly below the knee, depending on the shape of the leg.

left Subtle animal prints in high-quality fabrics are a classic. Paired with a slenderizing black wool crepe suit and a fine-gauge turtleneck top, this look is striking. The impeccable grooming of her hair, natural makeup application, sheer black hosiery, and black all-leather pumps give her a confident presence.

right A shorter jacket with distinctive detailing can add executive sophistication to a simple black top and knit skirt. A brighter color jacket requires lipstick and blush to balance a strong garment color. A subtle black leather belt with a gold buckle finishes the look.

■ Fashion Finesse describes the more flexible, personalized dressing style of both top-level and aspiring women in fashion and creative industries. Top-level women in many traditional companies also choose this more fashion-forward interpretation. Dana Buchman and DKNY are cut to fit a typically more body-conscious silhouette. Skirt lengths can vary from midcalf to above the knee, and pants show up here as well. Colorations are less traditional, ranging from subtly blended neutrals to bold combinations of tasteful brights.

All women's boardroom choices share these characteristics:

- Impeccable tailoring, with crisp edges, smooth hems, and gracefully rolled lapels
- Exceptional fabrics, including knits, silk, and fine wool
- Flawless fit, carefully customized to the individual's physique

Boardroom dressing is distinctive. It makes a personal statement. It is about quality, exceptional professionalism, and refinement.

Of course, clothing of this caliber is expensive. Boardroom-level women need to banish any lingering belief that wardrobe is a frivolous topic and make this important investment in their career image. Boardroom men routinely invest in custom suits and imported silk neckwear to announce their position and display their pride in themselves. Even the least fashion-conscious male executive can recognize instinctively when a female counterpart does—or fails to do—the same.

Clothes alone don't have style; you do. A client of ours has a large mirror on the wall at the bottom of her stairs, which she passes each day as she leaves for the office. "If I glance in the mirror and something stands out from the whole picture, like oversized earrings or a fussy scarf, I eliminate it or change it. I want people to notice me, not have their attention distracted by something I'm wearing."

Formalwear for Women

A boardroom-level career typically includes a number of formal occasions—company functions, political gatherings, and charity events. A closet full of memorable ball gowns is one way to meet this wardrobe need, but a collection of dressy separates is a more practical alternative. Just six or seven well-chosen pieces can combine into dozens of looks, appropriate for the entire range of dressier occasions. This cost-efficient approach lets you invest in the highest possible quality for each individual component.

Here is just one example of a formalwear grouping. Modify the plan to fit your own coloring, body type, and social schedule.

- Full-length dress in black silk charmeuse, fitted spaghetti strap bodice, front-draped skirt

- Fitted white lace overblouse with long sleeves, high neck, and peplum hemline
- Soft, full-leg black silk pants
- Short, black velveteen skirt
- Matching velveteen fitted jacket
- White angora sweater with openwork and jewel trim across shoulder area
- Brocade Chanel jacket, black background with dark green and gold motifs
- Gold metallic knit sweater

The dress looks elegant alone, or functions as a skirt with any of the other tops. The sweater, velveteen jacket, and brocade Chanel work with all the bottoms in the group. Both jackets can be buttoned up or worn open with the gold shell.

For even greater versatility, mix these pieces with your daytime wardrobe for less formal occasions:

- Pair the velveteen skirt or soft pants with any silk blouse for dinner out.
- Wear the gold sweater and brocade jacket with gabardine trousers for an open house.
- Consider the velveteen jacket with a pleated challis skirt for a symphony concert.
- Top black-velvet corduroy jeans with the gold sweater for a casual holiday look.

chapter five

accessories

> It has long been an axiom of mine that the little things are infinitely the most important.
>
> Sherlock Holmes

accessories are the icing on your wardrobe cake. They transform "everybody" clothes into a statement that communicates your unique message. Topnotch accessories are a wise investment of wardrobe dollars, because they often have a longer life span than the garments with which they are worn.

Accessories for Men

In the subtle world of men's business attire, small accessory items play a key role. The fine details can make or break a successful look, upgrading or downgrading the impact of even a fine suit.

"Wanna know if a guy is well dressed? Look down."

George Frazier, fashion journalist, *Esquire*

Shoes

Feet are not a particularly attractive anatomical feature, so all the more reason to shroud them in extremely elegant surroundings. Shoes should blend in with a man's total look rather than calling undue attention to themselves. Dark colors, such as black, dark brown, and cordovan, are most appropriate. Business shoes should have a lightweight look, with soles no more than ¼" thick and low, trim heels. The thinner the sole is, the lighter and more elegant the look.

The term *well-heeled* originally came from England. It reflected the ability of a man to re-heel his shoes on a regular basis. Only the more affluent were able to do this, thus the more global term well-heeled extended beyond the shoe and indicated a man's wealth.

Fit and comfort are critical. If your feet hurt from poorly fitted shoes, little else matters. If they pinch in the store, they will inflict great pain later on. Always try on both shoes, as your left and right may be slightly different sizes. Buy to fit the larger foot, and if necessary, add a pad in the shoe for the smaller foot. A properly fitted shoe allows "wiggle room" for the toes and fits snugly against the heel. Leather soles and heels also contribute to the comfort of a shoe by combining a natural cushioning action with natural absorbency.

"Spend your money on great shoes, because they can make or break your look."

Monet Cole, cofounder of Fashion-411.com

The upper portions of men's shoes are available in a variety of materials:

- Vinyl looks cheap and is uncomfortable to wear because it is neither flexible nor absorbent.
- Leather is the ideal material for business shoes. Learn to recognize these following variations:
  - **Cordovan** *is the most durable. It is made from the rump of a horse and has a distinctive reddish-brown color.*
  - **Kidskin** *is made from the hide of a young goat. Leather from smaller animals is softer and suppler, as well as more costly.*
  - **Calfskin***, obtained from young cows, is equally desirable for fine business shoes.*

- **Cowhide**, *from mature animals, is typically used for more casual styles because it is thicker and less elegant.*
- **Suede** *shoes are also casual but can work with tweedy suits or with sportcoat looks. Fine buckskin suede is made from the hide of a male deer, finished on the flesh side.*
- **Patent leather**—*finished with a high gloss—is reserved for evening shoes.*

The shoe's styling also determines whether it belongs with dressy or casual clothing. Lace-up oxfords have the most conservative business image and coordinate well with traditional business suits. The unadorned plain-toe lace-up style is the most conservative; it can even double as a formal shoe. The cap toe—with a single straight seam across the toe—comes in plain and perforated variations. In black or brown, it is a staple in a man's business wardrobe. A sleek version of the wingtip has a distinctive curved-toe design and decorative perforations. Slightly heavier than the cap toe, it works especially well with suits in tweeds, checks, or flannel fabrics.

Most men appreciate the convenience and elegance of slip-on shoes, available in a variety of styles from dressy to casual. Dressy slip-ons mimic the shape of their lace-up cousins. Available in plain toe, cap toe, or wingtip variations, they work well with conservative business attire.

Tassel loafers define the more relaxed end of the dress shoe continuum. Dressiest in black, the look is more casual in cordovan or brown. They can be worn with less formal suits as well as blazer and sportcoat combinations. Penny loafers (without the penny, of course) and loafers with distinctive metal buckles blend with business casual attire not with traditional business suits.

Sneakers, boating shoes, and other sport shoes don't belong at the office, even on Casual Friday. And cowboy boots are acceptable for business only in certain clearly defined regions of the country and then only in very specific industries.

A pair of fine leather shoes can represent an investment of several hundred dollars, but with good care they should last for many years. Always apply a coat of protective polish before the first wearing. Then use a leather-cleaning cream, and polish regularly. If you travel a great deal, find the best shoeshine technician at the airport and make it a ritual to get your shoes shined before a trip.

Be sure to rotate shoes, allowing each pair to rest at least one day between wearings.

Clean suede shoes with an art gum eraser, and gently brush the nap. Always use cedar shoetrees to maintain the shape between wearings and to deodorize. Have shoes re-heeled and resoled as soon as they begin to show wear. Continuing to wear them will speed the deterioration.

Socks

Besides cushioning the feet and absorbing perspiration, socks can enhance or detract from a polished appearance. They should be dark or neutral and are more interesting with subtle, coordinating patterns. Match the trousers when the trousers are dark and match the shoe when the trousers are khaki. Black, dark brown, and dark blue socks are staples. Charcoal gray, maroon, or a small pattern offers interest. White sport socks are out of place, even in a casual business environment.

"Your socks should never be funnier than you are."

Hal Rubenstein, author of *Paisley Goes with Nothing*

Natural fibers such as cotton and wool allow air to circulate, keeping the feet warmer in winter and cooler in summer. Look for styles with nylon-reinforced toes and heels for greater durability. The thinner the socks are, the dressier the look. Fine-ribbed cotton and wool are the best choices with classic business suits. Heavier knits are better balanced with tweed sportcoats or more casual wear.

Above all, socks must be long enough to avoid showing a naked band of hairy leg below the trouser hem when legs are crossed. Choose over-the-calf styles or calf-length socks with a nylon-blend top band to hold them in place.

Belts and Braces

A belt is essential to hold pants at the waistline and add definition to the overall look. Choose one about 1" wide with a subtle metal buckle. A properly fitted belt is long enough to fit your waist and fasten in the second hole.

A black belt in fine leather or more exotic skin, like alligator or croco-dile, is a business wardrobe basic. With more casual looks, consider brown or burgundy leather or woven leather. The belt color should relate to the color of the suit, the trouser, and especially the shoes.

Braces are an elegant alternative to a belt. These "grown-up suspenders" have leather tabs that attach to buttons inside the trouser waistband. By suspending the trousers from the shoulders, they allow the pants, especially pleated styles, to hang more attractively and eliminate the discomfort of a too-snug belt. Pants worn with braces should be at least ½" larger in the waistline.

Braces add a fashionable touch to a business look, even when the suit coat or blazer is removed. Made from 1¼" strips of rayon or silk in solid colors or conservative patterns, they should coordinate with, but never match, the necktie. The attachments should always be leather and button inside the trouser. Don't compromise your image by wearing clip-on sus-penders (too childlike and casual) or wearing both braces and a belt (too paranoid).

Handkerchiefs

Handkerchiefs serve two distinct purposes—fashionable and functional. For functional applications, choose white cotton and linen for softness and absorbency. Be sure to have a clean one every day—several if you are in the midst of a cold or allergy attack.

Tucked into a breast pocket, a handkerchief is the least expensive way to polish and upgrade a business suit. A crisp, fresh square of hand-rolled white linen is always correct. Colored-silk pocket squares cycle into and out of popularity and are best saved for after-business hours. Even when they are in style, it takes panache to wear one well. If you try it, stick to solid colors and small patterns. The pocket square should coordinate with, but never match, your tie. Pair a solid square with a patterned tie or vice versa.

Whether you choose white linen or colored silk, insert a pocket-handkerchief in one of three ways:

- Hold the center point of the square, letting the corners fall free. Run your other hand down the square, gathering in the fabric, to about the midpoint. Fold loosely, bringing the corner points and the center together, and tuck the resulting midpoint fold into your pocket. Fluff the exposed edges slightly.

- Fold the square diagonally, points slightly askew. Place a finger at the midpoint of the folded side. Bring one folded corner up toward the points, overlapping slightly. Repeat for the other folded corner. Fold each outer edge in again, and then tuck the handkerchief into your pocket with only the points exposed.
- Fold the handkerchief in half both lengthwise and crosswise, creating a four-layer smaller square. With the four free points toward you, fold the two outer corners toward the center. Fold the resulting "rectangle" in half again, and slip the final fold into your pocket, exposing the triangular point.

"If you must have your clothes monogrammed, do it where it can't be seen."

Hal Rubenstein, author of *Paisley Goes with Nothing*

Jewelry

Men's jewelry adds subtle punctuation to the total look but should never be a focal point. Watch, rings, cuff links, and collar pins should all be elegant and subtle.

There is no better business jewelry investment than a high-quality watch. Begin by looking at the costliest watch lines: Rolex, Cartier, Baume-et-Mercier, Ebel, Omega, Piaget, Raymond Weil, and Patek Philippe.

Study the design, the metals—gold, stainless, or platinum—how the numbers are displayed on the face of the watch, the weight, the size as it relates to your frame, and your immediate reaction to it. If you are able to invest, purchase the best you can afford. Otherwise, work to duplicate as many of the features of fine-quality watches in a price range you can afford.

The best in less-expensive business watches feature trim styling in costume gold or silver with a fine leather or good-quality metal band. Heavier styles are appropriate, too, especially with larger men. Avoid cheap-looking expansion bands, heavy sport watches, cartoon characters, or novelty designs.

Wedding bands and conservative signet rings are universally appropriate, but limited to one per hand. College rings and fraternity rings generate a wide variety of responses. In some circles they are considered a trademark of the young and inexperienced. In other situations, they can be effective for starting a conversation or establishing common ground with a new acquaintance. Evaluate your own situation carefully, and, if in doubt, leave the college ring in the jewelry box.

Cuff links, used to secure French shirt cuffs, should be small, conservative, and high quality. Avoid the type with a decorative front and clip back, because the cuff can be seen from both sides.

A collar pin adds a polished touch, tucking the collar edges close to the knot and arching the necktie slightly away from the shirtfront. Wear one with a straight-point or rounded collar, but not with a widespread or button-down style. Collar pins are available in three variations:

Cuff links: The cuff links on the left are acceptable. The cuff links on the right are a better choice because the links on either end are similar and therefore more elegant.

- A bar with one screw-on end that fits through stitched eyelets in the shirt collar. This is the easiest to use.
- The pin-through variety works with any short collar, eyelets or not. The holes close up when the shirt is laundered. This is the most difficult to use.
- The snap-on type initially looks fine, but it doesn't hold as securely and usually needs to be adjusted throughout the day.

Tie bars, tie tacks, and similar appliances are solidly out of fashion. Keep your necktie somewhat secure by tucking the narrow end through the loop, chain, or label on the backside of the wide end.

Glasses

Because they are worn almost continuously, selecting an attractive glasses frame is of primary importance. Frames that closely echo your hair color are nearly always flattering. Select a style that flatters your facial shape and your features. As a general rule, they should follow the natural line of the eyebrows.

- Slightly wider frames visually broaden a long, narrow face.
- Slightly narrower frames appear to slim a fuller facial structure.
- Angular styles look harmonious with angular facial features.
- Gently rounded frame shapes blend best with softly contoured features.
- Frames with a low bridge can shorten a long nose.
- Frames with a very high or transparent bridge lengthen a short nose.

Briefcase

Most briefcases need to accommodate an array of high-tech equipment—laptops, PDAs, cell phones, and sometimes cameras. A trim, tailored, 3" case looks far more stylish—and better organized—than a bulging, oversized one. Heavy leather is the best look if you can afford it. Otherwise, seek out a good-looking canvas briefcase with leather attachments. Black is the best color, followed by brown, and then burgundy.

Look for indications of quality such as genuine stitching rather than embossing, metal-reinforced corners, and rivets to secure the handles and hinges. The same service that polishes and repairs your shoes can also keep your briefcase well maintained.

Upper-level executives often consider it beneath them to drag around a large, crowded briefcase. They will generally opt for a top-quality leather portfolio. Portfolios made from canvas or nylon are increasingly popular. They work fine with casual business clothing, provided they look new and well maintained, but they don't coordinate as well with dressier business attire.

Wallet

The wallet should be made of top-quality leather in black or brown. It should never bulge with anything—even money. The oblong "secretary" style has more presence than a traditional square and maintains a trim appearance in your inside jacket pocket. Tucking a wallet in your back pants pocket can create a big lump and can more easily be lost or stolen, but sometimes that is the only place to put it. Some men prefer to keep it in their briefcase.

Outerwear

A classic tan trench coat that can be worn year-round is one of the best wardrobe investments. Its styling is dressy enough to wear with a suit, but relaxed enough to work equally well on casual day. With a zip-in liner, it can double as a winter coat in many climates.

The styling of the traditional trench coat dates back to World War I. Each detail of the coat had a utilitarian function rather than an aesthetic one. Little has been changed on this classic since the early 1900s, although the details such as the epaulets, button-over collar, and multiple pockets are now considered aesthetic ones.

Cotton or cotton-polyester blend in a water-repellent poplin, twill, or gabardine is a good choice. A better, but more expensive, choice is microfiber because it travels so well, sheds more water, and is actually warmer than cotton-poly blends. In either case, look for single- or double-breasted styling with a roomy cut to fit over suits and sportcoats. Tan is always a classic, safe color choice, but charcoal, black, and olive are more stylish alternatives. The long belt—even though it usually has a buckle—is meant to tie, not buckle at the waist. Below-the-knee length is the best-balanced proportion and the warmest choice.

An overcoat, if your climate or travels demand one, should be all wool in navy, charcoal gray, or black. If you don't mind more frequent dry cleaning, camel color is a rich-looking alternative. True camel hair, alone or blended with wool, is durable. Cashmere, although it feels wonderful, is more delicate. If you select this luxurious fabric, treat your coat with great care, and don't wad it up and stuff it into the overhead compartment on an airplane. Pull out the durable trench coat for "road warrior" assignments.

Double-breasted styles are warmer because of the double-layer front panel, but a single-breasted design with a concealed placket front is equally appropriate. The back vent should extend no higher than the curve of the seat. Longer vents offer less warmth and protection, and they look foolish flapping in the breeze.

Accessorize a coat with black or brown leather gloves and a dark-colored wool muffler. An alarming amount of body heat can escape through a bare head, so a good-looking wool cap is a logical complement to your outerwear ensemble.

Each businessman needs to work out his own personal style for protecting his shoes from the elements, but why ruin a pair of good-quality shoes when there are alternatives? Consider either plastic rubbers over leather shoes, warm boots, or waterproof shoes with rubber soles during rain, snow, or sleet.

A businessman's umbrella should be black or a small, dark pattern with a plain, good-quality handle. A generous size offers maximum protection, but bright, oversized golf umbrellas belong at the country club, not the office. Fold-away umbrellas are less elegant than the ones that don't fold, but perfectly acceptable, especially for travel.

Accessories for Women

As Rousseau said, "Taste is, so to speak, the microscope of judgment." Many wardrobe consultants advise clients to invest as much as half of their wardrobe budget in accessories. A modest outfit can triple its face value when worn with an excellent-quality handbag, shoes, and jewelry. In addition to their style-enhancing abilities, accessories often are long-term investments. A quality silk scarf, for instance, can last decades. And good jewelry with minimal care is nearly indestructible. Accessories also sidestep the issue of weight fluctuation. When did you last hear a woman say, "I've gained so much weight I can't squeeze into my watch"?

Shoes

Shoes are literally the foundation of your accessory wardrobe. Above all, they must be comfortable. How upbeat can you feel or look when your feet are in pain? They should also be subtle. You don't want to create a focal point at the polar opposite of your face.

At a recent conference for women entrepreneurs, a striking dark-haired woman was wearing a black wool skirt and fuchsia jacket. Sheer black nylons blended with the hemline, but she had chosen fuchsia shoes with 4" heels. She explained that the color lifted her spirits on a dreary day, but it lowered everyone else's attention . . . directly to her feet!

Real leather is a must, both for looks and comfort. It has a rich elegance that synthetics can't match, and it shapes with wearing, molding to fit the curves of your feet. Crocodile is extremely elegant, classic, and expensive.

Quality shoes are costly, so choose neutral colors to maximize your investment. Opt for shoes in black, navy, brown, or taupe, and perhaps burgundy if you can justify the purchase. Shoes in camel and rust coordinate with warm-colored clothing. Shoe color should match the hemline or be darker, so the entire look appears "grounded." White, ivory, and pastel shoes don't work in business. Fashion colors, such as red or purple, are usually impractical because they generally work with only one outfit. For an extremely chic appearance, matching the shoe with the exact color of the hemline can create a high-fashion look. However, avoid looking as if everything has been dipped in the same vat of dye—the dated "bridesmaid" look.

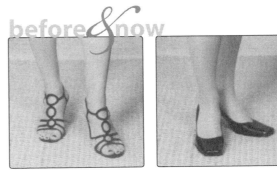

before Strappy sandals show too much foot. They also inhibit the stride. **now** Closed-toe leather pumps are always correct in business. They are slenderizing and professional. Black is the essential color.

For the most slimming, elongating look, coordinate the color value (light/ dark characteristic) of your shoes to your nylons. With a dark neutral hemline, you can match all three components, for example, navy skirt, sheer navy hose, navy shoes. With a brighter garment, choose midvalue neutral shoes and hose, such as taupe with coordinating neutral pumps.

A basic pump is the most versatile style. With a closed heel and toe, it works in any season and is equally appropriate with skirts or pants. It also is the most slenderizing and flattering shoe design. Approach slingback and open-toe styles with great caution.

Classic pumps will look subtly fashionable, trimmed with contrasting materials such as suede or patent. It gives added interest and attractively shortens a long, narrow shoe. Be careful about embellishing unadorned pumps with clip-on shoe decorations. They will generally tear a hole in the hosiery.

Look for heels between 1" and 3" high. They flatter your leg shape by elongating the calf muscle and slimming the ankle. They also give most women a more graceful walk than a very flat shoe. Wider, curved heels look more stable and current than very narrow ones, and blend more readily with longer skirt lengths and with pants. They also are much more comfortable to walk in.

With very casual clothing, a tailored woven leather loafer is an ideal match. A cordovan color blends readily with khaki, denim, and other casual colors and fabrics. Strappy sandals and very high heels are inappropriate for office wear. Their message is more social, even flirtatious. In fact, one survey done in the workplace reflected that the single component of women's attire that was rated "sexiest" by both genders was the revealing, high-heeled shoe.

Even the most upscale sneakers are never appropriate businesswear. If you absolutely must wear them for a lengthy cross-town hike to the office, change into a dressier shoe the moment you arrive. Or consider substituting a handsome, leather walking shoe for your travels. Image is a daylong affair. We have hundreds of opportunities in a single day to make either a strong or an ineffective impression. Why not give yourself every opportunity to be visually effective?

If you live in snow country, add a pair of practical, lined, and water-proofed boots to your wardrobe. Those black pumps won't keep you warm or dry after a blizzard. Wear the boots to and from the office, and carry your pumps in a tote or your briefcase. Don't wear the boots all day. They look too heavy and awkward with business dress, they make your feet swell, and they are a haven for foot odor.

Boots as a fashion and business mainstay for women began when Mademoiselle Chanel wore boots in the winter to cross between her apartment at the Ritz and her clothing salon in the rue Cambon.

Career footwear needs to be meticulously maintained. Have a repair shop put reinforced tips on every new pair of high heels. Rotate shoes so they can recover their shape between wearings. Polish shoes regularly, get to the airport early for your shoe maintenance, or drop them by the local shoeshine stand on your way to work.

Hosiery

Neutral-colored hosiery is the strongest and freshest look for business. A shade matching your skin tone is safest in very conservative industries.

Sheer and semi-opaque black and navy are wardrobe staples. Opaque black hosiery has become another wardrobe basic with shorter black skirts. Bright colors in opaque hose are inappropriate. Avoid skin-tone colors with an orange or greenish cast. Ashy neutrals look unattractive against the skin tones of most women of color.

With pants, select fine-gauge socks, pantyhose, or opaque tights. Dark colors that blend with shoes and/or hemline are still the best choice. Never, ever go barelegged to the office, no matter how tan your legs or how hot and muggy the weather. The entire look is unfinished and unbusinesslike. In fact, in corporate workshops on professional appearance, this is one of the top issues where management typically requests a review and renewed emphasis.

Pantyhose today can do more than just cover legs. Lycra-blend styles can slim, trim, and control bulges. Watch out for brands that end the Lycra abruptly at the upper thigh, creating an unattractive roll of flesh just below the control portion. Better brands diminish the Lycra content gradually down the leg, slimming thighs as well as tummies.

The advent of microfibers—minuscule strands of synthetic fibers—opened the door to nylons that are simultaneously sheer and sturdy. Until grocery-store brands incorporate microfiber, consider department store brands that will repay your investment with a smoother look and longer wear.

Experiment to find the brand that works best for your shape and your lifestyle. Then buy in quantity to avoid an early-morning crisis. Some brands even offer a subscription service—much like the old-fashioned milkman—that lets you establish a regular color and quantity assortment that is automatically shipped to you at designated intervals. (See the Resources section at the end of this book.)

Check your hose front and back before you leave the house. Runs and snags undermine the most polished image. Keep a spare pair in your favorite hosiery colors in a desk drawer or glove compartment for emergencies. If you keep nylons with minor runs to wear under pants, knot the legs loosely so you can distinguish them from the still-perfect pairs stored in the same drawer.

Belts

A skirt or pants waistband is generally not a fashion focal point, but a structure that looks best covered by a good-looking belt. First buy leather, suede, or skin belts about 1" wide in the same neutral colors as your shoe collection (black/navy/gray/taupe/burgundy with a cool-color wardrobe; camel/brown/rust with warm-color clothing). The belt should fit comfortably and securely over the garment's waistband when buckled in the second or third hole. A shoe repair shop can shorten a too-long belt and occasionally add holes to lengthen a small one.

Then build your collection of tailored fashion belts to suit your personal style. You also may choose one or two elegant metal buckles and a color assortment of interchangeable leather strips on which to wear them. Use a belt to add polish and pizzazz to an outfit and to balance your figure challenges, too.

The Ten Rules of Belting

1. Let a gold or silver belt buckle show under an unbuttoned jacket for the most slimming illusion.
2. Upgrade a dress or belted jacket by replacing the cheaper attached belt with a quality leather one.
3. Add a quality canvas or woven leather belt to polish a casual look.
4. Wear a narrow belt over a longer, shaped jacket for a fresh new look. Wear a shirt as a lightweight jacket, belted over casual pants and a turtleneck.
5. Match the belt to the garment's bodice color to lengthen a short-waisted figure.
6. Match the belt to the skirt or pants color to lengthen legs.
7. Select a belt color that contrasts with the garment to emphasize a trim waistline.
8. For a less curved figure, look for a matching color belt with an eye-catching buckle to focus attention to the center of the body, creating the illusion of a narrower waistline.
9. Avoid wider styles if you have a thick waist, short torso, or low, full bust line. The wider the waistline is, the narrower the belt.
10. The one sure way to destroy the beauty that a belt offers to an outfit is to fasten it too tightly so that it puckers or ruins the lines of the outfit. Worn too tightly, a belt will emphasize any tummy fullness or bulges above or below the waist.

Scarves

From a practical perspective, we aren't fans of scarves. They often add bulk and become messy and disheveled during the day. But from an aesthetic perspective, they are stunning as they tie an outfit together and add interest. The difficulty is finding the right colors, the correct size, and the proper knotting. If you enjoy scarves, these are options to consider:

- Unify an unmatched suit with a patterned scarf that repeats both the top and bottom colors, plus at least one additional accent shade.
- Update a garment in a less-flattering color by using either a softer or a brighter scarf near your face. If black is too harsh next to your face, select a scarf where the primary color is either white or cream with variations of black.
- Silk is the best fabric for scarves; it drapes more beautifully and ties into a smaller, more elegant knot that any other fabric.

Glasses

Because they are worn daily, be sure your glasses are flattering to your coloring and facial shape. Many men and women have a small wardrobe of eyeglasses. Black plastic and tortoiseshell are always appropriate. Smaller lens in interesting shapes generally look updated and chic. Try selecting frames in the same color family as your hair for your everyday pair. Then add a second pair in a two-tone laminate, like black and clear, or choose rimless.

When Liz Claiborne introduced her planos, glasses with clear noncorrective lenses, her research indicated that glasses implied that the wearer was richer and smarter than the nonwearer.

Don't neglect eye makeup behind glasses. Lenses for far-sightedness will magnify the eyes, so apply muted shadow colors with a light touch, and use a brighter lip color to balance the look. Lenses for near-sightedness minimize eyes, so compensate with slightly bolder shadows, more prominent liner, and a heavier coat of mascara.

Many men and women have enjoyed the benefits of LASIK eye surgery, which significantly improves eyesight. This procedure, however, doesn't always eliminate the need for glasses.

Jewelry

When a client of ours became a vice president in her firm, her first image upgrade was a fine watch. "It's the one thing everyone notices," she explains, "so you can't afford to wear something cheap. It is also an enduring investment so I can amortize the cost over twenty or more years."

Begin by looking at the costliest watch lines: Rolex, Cartier, Baume-et-Mercier, Ebel, Omega, Piaget, Raymond Weil, and Patek Philippe.

Study the design, the metals, how the numbers are displayed on the face of the watch, the weight, the size, the delicate or heavy lines, the band, and your immediate and emotional reaction to it. If you are able to invest, then purchase one of these elite, lifetime watches. There is no better business jewelry investment than an exquisite watch.

However, you can certainly go back to your realistic price range and select a watch that incorporates as many of those top-line design features as possible. The round face is the most classic. The tank shape is also a strong choice. Either a gold, white, or cream-colored face is a good choice. The black leather, suede, or crocodile watch bands are elegant. Or find a clasp-style metal band that combines yellow and white gold. Gold or silver bracelet bands are beautiful and enduring.

Fashion jewelry comes in three categories:

- Fine jewelry—precious metals and gemstones—is the upper echelon of quality. Such pieces represent a long-term investment and should be purchased and worn with care. Gold or sterling pieces can be fashionable for decades. Pearls are classic and worth the investment; however, smaller pearls rather than the standard size are more interesting. Many businesswomen wear diamonds during the day. Other than rings and stud earrings, however, most gemstone pieces are too dressy for the office.
- Bridge jewelry includes quality metal overlay, the finest faux pearls, and natural materials such as semiprecious stones and shells. Turquoise, lapis, malachite, mother-of-pearl, and paua shell have a quiet, tasteful beauty that far exceeds imitation gemstones. Glazed porcelain pieces reflect the colors of a wide variety of garments. The bridge category puts elegant statement pieces within reach of many budgets.
- Costume jewelry was given the mark of approval by Coco Chanel in the early 1900s. After losing several gems during a hectic day at

the shop, she took all her real jewelry to a jeweler and had excellent, paste imitations made of the real pieces. Then she put her real jewels in her safe and wore the copies.

Although it is a sought-after luxury to have all jewelry pieces in 14- or 18-karat, it isn't practical or obtainable for the great majority of business-people. There are hundreds of beautiful, classic costume pieces, especially earrings that add flair and sophistication. Many today are well made, with interesting design details. Some lines even offer a lifetime guarantee of quality. As in all things, it is better to invest in a few nicer items than to accumulate lots of pieces that are basically just "throw-away chic." Bracelets draw attention to lovely, manicured hands. But stay away from clunky bangles or noisy charm bracelets. Shaped cuff-style bracelets in precious metals or quality overlays fit smoothly onto the wrist and convey a tailored, polished message.

Rings should always be 14-karat gold, sterling, or platinum. Limit yourself to one per hand, but a matched wedding set counts as a single ring. Faceted gemstones are perfectly appropriate as are diamond solitaires, pavé diamonds, and baguettes in daytime rings. But leave the oversize dinner rings at home and skip the pinkie rings, too.

Earrings—only one per ear for most industries—are a must to polish a look and to hold attention near the face. Start your collection with a plain gold or silver pair and a pearl set (real or imitation). A button style that fits flat to your earlobe is more businesslike than a hoop. Avoid dangly styles that create distracting movement.

Career earrings should make a statement. But today's look is more compact; gold balls, hoops, or diamond studs have visual presence. Use a coin as a size guideline. Large earrings can range from the size of a dime up to the size of a nickel. If you wear glasses, keep earrings smaller and tailored in styling. Pierced are much more comfortable than clip-on styling.

A pin is a sure-fire way to add interest to a plain garment. Wear it high on your shoulder to lift and lengthen the silhouette. Often a pin placed on a lapel is too near the bust line for a graceful look. A geometric shape in your best metal will work with a variety of clothes. A wearable art piece, a well-constructed fabric flower on a designer suit, or a whimsical motif that relates to one of your hobbies or interests can be a great conversation starter. Pins for your business wardrobe should not be flashy, frilly, or jingly.

A simple strand of pearls adds elegance to business attire. The most versatile length is 18" to 20". Consider the three- or five-strand seed pearl necklace, too, for more options and elegance. If you can't afford the real thing, choose realistic imitations rather than anything oversized or brightly colored. White or pale pink pearls look best on women with cool coloring; creamier colors make warm-toned skin glow.

Business jewelry looks best when selected for aesthetic reasons, not sentimental ones.

"Remember, what is the rage today is a rag tomorrow. Shoes that should be worn by shot-putters, earrings the size of belt buckles, belt buckles the size of earrings—I have seen them all come and go. . . . I know this because I am a pig, and as a pig, I have always stood out."

Miss Piggy, *Miss Piggy's Guide to Life*

Purses/Briefcases

Carrying both a large purse and an oversize briefcase creates an overloaded, disorganized look. Select one or the other. With laptops, PDAs, and cell phones to accommodate, briefcases have become larger. If you choose a briefcase, slip in a small wallet-size purse to carry your personal essentials. If you opt for a purse, carry business papers in a leather notepad or trim portfolio.

Women's briefcases are available in an array of softened, feminized designs. A hard-edged, square-cornered, mannish style looks dated for women in most fields, and it's too heavy filled up with business essentials. Look for a soft-sided case made from genuine leather, preferably in black. It is an excellent briefcase choice because it blends with nearly any wardrobe color. Design details such as perforations, matching topstitching, woven sections, or trim in a contrasting material create a distinctive look.

If you opt for a purse, keep the size moderate (use a sheet of typing paper as a guideline) the style tailored, the color neutral, and the material genuine skin. Although a clutch style is perfectly appropriate, it may not be the most practical choice. A shoulder bag provides greater convenience and is more resistant to purse snatching. Look in a full-length mirror to properly adjust the strap. Some women like it right under the armpit, others about halfway down, but the bag should not rest on the widest part of the hip.

Straps incorporating a gold chain are dressier, as are thinner straps. Save the thicker shoulder straps for very casual bags.

Never overstuff your purse or briefcase. Edit the contents regularly, and carry only what you really need. Put the past years' pictures of the kids in an album. Store a duplicate lipstick in your desk drawer. Carry only a small package of tissues in your car. Reduce the number of credit cards you carry.

A quality purse or briefcase should last for years, so maintain it carefully. The same shop that handles your shoeshine can clean, moisturize, and polish your briefcase when it starts to look scuffed. Don't polish it with black polish. It will come off on your clothing.

Hats

Although some flamboyant entrepreneurs and women in creative fields wear them as a personal trademark, hats are inappropriate for the majority of businesswomen. They make a fairly profound fashion statement and are best reserved for social occasions. The exception is in very cold weather, where a hat is essential to conserve body heat. Select whatever style provides maximum protection with minimum damage to your hairstyle.

Outerwear

The classic trench coat in traditional tan or black has been a basic for years. Designers have updated the classic trench with visible stitching and other fashionable touches, and the traditional jacket has again come to the forefront of outerwear. There are many other styles that offer updated, feminine alternatives. Consider all wool, a cashmere blend, a muted metallic, or a black, shiny belted jacket for added flair.

Whatever the style, be sure the coat fits properly. Select a sleeve style roomy enough to slip on easily over a suit jacket and a hemline long enough to cover all your business skirts and dresses. If your climate demands a heavier winter coat, choose a midcalf tailored wrap or buttoned style. Camel hair, alone or blended with wool, can be attractive and durable. However, 100 percent cashmere, for all its beauty and luxurious feel, may be too fragile for hard everyday use. Black is a beautiful classic. Red also works for day-into-evening versatility. Winter white is lovely, but expensive to maintain. Generally a shade slightly deeper than your hair color is especially flattering.

For casual day, stay with the same classic styling and colors described. Parkas, down jackets, and other sporty outdoor looks don't belong at the office any day of the week.

A fur coat is a questionable choice for business, no matter how cold the weather. Whatever your political opinions on animal rights issues, why risk offending a colleague or potential client sympathetic to that cause? Yet many of our female clients in New York, Chicago, and other very cold cities put a full-length mink coat at the top of their list of essentials. The answer is to use good judgment in wearing animal fur, and have one other warm coat when the climate and other environmental factors demand nonanimal skins.

A pair of sleek leather gloves in black or brown should coordinate easily with your coat. For extra warmth, choose a pair with fur lining. Be sure gloves are long enough to reach beyond the edge of your coat sleeve. Stretchy one-size-fits-all knit gloves are generally too informal for businesswear.

A soft woolen challis scarf or muffler keeps the chill out while it polishes your look. Avoid any synthetic fiber, which will feel more clammy than cozy. Consider indulging yourself with the softness of cashmere in a scarf, where durability is less of an issue. A soft stripe or plaid in related colors will add interest to your solid-colored coat. Drape the scarf to cover the garment underneath, which may not blend as well with your coat color.

Behind the Scenes

Some of the most important accessories for women never see fashion daylight, but these supporting members of the wardrobe team can make or break a professional look. A properly fitted bra can shave years and pounds off a woman's figure. Well-informed salespeople are becoming a rarity, so many women unwittingly fit themselves into the wrong bra. The typical mistake—too large a band size and too small a cup—creates bulges at the armhole and upper edge. The right bra, on the other hand, can enhance a small bust line or minimize a full one. Contact a specialty bra or lingerie shop, or call your favorite department store to get the professional assistance you need.

Underwear, regardless of the style you prefer, should never show a ridge, bulge, or shadow line under your clothes. Look for styles finished with flat lacy elastic instead of the thicker cord elastic. Or consider a panty/pantyhose combination.

Lined skirts don't require a slip, but if you wear one under dresses or soft skirts, be sure it is short enough not to show, but long enough to reach the top of the skirt's hem, preventing a shadow effect.

Shoulder pads work wonders to establish a strong, assertive look and balance upper-body to lower-body proportions. Exaggerated "fullback" looks went out of style decades ago, but a natural squared look is always in style. Jackets, of course, have the padding built in. With more casual knit tops, cotton shirts, and cardigan sweaters, you may need to add your own. Contoured foam pads conform to your shoulder shape and gently cling to the garment fabric, so they can be used interchangeably in a number of garments. Some styles include a flap on the underside to fit around your bra strap for added stability.

A Final Note for Women

Without exception, cheap handbags, acrylic scarves, plastic jewelry, and bargain-priced shoes will diminish everything else that you own. They will be the first to be thrown away or given away in a closet cleaning. If they stay in your wardrobe, they will never add anything; they can only subtract both from your garments and your bank balance. The best rule in purchasing accessories is that none of us can afford to buy cheaply.

grooming

Finally, be increasingly fastidious about your personal grooming . . . it is unattractive on the young and positively shocking on older people.

Geneviève Antoine Dariaux, former directrice
of Nina Ricci in Paris and author of *Elegance*

grooming is an irrefutable signal to the world indicating how you value yourself. You can spend a small fortune on clothing and undermine the entire effect with greasy hair, chipped nails, or stained teeth. Grooming is made up of dozens of small details, but they all come together to make one powerful statement. If you value yourself enough to pay attention to those details, others are more likely to value you, too. Some grooming issues are gender-specific. Others such as hand care, dental hygiene, and controlling perspiration are important for every professional.

Hands

Hands are a highly visible part of your professional image every time you shake hands, sign a contract, demonstrate software, or pass the salt. Keep them scrupulously clean. If your hobby is gardening or tinkering with cars, use protective gloves or push bar soap underneath the nails before starting a messy project. This prevents tough stains around and under your nails.

Frequent application of hand cream will prevent dryness and chapping. So will the consistent wearing of gloves in cold weather. Dry hands look as bad as they feel. Try to get a manicure weekly, either professionally or in your own home. Having a standing appointment for a professional manicure is a good way to acknowledge yourself and carve out an hour for light business reading, meditating, or just being silent. Otherwise, create a regular time for nail care in your home.

For men, one of the marks of a true gentleman is well-groomed hands with short, clean nails and no roughness of the cuticle or skin. Lightly buffed nails are an option, as is clear nail polish.

Scarlett O'Hara was wrong on at least one count. If she wanted to perpetuate the idea that she was a lady of leisure, not of labor, she should have worn gloves to cover her callused, hardworking hands when she visited Rhett Butler in jail after the war. People do notice hands.

For women, hands are equally important and require a little more attention. Short, bitten nails, ragged cuticles, hardened calluses, and chipped polish detract dramatically from everything else. So do excessively long, acrylic nails, as well as oddball colors such as purple, yellow, and blue. Airbrushed designs and nail jewelry may be fashionable at times, but there is no place for them in a work setting.

The ability to grow long, strong nails is part genetic and part regular maintenance. There are a number of products available that will strengthen nails and allow many women to transition from silk wrap or acrylic nails to their own natural nails. For other women, these products just don't work. Part of the reason is the shape of the nail bed. A very flat nail bed doesn't produce a curved, strong nail. A more rounded nail bed will produce nail growth that is more resilient to hard surface contact without breaking.

Whether you opt for natural or acrylic nails, there are three guidelines:

1. Nails need to match in length and be approximately ⅛" to ½" beyond the tips of the fingers.
2. Nails can be buffed or polished. A high, buffed gloss is beautiful and strengthening. A white-tipped French manicure looks fresh,

clean, and sophisticated but needs to be applied by a professional. Polish can be clear, a lightly tinted pink, or peach. Shades of rose, pink, coral, or red can work but are not as versatile. Lighter colors are also much easier to maintain and appear fresher. Darker colors require more frequent touchups.

3. Create a regular nail care schedule and stick to it religiously.

Teeth

Americans are among the most teeth-conscious people on earth. We take for granted the general availability of high-quality dental care; therefore, we feel surprise or even revulsion when someone has unhealthy, unattractive teeth.

Basic dental hygiene is essential. Brush at least twice a day. Many dentists recommend the variety of electric toothbrushes readily available. If you haven't already developed the flossing habit, start now. You will probably be able to keep your own teeth your entire life if you floss regularly because gum disease, not tooth decay, is responsible for most tooth loss. Dentists indicate it is even more important than brushing. Flossing will also eliminate 90 percent of mouth odor because decayed food is removed more efficiently. Keep an extra toothbrush and toothpaste in your desk drawer to use after lunch or before an important meeting. Complete your dental care program with twice-yearly professional cleaning.

If you have teeth that regularly retain broccoli, pepper, parsley or other foods, be sure to keep toothpicks or floss with you to use privately in the restroom immediately after eating. Nothing spoils the impact of your image quicker than having some spinach stuck between your teeth during a business lunch.

Orthodontics has come a long way since the days of "tin grins." Adults who need braces to correct overbite problems or crooked teeth appreciate the new designs of braces made from clear materials that are virtually invisible. The results are well worth the investment. One client discovered that his company's new dental plan would pay for the braces he had wanted since his teens. The two-year process not only improved his teeth dramatically, but in the process reshaped his entire face into more pleasing contours. A two-year investment is well worth a lifetime of straight teeth and the elimination of headaches, chewing problems, and other issues that come from the misalignment of the teeth and jaw.

Bleaching can correct serious discoloration. Used extensively by celebrities around the world, whitening has gained popularity with the general population. Bleaching products are available from drugstores, but your dentist can provide more permanent bleaching. For more damaged teeth, bonding, porcelain veneers, or crowns may be the answer. These procedures actually create the appearance of new teeth. The procedures range from $100 to $800 per tooth, but the results can look perfectly natural when done by an experienced dentist with aesthetic awareness. In some cases dental insurance will pay for all or part of the cost. Even if insurance doesn't cover the cost, improving the appearance of problem teeth is a permanent and visible investment in your professional future.

Body Odor

A daily shower or bath is an obvious part of everyone's personal routine. It provides wonderful emotional benefits as well. Even if you don't perspire excessively, a good underarm deodorant is a must. To control more difficult odor problems, clean under your arms with an astringent, which kills bacteria. Add an antiperspirant and a deodorant body powder. For both men and women, keeping underarm hair shaved or closely trimmed eliminates a breeding ground for bacteria. Body odor will be intensified by caffeine, spicy foods, and stressful situations.

"There must be a few things a hot bath won't cure, but there aren't many."

Sarah Ban Breathnach, author of *Simple Abundance*

Wearing natural-fiber garments that allow air to circulate and perspiration to evaporate will also cut down on wetness and the resulting odor. Hang clothes outside of the closet to air out. Consider absorbent underarm shields when perspiration and the subsequent staining are particular problems.

Grooming Basics for Men

Good grooming is as important for men as for women, and now men have a wide range of cosmetics products and hairstyle options once available only to women. Lax grooming standards project an image that implies a person might be inattentive to professional details as well.

Facial Hair

Overwhelmingly the most-asked question from men in our seminars relates to hair—on the head and on the face. Although standards have relaxed somewhat over the years, our advice still stands: the safest look for a businessman is a clean-shaven face. Everyone reacts positively to this look, whereas many people have negative reactions toward men with mustaches and beards. Facial hair may imply rebellion against authority, appear to cover up or mask facial expressions, or simply detract from a man's appearance. It is a natural harbor for food, lint, and anything else it can attract.

Going . . .

Gone!

Going . . .

Gone!

The standard is not the same for every man and every field of work. The arts, advertising, social services, and academia are far more accepting of well-groomed facial hair. But the same look, especially a beard, could seriously undermine the credibility of a banker, CPA, salesperson, or investment broker.

There are other considerations to the wearing of facial hair as well. A man with a receding chin, a weak upper lip, or a cleft palate could minimize these characteristics with a beard or mustache. Some men gain a distinguished look from a short, extremely well-trimmed beard framing their face. Other young executives can look more mature with facial hair. In fact, several well-known consulting firms encourage their employees to grow mustaches, if they are thick and well groomed, to counteract their youthful appearance.

The clean-shaven look is always safest and usually the most attractive in business for the majority of men.

Under any circumstances, however, a beard or mustache must be attractive and meticulously groomed to be acceptable:

- A scrawny, sparse, or light-colored growth won't enhance anyone's appearance.
- Facial hair that grows in a dramatically different color than the hair on the head can look odd and distracting.
- Unorthodox styles such as the "soul patch," goatees, and "Fu Manchu" beards are unacceptable in all traditional business environments.
- A mustache or beard must be shampooed regularly.

With facial hair, extra care must be used when eating. Wipe your mouth after every bite; few sights are more unappealing than food trapped on a hairy upper lip.

Hair

An out-of-date hairstyle suggests that a man is out of touch with new developments in other areas as well. Check men's fashion magazines about once a year, and if you can't find at least one photo of a style similar to yours, it's time for an update. Like most things, you get what you pay for. An $8 haircut is probably going to look like it.

Since biblical times, hair has established itself as important and almost mystical in its power. Samson lost his strength when he lost his hair. His strength was regained when his hair grew back.

The specific gender of your stylist has no bearing on the quality of the haircut, but typically a hair professional whose clients are mostly of a single gender has more highly developed skills. A good stylist will consider facial shape and hair texture as well as current hair fashions. Make a standing appointment at three- to four-week intervals to maintain a consistent look. If you are looking for a good stylist, observe the styling of your coworkers, clients, customers, or best friends. When you find a cut that you admire, compliment that person and ask where he gets his hair cut.

Ask the stylist's advice about hair products, such as gel or spray to keep unruly hair under control. You also will need a shampoo and a conditioner formulated for daily use with your hair type.

After each shampoo, gently blot out excess moisture. Hair is weakest when wet, so excess rubbing with a towel can cause breakage. Then comb it into shape and let the hair air-dry, or blow it dry on a medium or low heat setting to define the shape and add fullness. Excessive heat can dry or damage hair. End the blow-drying with a few moments of cool air to set the style and close the cuticle on the hair shaft.

Nothing is more ridiculous than the comb-over. Trying to replace hair on top of the head by creatively moving it from another part of the head just doesn't fool anyone. A natural hairline is a vastly more self-confident choice.

before&now

before While this look can work for casual situations, it conveys a laid-back, possibly too easygoing appearance that may prohibit significant advancement. **now** Sharp and well groomed, his hair and clean-shaven appearance will open doors and promote opportunity. He has the polish required as a high-potential candidate in any organization.

There is nothing inherently unattractive about baldness. It is not fatal, professionally or socially. Many very successful and attractive men carry off this look with distinction. The best choice is a short, neat, well-trimmed style, working with whatever amount of hair you have. Don't wait months between haircuts believing that it won't matter and no one will notice. Less hair requires regular maintenance, too.

If you are determined to supplement the hair quantity that nature supplies you, be a cautious consumer. The market is filled with toupees, chemical treatments, hair transplants, and hair replacement "systems." Thoroughly investigate any product and the company that provides it. Insist on talking with satisfied customers before you make a final decision. Expect to pay a high price for any option with a natural look.

"An up-to-date, precision haircut can contribute to a youthful appearance and sometimes disguise thinning hair. Recently, one of my friends, a thirty-something, balding attorney, went on a ten-day European cruise. When he returned, his office was buzzing because he looked great and appeared to have more hair. Someone even asked if he had hair transplants. He laughed and explained while on the ship, he went to get a "trim." Being a friendly, talkative guy, he didn't really notice his trim was becoming a new, more flattering hairstyle that camouflaged his thinning hair—until it was finished. His wife noticed immediately, as did his friends and colleagues, because he projected a more confident and youthful look."

Marge Mastromarchi, corporate image consultant

Hair Color

A dusting of gray at the temples is widely considered to give a man a distinguished look. However, when the gray is an unflattering shade of yellow or creates an aged appearance, modern hair-coloring products can work wonders.

Work with a professional to get the color right; then consider the savings and convenience of maintaining the look yourself at home. There are a number of in-home products that color gray with several different subtle shades. This will eliminate gray without creating a flat, all-one-color "helmet" look.

Hair-coloring products come in three varieties:

- A rinse washes away with the next shampoo or can run when you perspire.
- A semipermanent color lasts through six to eight shampoos, an ideal way to experiment with color.
- Permanent color stays on the hair until it grows out. The only upkeep this option requires is to color the new growth about every four to six weeks.

Eyebrows and Nose Hair

Unruly eyebrows or brows that grow together into one continuous line across the forehead create a Neanderthal appearance and a facial expression that seems perpetually angry. Enhance your appearance by thinning and controlling them in one of these ways:

- Undergo electrolysis to remove the excess hairs permanently.
- Keep a regular appointment with a cosmetologist to wax and shape your brows.
- Tweeze the extra hairs yourself. Warm and moisturize the skin, then pluck with a quick motion using sturdy tweezers. Rub baby teething gel on the area to deaden the skin and minimize discomfort.
- If occasional hairs are very long, comb them up toward your forehead and trim them individually, or have your stylist do it.
- If your brows are unruly, brush a clear styling gel, available at cosmetic counters, through brows to hold them in a controlled shape.

Few people will tell you that your hair, either inside or on top of your nose, is unappealing. But the truth is, it can be extremely unattractive and distracting. If you prefer home maintenance, tweeze on the top of the nose and trim on the inside. Also consider going to a salon that offers those services.

Skin Care

Men have a built-in advantage in skin care because daily shaving is a natural exfoliator, regularly removing dead, dry cells from the skin's surface.

Some men experience razor burn, an irritation caused by soap or shaving cream residue on the skin. Correct the situation by changing brands of shaving cream/gel or razor blades and carefully rinsing thoroughly after each shave. Triple-blade razors also help reduce skin irritation. The choice of electric or safety razors is strictly a matter of personal preference. Some men with thick, curly facial hair often prefer electric shavers—it's easier on their skin. Men with thick, dark hair may want to keep an extra razor at the office to get rid of five o'clock shadow before an evening business event.

A facial cleanser or soap and a light moisturizer formulated for your skin type (dry, normal, oily, or combination) are the most important skin care products for the average businessman. For troublesome conditions, such as acne or ingrown hairs, consult a dermatologist or an aesthetician. If you have facial scarring from adolescent acne problems or want to get rid of wrinkles and sun splotches, investigate laser resurfacing or micro-dermabrasion treatments. They can remove or dramatically minimize scars, pockmarks, wrinkles, and discoloration. There is a wide range of healing time from skin treatments—some are so unobtrusive that you will be back in the office within a few hours; others will require a week or more of healing.

Fragrance

Wear colognes and heavily scented after-shave products with a light touch. Your own nose, accustomed to the scent, is not an accurate judge of how much is too much. You can't go wrong without a fragrance, but you can make a mistake with one that is overpowering or offensive to a client.

Grooming Basics for Women

Hair

Creating the most attractive hairstyle is like creating a masterful piece in your wardrobe; it has to fit your face, be appropriate to your hair's texture, and fit your pocketbook and your time resources in the morning. A chiffon business suit would never work, no matter how hard you try! If you are spending more than twenty minutes in the morning on your hair or are constantly unhappy with its appearance, here are some ideas and guidance.

In the business world, an effective hairstyle:

- Is extremely well cut and shaped
- Looks natural and is never an artificial, overly sprayed "do"
- Flatters the individual's facial shape
- Is a color that looks natural and is flattering to the skin tone
- Requires minimum maintenance in the morning

A precision cut is the key to a hairstyle that works. If your current stylist isn't producing that precision, shop around for one who can. Ask for recommendations from women whose hair you admire, especially if their hair's characteristics are similar to your own. If you are the cautious type, make an initial appointment for a shampoo and style, just to get acquainted. Observe the stylist's other clients, as well as your own results. If you are comfortable with the stylist's reputation, then move ahead with a cut and color.

before&now

before With casual, messy hair and no makeup, this look won't create career opportunities. **now** Polished and professional, her makeup and hair contribute to her confidence and attractiveness.

In determining the cut, be sure the stylist is as informed about you as possible. Have him or her analyze your hair while it is dry. If you have changed your hair fairly frequently over the years, bring along photos that reflect these changes, and together you can determine which styles worked and why. You can also bring along photos from magazines of styles you like, but recognize that they are only guidelines. Before picking up the scissors, your stylist should understand:

- How much time and money you are willing to spend on your hair
- How adept (or clumsy) you are with dryers, round brushes, curling irons, and other styling tools
- How often you're willing to come in for a trim or color
- How conservative or creative your career field is
- What you usually wear for work
- What past cuts you've loved or hated

before&now

before Education and refinement are telegraphed in many ways. One is through attention to hair, makeup, and general grooming details. Here, her hair is too unsophisticated and she needs the understated elegance of well-applied makeup. **now** Smooth and refined, her cut, color, and styling are well complemented by natural makeup that enhances her eyes and smoothes out her skin.

The exact length for business hair is a matter of personal taste as long as you avoid inappropriate extremes.

Longtime *Vogue* editor Diana Vreeland described beauty simply as consistency. The easiest style to maintain day after day is one that works with your hair's natural tendencies. Forcing your unwilling hair into submission every morning is a battle you simply can't win.

> "I don't know any woman personally who really loves her hair, just women who cope. Hair is a living, powerful, mercurial, metaphysical energy force to be respected, reckoned with, and reconciled to. Hair humbles us, and we need to make peace with it."
>
> Sarah Ban Breathnach, author of *Simple Abundance*

Hairstyles can visually balance facial contours. A very long, narrow face looks fuller and more graceful with a medium-length haircut, soft bangs, and side fullness. A round face appears thinner in a cut with narrow sides and fullness on top.

before&now

before This hairstyle has all the lines going down, which creates a somewhat matronly look. Although she has naturally attractive features, makeup will make a huge difference **now** Fresh, fun hair, more defined eyebrows, soft eyeliner, and neutral lipstick create a winning and successful look.

Once you have established a cut you love, adopt a regular schedule for maintenance. Book your next haircut before you leave the salon, rather than waiting until you desperately need a trim. Many salons offer their regular customers no-cost bang or nape trims to keep hair looking tidy between cuts.

Shampoo

Wash and condition your hair as often as needed to keep it looking fresh. Use a quality shampoo, formulated for your hair type. Hair is weakest when wet, so lather just once and rinse thoroughly. Change shampoo and conditioner brands periodically to eliminate any problem with a buildup of ingredients on your hair.

Use a light, non-oily conditioner after each shampoo to protect the hair, add shine, and combat static electricity. Many conditioners work best with heat. Twice a month, wrap your head with a warm, moist towel or sit under the dryer for a few minutes before rinsing out the conditioner. The cuticles of the hair shafts will open up and allow better penetration.

before&now

before A wispier bang and more height at the crown will dramatically change the shape of her face. Makeup will give her a glow and freshness. **now** A great haircut is one of the best investments a professional can make. The changes in styling and makeup are dramatic.

Hair Color

"Does she or doesn't she?" Only her hairdresser may know for sure, but it's a pretty safe bet she does. In fact, over 80 percent of American women color their hair at home or in salons. That percentage will continue to increase.

Some hair color changes add lively highlights to dull natural colors, but the most common objective is to cover gray. George Patzer, a marketing professor at the University of Northern Iowa, has conducted several studies on physical attractiveness. "Like it or not, gray hair still has a negative impact on how a person is perceived," he concludes. "In many people's minds, gray equals old and old equals incompetent."

Hairstylists remind us that roots are what's down inside your scalp, not what's showing.

Selecting the right color and the right process is essential. Most experts agree that the most natural look comes from staying within two or three shades of your own hair color. Our skin and eyes become paler in color as our hair grays. If your hair is more than 50 percent gray, avoid a harsh look by choosing a new color about two shades lighter than the natural color you remember from years past. In any case, be sure a new color or highlight blends with the other elements of your coloring. Choose more golden or reddish tones if your skin and eyes are warm, more ash tones if your coloring is cool.

Whether you choose salon coloring or prefer to color your hair at home, you have several processes from which to choose:

- If your hair is 10 percent to 20 percent gray, try a semipermanent color. These products contain virtually no peroxide, so they gently coat the hair shaft to enrich your natural color while blending in gray. They fade in three to four weeks, avoiding visible regrowth.
- If your hair is about a third gray, opt for a long-lasting semipermanent color. A small amount of peroxide makes their color last longer—five to six weeks.
- To cover half or more gray usually requires a permanent color product that penetrates all the way to the cortex (center) of each hair. The color won't wash out, but will require touchups for regrowth. Don't wait too long between touchups thinking that no one will see the

regrowth on your crown. Anyone standing up while you are seated will see the gray hair before you do.

- Highlighting the hair usually incorporates using aluminum foil and sectioning off small amounts of hair. On each section, a lighter or contrasting color is applied. This produces the most natural, lightened look but requires more time and is more expensive than one-color processing. However because regrowth tends to look very natural, touchups are needed only every few months.
- Low-lighting the hair also incorporates foils and is very effective for gray or white hair. On the sectioned-off hair, a darker, not a lighter, color is applied. This produces a very natural effect to cover gray hair.

When you buy an at-home coloring product, realize that "what you see is not necessarily what you get." The photo on the box shows the result of applying that product to hair with all its natural pigment removed. Consult the manufacturer's chart to see the approximate result of using that product over your current hair color.

"Your hair isn't a toy; don't play with it."
"Clean is always sexy."
"The wind should be able to move your hair."

Paula Ganzi Licata, journalist

Because a textured hair shaft is more susceptible to breakage and damage, African-American women need to use extra-gentle ethnic lines of hair-coloring products. They also should seek out stylists who have extensive experience in textured hair.

For home hair coloring, follow the instructions to the letter. Don't skip the recommended test strand. It's the only way to determine exactly how long to leave the color on your hair. And do a skin-patch test to ensure you're not allergic to chemicals in the product.

Color-enhanced hair requires special care. Special shampoo and conditioning products are designed to clean the hair without stripping away color. Rinse hair with a paste of baking soda and water after swimming; then shampoo it to remove damaging salt and chlorine. Switch to a wide-toothed comb to untangle wet hair without unnecessary stress and breakage.

Perms and Thermal Restructuring

Tight, frizzy perms are a very dated look. For more body and volume, consider using color, which widens the hair shaft and makes the hair appear fuller, as do volumizing products sold at salons and any drugstore. Curling irons, Velcro rollers, and larger, round brushes also produce the look of more hair. Most salons and pharmacies carry quality styling sprays and gels that add body and texture.

However, if you are absolutely committed to a permanent, consider a softer body wave for enhancing and thickening the hair. Because of the strong chemicals involved, have a salon professional do the permanent. The expertise of a trained stylist is worth the investment. Spend the extra time to have your stylist teach you to style your newly textured hair. You don't want to end up with a frizzy, haystack look.

On the other hand, thermal restructuring will take thick, curly, bushy hair and literally turn it into soft, straight hair that is humidity resistant. The process takes about eight hours and costs about $800, but the results are dramatic, and the time saved each morning is equally dramatic.

Skin Care

It is said that women in their twenties have the skin God gave them; women in their thirties have the skin their genes gave them; and women over forty have the skin they deserve, based on how they have cared for it and the amount of sun they were exposed to.

You are never too young . . . or too old to begin taking care of your skin.

Clean, healthy skin is the best thing you can "wear" on your face—work time or any time. Because we are viewed from the neck up more than 75 percent of the time, it makes sense to pay attention to the way our faces look. The most elaborate makeup application can't compensate for skin that is poorly cared for.

Each of the four skin types—dry, normal, oily, and combination—has its own characteristics and advantages. Normal skin in relatively trouble-free, but it shouldn't be neglected or taken for granted. Normal skin tends to dry out with age, so it's wise to pay attention to potential trouble spots—

around the eyes and at the corners of the mouth—before they show the first signs of wrinkles.

Oily skin is more prone to blemishes, but it wrinkles less easily. A common mistake is to overcleanse oily skin with harsh alkaline soaps that can destroy the skin's natural protective acid mantle. (Attempts to dry the surface of oily skin will send a message to the brain that something is wrong and more oil is needed.) The result is a too-alkaline breeding ground for bacteria that will aggravate the skin's propensity to blemishes. Instead, apply a slightly acidic cleanser with your fingers or a fresh washcloth.

Dry skin, a natural consequence of aging, is a problem for many women over thirty. The skin gradually loses moisture and natural oils. Skin care products containing humectants draw moisture from the air onto the skin, and emollients keep the skin soft.

Combination skin includes patches of dry, irritated skin, coupled with patches of oily skin usually around the area of the face known as the T-zone—between the eyebrows, down the nose. There are now many products dedicated to combination skin, but your best bet is to choose something formulated for sensitive skin, with few fragrances or additives.

A quality skin care regimen is really just four simple steps:

- Cleansing morning and night removes makeup, environmental pollutants, and the oil, perspiration, and debris from your skin's metabolism. Bath soap can dry the skin and leaves a filmy residue much like the kind you see on your shower walls. Choose a water-soluble cream, lotion, or complexion bar that lifts dirt, and then rinses away with warm water.
- Toning follows cleansing, to close pores and re-establish the skin's normal protective pH balance, which is disrupted by the cleansing process. Choose a toner (or astringent) matched to your skin type, apply with a cotton pad, and enjoy the fresh, tingly feeling.
- Exfoliating removes dead cells from the skin's surface, either periodically with an abrasive scrub or daily with one of the new alpha-hydroxy acid products.
- Moisturizing softens the skin and attracts moisture from the air to help keep skin supple and wrinkle-free. Even oily skin usually needs a light oil-free moisturizer.

If you find yourself too exhausted at bedtime to follow a conscientious skin regimen, try doing the whole process earlier in the evening, perhaps after dinner. At the very least, you should be cleansing your skin and using daily facial moisturizer.

Which brand of skin care products should you use? The options are extensive and impressive, but cost is not always a sure indicator of results. All manufacturers shop in the same "supermarket" for their ingredients, and the FDA monitors the standards for purity, quality, and truth in labeling. The real success of any skin care line is the regularity with which it is used, along with taking the time to match the products with your skin type.

Shop for a coordinated group of products that offers a sensible strategy (cleanser, toner, exfoliant, and moisturizer both for the face and underneath the eyes) at a price you are willing to pay. These products need to be replaced more frequently than color products such as eye shadows, blush, and lipstick, so consider the overall investment. Most department store brands have samples you can test for a few days before buying an entire system.

> "A common occurrence for women in their forties is for their skin to gradually become blotchy and oily, even if it wasn't before. Sometimes 'adult acne' occurs. This is a result of skin cell turnover slowing down, and dead skin cells, makeup, and debris clog the pores. These changes in the skin are based on hormone changes and are aggravated by stress. This is when exfoliants, such as fruit acids and enzymes, can help speed up cell turnover and help keep the skin clear."
>
> Adele Casanova, president of The Winning Edge

Anti-aging
Skin aging incorporates five distinctive factors:

- Intrinsic aging—loss of skin resilience, which begins about age seventy
- Sleep lines—creases from pressing the face against a pillow
- Gravity—skin pulled downward and drooping
- Expression lines—creases from repetitive smiling, frowning, and squinting
- Photoaging—damage to skin caused by sun exposure, believed to be the overwhelming cause of visible aging in American women today

Face-lifts, collagen injections, Botox, laser resurfacing, and chemical peels are just some of the weapons in the dermatologist's anti-aging arsenal. Three options to minimize aging also are widely available:

- Sun protection is essential on an everyday basis, not just for picnics or a trip to the beach. Sunscreen products block the ultraviolet rays that cause skin damage, aging, and cancer. Many product lines incorporate a sunscreen into a moisturizer or a makeup base, ensuring daily application.

- Retin A, approved in 1971 as a prescription treatment for acne, is now also approved as a nonprescription treatment for photoaging skin. It stimulates the production of collagen proteins to repair damaged skin. On the minus side, Retin A also causes irritation and redness, and increases sun sensitivity.

- Alpha-hydroxy acids (AHAs), particularly glycolic acid, release the chemical bonds that hold dead cells onto the skin's surface so the skin can nourish itself more effectively and replenish itself more quickly. As a result, skin looks smoother, fine lines are minimized, and uneven pigmentation is diminished. Some dermatologists also believe that AHAs "appear to regenerate collagen and elastin proteins." Look for AHAs on the labels of cleansers, moisturizers, and other skin care products.

"The most beautiful makeup of a woman is passion. But cosmetics are easier to buy."

Yves Saint Laurent, fashion designer

Makeup

There is no such thing as a woman who doesn't look better with makeup. Makeup conceals flaws, accents attractive features, creates a creamy, polished look, and should be worn by every businesswoman every day. Too often, in pursuit of a "natural look," career women skip makeup altogether. They see other women with garish, overstated makeup and assume that's the only way cosmetics can look. In fact, well-chosen colors, deftly applied, look more "natural" than a woman's naked face.

Some women omit makeup simply because they don't know how to apply it and don't know where to turn for training. The typical department-store makeover is geared to product sales rather than education. But many salons, spas, and image consultants offer a true makeup lesson, in which the client applies cosmetics under the instructor's guidance. The lesson normally includes an illustrated worksheet that itemizes the color choices and application steps. Like any new skill, makeup application may feel awkward at first, so consider the first seven to ten days as practice time.

Marge Mastromarchi, president of Training Dynamics, Inc., states, "As an image consultant for over ten years, I have worked with many professional women striving to balance their business, social, and personal lives. The truly smart ones were clever enough to uncover one of the secrets to appearing healthy, energetic, and in control—the right makeup! A few color and camouflage techniques can quickly brighten our appearance and our attitude. When a woman projects a healthy, positive image to herself and others, her whole presence speaks 'success.' Appropriately applied makeup is an easy way to give ourselves a boost and project an image of competence and youthful energy at any age." A *USA Today* poll listed the number-one image mistake for women as "too much makeup" and the number-two mistake as—you guessed it— "too little makeup."

There are hundreds of variations on makeup techniques. The following steps create a conservative business face in seven to ten minutes. A polished look requires two components:

- Create a neutral background by perfecting skin tones with a matching base, apply a concealer if necessary, followed by powder after all other products have been applied.
- Emphasize features with eye shadow, mascara, pencils, blush, and lip color. There's nothing wrong with owning an extensive palette of makeup colors, but a single assortment chosen to complement your personal coloring can meet all your needs efficiently.

Base (foundation) conceals blotches, discoloration, and imperfections, so the skin becomes a proper background for the rest of your makeup.

Choose a shade matched closely to your natural skin color. Dot it onto your forehead, cheeks, nose, and chin, then blend sideways, with fingers, not a sponge, from midpoints on the face to the hairline or jaw line. (Sponges absorb too much product and fingers allow a better application.) If you prefer not to wear foundation, different cosmetic lines offer alternatives in the form of powder/cream combinations that are light and long-lasting. The key to using any foundation effectively is to make sure you blend beyond your jaw line. Makeup can look too obvious if it stops before the jaw line, creating a contrast against the natural skin tone.

If you need to cover blemishes and lighten under-eye circles, purchase a concealer brush and use your foundation as your concealer. It is much more natural.

Blush adds a healthy glow and defines facial contours. Cream blush works best on dry or normal skin, powder blush on oily or combination

before&now

before It is rare that a woman is more attractive without makeup. Almost every woman gains a great advantage in confidence and composure with the color and the enhancement of naturally applied makeup. Color comes from lipstick and blush; enhancement comes from brow pencil, eyeliner, and mascara. Camouflage comes from eye shadow and foundation. **now** Sophisticated and confident, six products—foundation, blush, eye shadow, eyeliner, mascara, and lipstick—applied with good quality brushes, take about seven to ten minutes to put on each morning. The effect lasts all day!

skin. Choose colors based on your personal undertones. Golden, tawny, and peachy shades work well on warm undertone coloring. For cool undertone, choose pink, burgundy, or plum. Strong personal coloring can support a brighter blush color, but soft delicate coloring demands a paler blush shade. Apply blush high on the cheekbones to visually lift the face and frame the eye area, or move it across the nose to create a healthy, "sun-kissed" look on pale skin. Women of color generally need golden undertones. Blend carefully, so you see a subtle glow of color rather than an obvious stripe. Reapply pressed powder over blush to blend and soften.

Eyes

Eyes are a natural focal point of the face—a center of communications. Enhancing them not only makes a woman more attractive, but also encourages others to make eye contact more readily and sustain eye contact longer.

Begin with a base of neutral shadow color closely matched to your skin tone. Applying a shadow primer on the eyelid before applying shadow protects the skin from the drying properties of powder eye shadows and keeps the shadows looking fresh longer. Choose a shadow in a matte finish rather than frosted or glittery. Apply it to the entire lid, lashes to brow, with a natural brush or a sponge applicator. Accent the crease with a darker neutral shade applied just below the brow bone. The color should be in the same family as your base shadow. For extra emphasis, add a color accent at the outer corner of the eye. Select either a softened version of your eye color or its complement (color wheel opposite). For example:

Eye color	Repeat	Complement
Blue	Dusty gray-blue	Burgundy or copper
Golden brown	Bronze	Smoky plum
Yellow-green	Olive	Plum

Keep all eye shadow colors muted and dusty rather than bright. Women of color might want to use more intense shades than those with paler coloring.

The single, most important step in applying eye shadow is to blend the colors together well. Use a shadow brush or sponge applicator lightly coated with the base shadow to blend the other colors. The finished effect should show shading and contours, rather than distinct areas of specific colors. If you achieve a "sleepy/bedroom" look, you have probably gone too far in your eye makeup application.

A soft pencil liner adds definition to the eyes. Select a neutral color such as charcoal gray or chestnut brown. Sketch along the base of the upper lashes from inner corner to the outer corner. Buff the color line slightly with a cotton swab to soften the look or use eye shadow and a very fine bone bristle brush. Many makeup lines now offer special two-in-one designs with eyeliner and a "smudge tip" on one stick. This helps soften the liner and eliminates the need for cotton swabs.

Curling gives a fuller appearance to lashes and opens up the eye area. Position a clean lash curler right at the base of dry lashes (wet lashes are more susceptible to breakage), and squeeze gently for ten seconds.

Finish lashes with two or three thin coats of mascara. Black is fine for women with very dark hair, but most blonds, brunettes, and redheads look more natural wearing dark brown. Skip brightly colored novelty mascara. How natural can royal blue lashes look? Stroke mascara lightly and evenly from lash base to tip on top lashes. Without adding mascara to the applicator, stroke a very light coat onto lower lashes.

Mascara is the most contamination-prone of all cosmetic products. Replace yours at least every ninety days. Save the applicator from the discarded tube, rinse it thoroughly with antibacterial soap, and use it to separate the lashes and remove any clumps of wet mascara.

Brows form a natural frame for the eye and lend expression to the entire face. The best brow look is a natural one, but sometimes nature needs a helping hand. Judiciously tweeze any stragglers below the arch or across the bridge of your nose. An application of baby teething gel will numb the brow area and make tweezing less uncomfortable. If you have some long, unruly hairs, brush them straight up and trim them individually to a more manageable length. Salon waxing is an alternative for a very clean brow look.

Fill in sparse areas or add color to pale brows with a light application of brown eye shadow, or using a special eyebrow pencil. Choose a matching shade to blend with darker brows. Women with blond, white, or gray hair should choose a color just slightly darker than their hair. Brush the color on with a brow brush, using short feathery strokes.

Lips

Lips are second only to eyes in creating your "look," yet many women fail to appreciate the potential. A surprising number balk at wearing lipstick at all because it is so visual, not blended like other cosmetics. Other women apply lipstick in the morning, and then never bother to reapply it. Yet without lipstick, half the face seems to disappear.

Using a lip pencil every time you apply lipstick will make the lipstick appear to stay on, even after eating. Putting a touch of foundation or powder on your lips prior to applying lipstick will also help hold the color. New products on the market literally stay all day, only requiring the addition of clear lip-gloss.

The extra effort required to keep lipstick fresh pays off in a brighter, more attractive face and moister, less chapped lips. It also defines the mouth, which is where people often focus when you are speaking. If you still feel uncomfortable wearing lipstick, try a colored lip-gloss (without a high-shine finish) to achieve the same look. Coordinate your lip color with your personal color undertones and your level of brightness:

	Cool Undertones	Warm Undertones
Light	Pink, plum, light red-pink, light browns	Coral, peach, light warm red, golden browns
Dark/Bright	Bright pink, burgundy, blue-red, rich browns	Bronze, rust, warm red, tawny browns

A lip liner just slightly darker than your lipstick gives more precise shape and enhances staying power. Sketch in the natural lip outline, then fill in the lip area with small cross-strokes and blend with your pinkie. Apply lipstick with a lip brush for better control and a lighter coating. Applying your foundation to your lips before applying lipstick will also ensure that your lipstick does not fade as quickly.

When women don't wear makeup, most generally avoid looking at themselves in a reflection. When they do wear makeup, they generally enjoy looking in the mirror. So it isn't really a matter of vanity. It is a matter of self-care and self-esteem.

Keep a spare lipstick in your desk drawer and another in your briefcase for discreet midday touchups. Of course, never apply lipstick during a meeting or at your restaurant table.

Fragrance

Fragrances evoke strong emotional responses. Part of the reason is that the olfactory sense is located in the right side of the brain, the part that controls emotions and creativity. Aromatherapy has been studied for centuries and claims to help ease stress and enhance feelings of well-being.

Many businesswomen feel undressed without their favorite daytime fragrance. They consider it the finishing touch—their feminine, invisible, elegant signature. Others avoid fragrance because they don't enjoy it or others around them don't enjoy it.

An acquaintance of ours wore an expensive new fragrance to work and was flattered when an important new client commented on it, even mentioning the perfume by name. She was flattered, that is, until the client mumbled with obvious distaste, "My ex-wife wore that every day."

The safest advice is not to wear any fragrance for business, but that's not a lot of fun. Consider choosing a light, fresh scent, and apply it very sparingly. Apply the fragrance before you dress to avoid staining or damaging fine fabrics. And air your clothes after wearing so that today's fragrance doesn't cling to the jacket and clash with next Wednesday's new cologne. Many bath products, skin care items, and hair products have distinctive fragrances. Search out fragrance-free brands to avoid a clash of multiple smells.

"For the sense of smell, almost more than any other, has the power to recall memories, and it's a pity that we use it so little."

Rachel Carson

part three

business casual dress

chapter seven

the new business casual look

I base my fashion taste on what doesn't itch.

Gilda Radner

today, the ins and outs of business dressing are being discussed more energetically than ever, stimulated by the trend of dress-down days and business casual weeks. The corporate world is loosening its tie and rolling up its sleeves, and it is clear that casual business dress is here to stay.

The trend has its roots in the 1980s and 1990s in Silicon Valley, where youthful computer geniuses saw no need to conform to traditional ideas about business wardrobe. As the influence of their cutting-edge technology expanded within the larger business community, so did the influence of their clothing choices.

More employees telecommute, working from in-home computer hookups. More professionals communicate via e-mail rather than face-to-face. The need to dress up every day appears to be less important.

Manufacturers of casual clothing happily jumped on this popular bandwagon. Levi Strauss, maker of the popular Dockers brand, commissioned Evans Research to document the trend over a decade ago. The results, showing that nearly two-thirds of companies surveyed allowed casual dress at least occasionally, became the basis for countless newspaper and magazine articles heralding the revolution in business dress.

Dayton-Hudson's Target stores offered a free training video to help companies communicate their casual-day expectations to groups of employees.

And when traditional suited organizations such as IBM and Fannie Mae announced their shift to business casual, the trend was solidified.

When General Motors established its Saturn division in 1983, they eliminated hourly wages, time clocks, VIP parking spaces, the executive cafeteria, and traditional business dress. All Saturn employees dress similarly in business casual.

The list of supporters continues to grow, including American Express, Chase Manhattan, Citibank, and General Electric. Evans Research's second study in the mid-nineties, also commissioned by Levi Strauss, showed that 90 percent of the firms surveyed allowed casual dress in some form, either for special charity days, during the summer months, on Fridays, or full-time.

Of course, those statistics don't spotlight the companies that have cut back or dropped casual days when too many employees thought "casual" meant dirty jeans and sweatshirts or sundresses and sandals. However, the Evans survey seems to show overwhelming support for casual dress among human resource managers:

- 85 percent believe it improves employee morale
- 82 percent say it reduces status distinctions
- 72 percent feel it saves employees money
- 45 percent believe it improves productivity

Like any new business trend, corporate casual has its fans and its foes:

"This is one of the best employee perks that we could ever offer. Our employees love it and it doesn't cost us a penny."

Dewitt "Buzz" Mitchell, president of Daniels Communication

"It appears as though productivity has increased significantly since we implemented business casual. Employees are much more relaxed and comfortable. They seem to make better business decisions and relate to people in a more open and less formal way."

Mia Cole, business manager, Fannie Mae

"I love the business casual look for the way it combines unattractive with unprofessional while diminishing neither."

—Dilbert, cartoon

For every professional who feels more productive in casual attire, there is another who feels less confident and less professionally dressed. Some employees appreciate the savings of buying less-structured clothing; others resent having to maintain separate business wardrobes for traditional and casual occasions.

The comfort of casual clothing can make employees feel more productive, but employers worry that people will take the casual trend to inappropriate extremes. Without a doubt, casual dressing allows for greater flexibility in wardrobe choices, but for many the increased range of choices leads to confusion and insecurity about just what is appropriate.

"Dress-down Friday offends me," says natty novelist Tom Wolfe. "There's only one way to stop it: dress-down one-upmanship. Show up in a tweed hacking jacket with slanted pockets, flannel trousers—not charcoal but mustard—a pair of suede brogues with tobacco-brown leather toes, a Sea Island cotton shirt—one of the most expensive fabrics in the world—an ascot from Brooks Brothers or Paul Stuart, and to keep the ascot from falling, an antique silver stickpin from James Robinson."

Fortune magazine replies . . . "Alas, Tom, not in our lifetime."

Pros	Cons
Boosts employee morale	May feel less professionally dressed
Usually less costly	May need a second business wardrobe
Can be more comfortable	May be taken to the extreme
Offers greater flexibility in wardrobe choices	Confusion and uncertainty about appropriate wardrobe
Less visual distinction between managers if everyone adheres to the same level of dressing	Lack of visual credibility

An interesting paradox has occurred in many corporations that sought to introduce business casual to lessen status distinction. Visually, there is actually more distinction between managers and support staff when they wear very different items of traditional and casual clothing. For example, the upper levels of management will generally continue to wear traditional business attire or elegant business casual, while the rest of the company wears baseline or mainstream business casual. Prior to the introduction of business casual, men and women from all ranks wore mainly business suits, so the line between upper-level management and all other levels was less visible.

Susan Morem, author of the book *How to Gain the Professional Edge* and the "Business Casual" corporate training video, has consulted with many companies on their casual dress codes. While many organizations are enthused about joining the growing number of companies that offer the opportunity to dress down, one very important factor is often overlooked—the customer. While the studies show many benefits for employees who are able to dress casually, many customers disapprove and dislike doing business with casually dressed employees. Not only does it make it difficult to distinguish between the employee who is working and other customers, but some customers have complained and threatened to take their business to a more professionally dressed competitor.

Ms. Morem states, "I was called to help a bank as they struggled to redefine their Casual Friday dress code. They hadn't been concerned until they received a call from a disgruntled customer who took the time to call and complain about the too-casual appearance of the teller she had to deal with. It was distasteful for her to conduct financial matters with someone who looked as though they ought to be lounging instead of working. Of course, it is impossible to know how many other customers may have been offended or even taken their business elsewhere for the same reason."

Whatever your personal level of enthusiasm for casual dressing, understanding it is a must in today's business climate. Your visual image communicates its message constantly, in denim, Dockers, or a double-breasted blazer. The wider range of looks—and related messages—in business casual creates too many error opportunities to leave the matter to chance.

Companies have very good reasons to avoid letting their casual-day dress drift too far down the scale. One employee benefits firm we worked with had just lost a huge contract to a competitor after the prospective client made site visits to both firms. Some time later, the company president initiated an off-the-record chat with the CEO of the client firm. The CEO confided that his final decision hinged on the fact that the competitor's employees "just looked and acted more professional, more businesslike." Not surprisingly, the benefits firm promptly instituted a written dress policy and a series of training sessions to clarify the policy to employees.

Of course, a sudden shift to a casual dress code can send everyone scrambling. Many professionals spend so much effort on a traditional business wardrobe that their at-home clothing looks as if it came from the bottom of the hamper. Avoid the temptation to adapt your gardening pants, exercise wear, or car-washing attire to the office, even for business casual occasions. Instead, acquire a small assortment of top-quality, casual garments and then add more items as you need them.

Begin by checking your company's written policy, but beware of applying it verbatim. We have consulted on the development of countless dress codes and assure you that often the finished policy reflects management's absolute minimum standard, not what they would prefer to see around the office.

One prominent bank circulated a casual-day policy that excluded only three things:

- Jeans with holes or tears
- T-shirts printed with obscene sayings
- Bedroom slippers or thong sandals

Would it be a smart career move for some up-and-coming bank manager to arrive wearing:

- Stained—but intact—jeans
- A T-shirt proclaiming "Bozo the Clown for President"
- A pair of thick white socks and Birkenstocks

Only if he or she wants a professional future as minimal as the image that costume conveys.

Frankie Walters, a corporate image consultant, was asked to establish guidelines for a major corporation implementing Casual Friday attire. The guidelines were communicated in a company-wide memo stating that tank tops, midriffs, jeans, and athletic shoes were inappropriate. Interpretation ranged from "at-home casual"—gray fleece workout sweats accompanied with dirty pink fluffy slippers to "casual chic attire"—a camel blazer, navy silk knit shell, pleated wool gabardine slacks, and low-heeled pumps.

This scenario prompted the corporation to define more clearly a Casual Friday look that best represented their global image. The company suggested that each individual determine what attire was appropriate based on the following considerations:

- Who are you? (What is your position within the company?)
- What are your duties that day?
- Who are you meeting?
- Where is the meeting?

Often your best visual guideline for "how-casual-is-casual" comes from observing superiors and respected peers, especially those who were involved in developing the written dress policy. They understand exactly what management expects to see and probably feel a responsibility to model that preferred look as an example for others.

Consider all the variables of your situation. Certain geographic areas, lines of business, departments, and personalities lend themselves to a more relaxed interpretation of "casual" than others.

- West Coast? East Coast? Midwest?
- Metropolitan area? Smaller city? Small town?
- Finance? Sales? Creative work?
- Traditionalist? Technology wizard? Wheeler-dealer? Maverick?
- Attire your boss wears.
- Attire your clients wear.
- How much you may travel to areas or client sites where dress codes differ from your own.

When you're unsure of the host's dress code, whether the occasion is social or business, ask. No one is apt to be offended, and many would be complimented that you care enough to make an inquiry.

What's Casual?

There is no single, clear-cut casual look for all situations. We can arbitrarily define three levels of casual business attire, but they actually represent points along a continuum. There is variety within each category, and the top end of one level blends into the bottom end of the level above.

Your company's dress policy—written or implied—may dictate which level you select. Or you may vary your look according to the specific occasion or companions. Some executives even forgo casual-day dressing if they have an important meeting or client lunch on a given day. As one executive puts it, "My company doesn't dictate how I dress . . . my customers do."

"In an era of corporate downsizing, is 'down-dressing' a good idea? Might not managers, given a choice between two workers to retain, subconsciously choose to keep the one who looks more professional?"

—Marilyn Gardner, *Christian Science Monitor*

"Baseline casual" is the most relaxed look acceptable for business situations. This look—jeans, chinos, or dressy cargo pants with a collared knit shirt—works on casual day in companies whose standard dress code is already rather informal. In a more formal company, you might choose a baseline casual look only for very informal occasions such as clean-out-the-files day or a conference held in a wilderness lodge, but never for regular wear.

"Mainstream casual" is a safe, middle-of-the-road interpretation for day-to-day business activities. For men, this more pulled-together look features pleated wool, cotton, or microfiber trousers, a pressed cotton sport shirt with long sleeves, a polo-style cotton shirt, or a sweater in cooler weather. For women, quality wool, cotton, knit, or microfiber trousers or skirt, a coordinating top or fine-gauge sweater, and third-layer vest, jacket, or cardigan will work.

"Executive casual" is the best choice for managers and executives (or those who aspire to be), especially in high-profile companies and departments. Tailored separates in this category work well for important internal meetings or presentations that fall on casual day. For women it is a matching or coordinated pantsuit; for men a high-quality, lightweight wool trouser and blazer, a pressed cotton shirt, and possibly a more casual tie. A person wearing this look still maintains a commanding visual presence, even when casually dressed.

Business Casual and Traditional Attire

The following chart summarizes the continuum from casual to boardroom attire:

❧ Category	Guidelines for Men	Guidelines for Women
Baseline casual	Denim, cotton, or corduroy pants	Denim, cotton, or corduroy pants or skirts
	Knit or plaid shirts, short or long sleeves	Knit shirts or cotton blouses
	Casual shoes/accessories	Casual closed-toed shoes/accessories
Mainstream casual	Higher-quality khakis, microfiber or gabardine pants	Wool, blend, or manufactured fabric skirts
	Solid-colored or subtly patterned pressed shirts, pressed cotton shirts	Coordinating blouses or tops
	Polo-style shirt, long or short sleeves	Long or short sleeves, sweaters, cardigans, contrasting vests
	Pullover sweaters, contrasting vests or cardigans	
	Leather loafers	Flat leather shoes
	Casual, coordinated accessories	Casual, coordinated accessories
Executive casual	Cuffed, lightweight wool trousers	High-quality pantsuits
	Long-sleeved, well-pressed shirts	Silk or cotton blouses
	Fine-gauge cotton or silk sweaters	Fine-gauge cotton or silk shells
	Coordinated sportcoats/blazers	
	Woven leather loafers	Quality low-heeled pumps
	High-quality accessories	High-quality accessories
Traditional business	Medium-to-dark wool suits	Skirted suits or tailored separates or tailored business dresses
	White or blue business shirts with button-down or straight collar	Silk, knit, and cotton blouses or fine-gauge sweaters
	Quality accessories: ties, belts, shoes, jewelry	Quality accessories: scarves, belts, shoes, jewelry

(continued)

(continued)

❧ Category	Guidelines for Men	Guidelines for Women
Boardroom attire	Highest-quality wool suits with pleated trousers	Highest-quality skirted suits in wool, silk, or other fine fabric
	White business shirts in superior quality cotton, straight collar, optional French cuffs	Highest quality silk blouses, long sleeves, or sleeveless knit shells
		Optional leather belts
	Highest-quality silk power ties	Optional silk scarves
	Highest-quality gold or stainless watch and jewelry	Highest-quality gold or stainless watch and jewelry

Whichever category you select, some clothing items should never see the inside of your office—even though increasingly relaxed written dress policies may fail to exclude some of them:

Women
Tattered, frayed, or wrinkled jeans
Sweat pants or jogging pants
Leggings or Spandex pants
Casual shorts
Leather pants
Ultrashort skirts
T-shirts with logos
Anything with a printed slogan
Tank tops or camisoles
Cropped (above-the-waist) tops
Sweatshirts
See-through voile or chiffon blouses
Sneakers or sandals

Men
Tattered, frayed, or wrinkled jeans
Sweat pants or jogging pants
Shorts, including biking shorts
High-water pants
T-shirts with logos
Anything with a printed slogan
Tank tops
Cropped (above-the-waist) tops
Sweatshirts
Garish print sport shirts
Sport team jackets
Hiking boots
Sneakers or sandals

"Some things do not alter with time and technology. Dressing up to go to work always has—and always will—reflect professional discipline and a respect for the job or the client at hand. Even on Fridays."

Deirdre McMurdy, author

A casual business look, at any level, should always include:

- High-quality garments in good repair
- Appropriate hosiery, socks, and underwear
- Well-maintained footwear
- Coordinated accessories: belt, jewelry, makeup
- Clean, styled hair

Many organizations allow casual dress every day from Memorial Day to Labor Day and revert to traditional business dress during the winter months. Doing things differently can stimulate interest. The famous Hawthorne Study in the early 1900s follows this same idea. A factory determined that they could increase productivity if they brightened the lights. They let the employees know this and implemented the change. Productivity went up. Then it was determined several months later that the lights were too bright and it would increase productivity more if the lights were dimmed. Again, they informed the employees, and productivity went up yet again.

So the answer to whether business casual is more effective than traditional attire or vice versa is simply that both work. A large part of the reason is that in implementing both options, employees are acknowledged and validated.

"When the emphasis is placed on business for business casual, there is less chance for error."

Janet Crowe, Professional Impression

chapter eight

baseline casual dress

> Every generation laughs at the old fashions, but follows religiously the new.
>
> Henry David Thoreau

baseline casual is a viable dress-down option for men and women who work in a profession or company with a relaxed everyday dress standard. Even men in fields that are traditionally more dressed-up need a selection of baseline casual clothing for specific occasions:

- Clean-out-the-files-at-the-office day
- An executive retreat in a rustic location
- Taking a client to a baseball game
- The company picnic

An understanding of baseline casual must be grounded in an understanding of what it is not. Designer Barry Bricken's quote in *GQ* magazine describes it well: "It's not a yacht look, a cowboy look, a golf look, a lumberjack look, a ski-resort look—it isn't any of those."

Even at this most relaxed level, business casual still is more about business than about casual. A baseline casual look can't be thrown together with little or no thought. It requires an understanding of style options, fabrics, construction quality, and fit standards. It is an important component of professional credibility.

A client who owns a successful construction company recognizes that image plays a critical role in how you are perceived regardless of the level of formality of your dress. "Image isn't just about looking good," he says. "It is about being perceived as trustworthy and believable. Casual dress is the nature of our company. To stay competitive we focus on all our resources. The most important resource is our people. We've had uniforms made for our employees rather than having them wear jeans and T-shirts. Because we are a vital part of the community, we are in the spotlight. We have to look like a professional business. We can't give the impression that we make snap decisions, do sloppy work, or scramble to keep things together. We've learned the value of perception and image."

Although the items in a baseline casual wardrobe need not be terribly expensive, don't assume that low-budget choices that shrink, pill up, and fit poorly will fill the bill. The twin clichés "Quality shows" and "You get what you pay for" are as true in this category as they are for boardroom attire.

Shopping for casual business wear is easy. Virtually every department store, quality discount store, and many sportswear specialty stores offer wide varieties of business casual dress. Open a store charge account, and you'll receive mail notices about new arrivals and upcoming sales. Determine your most important purchases, and evaluate how well the store's merchandise fits your requirements.

Online shopping is an ideal way to build your casual business wardrobe, and it offers some genuine advantages:

- Most Web sites provide a customer service number where a representative will describe the merchandise, pointing out details of fabric quality, construction, and fit that a harried retail store salesperson wouldn't know.
- Most online merchandise is available in extensive sizes and color ranges, and some Web sites provide the option of viewing the garment in each of the various color choices with a click of the mouse.
- Some companies will even hem pants to your requested length for no additional charge.
- You can reorder old favorites without a trip to the mall.

If you catalog-shop, consider stocking up on basics such as trousers and polo shirts from the sale catalog. The merchandise is the same as in the regular catalog, but availability is limited, so order the same day the catalog arrives. When placing a sale order, ask about favorites from the company's regular catalog. They may also be available at sale pricing, but in quantities too limited to warrant a listing in the sale book.

You may occasionally be unsure about which size to order from a catalog. Try ordering both of the sizes in question, then returning the one that isn't right. Some catalog companies pay return postage and you don't have to wait to begin wearing the right-size garment or risk it being out of stock.

Off-price shopping is a viable option for people with more time than money to devote to wardrobe development. Here's how Marshall's, Syms, Loehmann's, and other large promotional retailers operate:

- A manufacturer cuts 1,000 of a particular design but sells only 900 to his regular wholesale customers. The leftover 100 are offered to an off-price retailer at a greatly reduced cost.
- The store operates in a no-frills environment with minimal staff to keep expenses low.
- Both savings elements (low wholesale, low overhead) are passed on to the customer.

The selection in an off-price store will not include every size of an item, or every item in a coordinate grouping. You'll have to do your own searching, because sales help is almost nonexistent. You'll also need to check the store regularly, because new merchandise arrives nearly every day, but the savings can be well worth the time invested.

Consider these cautions before you try off-price shopping:

- Check store policies. Some accept only cash payment, no checks or credit cards. Others offer no cash refunds, only a store credit for returns.
- Learn how to recognize quality, because the inventory is usually a mix of first-quality merchandise and irregulars, top designers, and poorly made bargain-basement brands.

- Don't get carried away by discount prices. An off-price item is a bargain only if you like it well enough that you would have bought it at full price. Your business associates will never see the markdown, but everyone will notice a great garment—or a shoddy one.
- Check the style. Styles may be one to two years old by the time they reach an off-price store. The average fashion cycle in menswear is seven to eight years, so you may sacrifice up to a quarter of the garment's wearable life. Women's fashions cycle even more quickly.

Baseline Casual Dress for Men

You've undoubtedly heard the expression "Be careful what you wish for . . . you just might get it." Businessmen who wished for freedom from a coat and tie are questioning the wisdom of that wish now that it has been granted.

Even men who thrive on change and chaos in the corporate world are sometimes befuddled by the chaos that changing business dress codes have brought to their closets. No wonder. Since the demise of the 1960s leisure suits and Nehru jackets, businessmen have dressed by a simple unchanging formula—one that was influenced by President John F. Kennedy and his clearly presidential presence—a dark, well-cut, all-wool suit; a starched white, all-cotton shirt; and an all-silk red tie.

In its infancy, business casual simply introduced a second formula: khaki pants and a polo shirt. But businessmen were fairly quick to recognize that this new formula wasn't enough. Business dressing today is situational. A typical career spans a range of activities and environments, each with its own dress expectation. Similarly, a business wardrobe needs to include choices for each degree of formality—or informality.

A frequent question from our seminar groups is, "What about jeans?" Our answer isn't always popular, but it is consistent. All-American, rugged, and beloved, jeans are a great choice for climbing a mountain . . . but a questionable choice for climbing the corporate ladder.

Of course, we acknowledge that there are exceptions. A few men, usually young, trim men, can pair jeans with a tweedy blazer and pull off a polished look, especially appropriate for creative professions such as architecture, advertising, and the arts. But a more mature man, especially with a paunch, is likely to look like . . . well . . . a paunchy guy in jeans.

It isn't always easy to assess which category you belong to, as most men alternate between being their own worst critics one day and unreasonably forgiving the next. Try one of these tactics to get a realistic assessment of your appearance in jeans:

- Have someone snap a few candid photos of you in jeans, then evaluate the message that the look conveys.
- Study another man with a build similar to your own. Picture him in jeans and decide if that's a look you'd like to duplicate.

Should you decide to make jeans part of your baseline casual wardrobe, keep these points in mind:

- Jeans for the office must be in mint condition—not torn, frayed, or faded—always clean, and pressed.
- The fit should be customized for your build. Terminology varies from one manufacturer to the next, but in general, slim jeans are cut for narrow bodies; regular cut is eased somewhat through the seat and thighs; relaxed cut is full through the seat and thighs. Boot cut jeans are cut so that they fall over the shoes in a smooth line. They are a popular and trendy alternative, but beware of the boot cut leg that borders on flare, or that is too tight in the seat.
- Unless the jeans are marked "prewashed," buy them slightly larger than you need to allow for shrinkage.
- After washing twice to remove any shrinkage, hem the jeans to the proper length. Never roll up excess length or allow it to bunch up around your ankles.

If jeans are not your best look, build your baseline wardrobe around casual khaki or corduroy pants instead. Khaki twill or chino makes durable casual pants. Compared to a polyester-cotton blend, an all-cotton fabric is more prone to wrinkles, but also lets air circulate between the fibers to keep your body cooler in hot weather. All-cotton pants also look a great deal cooler, image-wise. The smoothest, softest fabrics are made from combed cotton. Combing is an extra sorting process that separates the longest, sturdiest, most-lustrous cotton fibers from the less-desirable shorter ones.

Quality pant fabrics should feel naturally full-bodied. Some manufacturers try to conceal a flimsy fabric by coating it with sizing, a starch-like solution that seems to add body, but disappears with the first washing. A pair of pants with a "too-good-to-be-true" price tag may have been sized. Test the fabric by rubbing a section vigorously between your hands and looking for a fine white powdery substance.

Corduroy is a perennial favorite for fall and winter pants. It is occasionally a hot fashion item, but even in off-years, it can be a staple. Corduroy is a cotton or cotton-polyester blend fabric characterized by lengthwise stripes (wales) of surface fuzz called nap. Corduroy's nap has a definite direction. Run your hand over the surface to feel the nap, smooth in one direction and rough in the other. Check a corduroy garment to be sure all pieces are cut in the same direction; if not, the garment sections will appear to be different colors.

Corduroy is categorized by the number of wales per inch. Twelve-wale (also called fine-wale) corduroy is traditional and fairly lightweight. Eight-wale is slightly heavier with a glossy surface. If you wash and iron corduroy pants at home, press from the wrong side to avoid flattening the nap.

Certain distinctive design details define a pair of casual pants:

- More visible topstitching
- Welted seams (one seam edge is wrapped over the other and top-stitched in place)
- Quarter-top pockets (angled front pockets extending one-quarter of the distance to center front)
- Rear patch pocket or topstitched welt pocket
- Topstitched hem
- Bar tack pockets

Casual pants can be pleated or flat-front styling. A pleated front is more forgiving, cut fuller through the thigh area. Be sure the cut is roomy enough that the pleats aren't pulled open. A flat front creates a sleeker appearance, but demands a flat, firm physique.

Most manufacturers offer their casual pants in regular or long rise (distance from waist to crotch seam). Try long-rise pants if you are over six-foot-one or have a high-waisted build. More manufacturers—recognizing that another baby boomer turns fifty every five seconds—are adding small sections of elastic in the side area of waistbands for a more comfortable fit.

The most obvious top for a baseline casual look is a knit polo shirt. Although widely associated with designer Ralph Lauren's successful Polo brand, the term is used generically to describe any knit pullover with a front placket and knit collar. Various brands range in price from $8 to $80, so it is important to understand the features of a quality shirt and recognize the true value behind the price.

Fabric is one major component of garment quality:

- Cotton knits are cooler to wear but generally shrink with the initial washing and drying; cotton-polyester blends shrink less but don't feel as soft or comfortable.
- Jersey is a knit constructed from a single layer of loops and is sometimes thinner than other knits. You can recognize jersey by its appearance (fine lengthwise ridges on the right side, crosswise ridges on the wrong side) and by its tendency to curl to the right side along the hem edge when stretched. Most striped knits are jerseys. Jersey has an annoying tendency to twist off-grain after washing, skewing the garment's side seams and hemline.
- Interlock knit is literally made from two layers of interlocking loops. That construction gives an interlock a loftier hand and softer stretch and eliminates curling edges. An interlock has no visible right or wrong side and retains its shape well through many washings.
- Pique knit features a surface texture of tiny indentations. The nicest piques are double-knit rather than jersey construction. Pique is also called Lacoste knit, named for the famous tennis-wear line that uses this fabric extensively.
- Fine-gauge sweater knits are popular for cool-weather polo shirts. Slightly thicker than the typical T-shirt fabrics, they perform much like any other sweater knit.

Some tips for wearing these fabrics:

- For business, skip knit tops made from silky, shiny knits, sweatshirt fleece, or waffle-textured fabric similar to long underwear.
- Knits are described by the weight of one yard of the fabric. A weight of five to six ounces per yard is a good-quality fabric.

■ Virtually all cotton or blended knits will shrink in washing. Unless the garment is labeled "prewashed," buy a larger size to allow for shrinkage, especially in the length.

In a quality polo shirt the shoulder and neckline seams will be covered with a tape to prevent stretching with wear and eliminate irritation from the seams rubbing your skin. Stroke the taped section against your forearm to test for softness.

Turtlenecks, especially mock turtlenecks where the collar doesn't turn down, can also fit men's baseline category. They are usually worn under a plaid shirt or casual vest in cooler weather. A regular or mock turtle-neck can also be worn with a sportcoat or blazer from the mainstream or executive casual wardrobe. Better-quality turtlenecks are made from cotton interlock or fine-gauge sweater knit. The rib trim at the wrists and neckline will hold its shape best if it is made from a blend of cotton and Lycra. A neckband that is knitted tubular, rather than cut and seamed to size, looks more elegant and feels more comfortable as well.

Denim shirts fit into the baseline category if your workplace permits. Like jeans, shirts in denim need to be clean, pressed, and free of fading, stains, or fraying.

Plaid sport shirts—especially multicolor plaids such as madras and tar-tans—are right at home in a baseline casual look. Look for yarn-dyed plaids, in which threads of various colors are woven together to form sophisti-cated shadings. Plaid designs that are simply printed onto the surface of a solid-colored fabric shout "cheap." Printed plaids have an obvious right and wrong side, while yarn-dyed or woven plaids look the same on both sides.

Business plaid shirts—even casual ones—are made from refined fabrics such as broadcloth and very lightly brushed cotton twill. Avoid heavy, fuzzy flannel shirts that look more at home on a camping trip than at the office.

Sewing a quality shirt from plaid fabric is challenging because the plaid must match and balance. Matching means that the horizontal bars of color must align with bars of the same size and color at major areas like the side seams and center front. Balance means that the same dominant vertical color band should appear to the right and left of the center placket, down the center of both sleeves, on both cuffs, and so on. A plaid shirt that isn't matched and balanced will look oddly askew, even if the viewer can't pin-point what's amiss.

Baseline casual is a category in which short-sleeved shirts are acceptable for business. Except for a few obvious regional exceptions, avoid Western yokes and detailing, tropical prints, satin shirts, sports jerseys, and other specialized shirt styles.

In cooler weather you may want to top your baseline casual outfit with one of these jackets:

- An unstructured sportcoat, made by sportswear companies rather than suit manufacturers, features softer construction with less interfacing, padding, and lining. Watch quality carefully to avoid choosing a jacket that will look like a dishrag after a few wearings.
- A classic trench coat works with virtually all categories of casual and traditional business apparel.
- A corduroy jacket should have tailored styling and below-the-buttocks length.
- A waist-length bomber jacket in tan cotton twill or leather is the most casual jacket you should consider for the office.

No matter what the weather conditions, don't expect to be taken seriously in a sports team jacket or anything in shearling or lumberjack plaid fleece.

Finish your baseline casual look with a leather, braided leather, or canvas belt, dark casual socks, and loafers. Save the white socks, sneakers, and hiking shoes for the appropriate sports activities, and save your lace-up shoes to wear with clothing in the basic business category.

A few pieces of clothing can yield many baseline casual looks if the colors are well coordinated. Buy more items if you dress this casually on a day-to-day basis.

A Suggested Baseline Casual Wardrobe for Men

- Trousers (suggested number: 3 pairs)
  - *Regular (not faded or torn) denim jeans*
  - *Blue, black, or brown 100 percent cotton trousers*
  - *Khaki, olive, tan, or taupe 100 percent cotton twill trousers*

- Shirts (suggested number: 6)
  - *Solid-colored burgundy, blue, olive, brown, or rust plaid cotton shirt*
  - *Blue, black, olive, or hunter green cotton fine-ribbed turtleneck*
  - *Solid-colored burgundy, black, blue, olive, brown, or rust polo shirt*

- Sweaters (suggested number: 2)
  - *Solid navy or black crew-neck sweater to coordinate with trousers*
  - *Crew- or V-neck sweater in multiple colors to coordinate with trousers*

- Belts (suggested number: 1)
  - *Black or brown leather belt to coordinate with shoes*

- Shoes (suggested number: 1 pair)
  - *Suede or leather shoes in brown or black with rubber soles*

Baseline Casual Dress for Women

The bottom rung of the casual-dressing ladder can be a precarious spot for businesswomen. It may not be fair, but females still tend to derive much of their visual credibility from professional clothing. A male executive dressed casually can still look like a male executive dressed casually. But a female executive in jeans and a polo shirt is more likely to be mistaken for someone far lower on the organization chart.

Of course, you could just refuse to dress casually in the office. But as several of our clients have quickly discovered, showing up every casual day in your favorite boardroom-level suit can quickly label you as someone who isn't a team player or can't adapt to change.

Should you wear jeans to the office? No matter what the dress code says, we advise women not to do so. Denim pants may be the most durable garment on the planet and as all-American as apple pie, but jeans also have a decades-old marketing campaign that portrays them as sexy packaging for women's derrières.

Today, jeans tend to be cut as low-rise as possible, with tight-fitting seats and flared ankles. This may be great—perhaps—for a weekend look, but hardly the impression most career women want to leave with their bosses, subordinates, clients, or peers.

For fit and figure flattery, jeans are really a no-win option in the business world. Their abundance of horizontal design lines is unflattering to all but the best figures. Women built to wear jeans well risk looking too seductive, and less shapely women can easily appear overweight or sloppy.

If you love the look and feel of denim and it is acceptable in your workplace, substitute a denim skirt (knee-length or longer) for jeans. The look is still casual, but retains a measure of dignity and professionalism. Denim clothing looks slightly more dressed-up in alternative colors, such as black or a natural cream color instead of the usual blue.

Traditional cotton denim is usually heavy and stiff and becomes soft and comfortable only after multiple washings have faded its original color. The softest and most luxurious denim fabric is made from Tencel, a synthetic fiber manufactured from plant cellulose. Its plant origins make the fiber as absorbent and breathable as cotton, while its synthetic characteristics add excellent wrinkle resistance and colorfastness. Tencel's softness makes it ideal for blouses that are comfortable and bulk-free. Many pants styles other than jeans can work fine for baseline casual occasions. The key elements are a tailored look and quality fabric. Many denim clothing items now come with elastic or Lycra built in for easier stretch and greater comfort.

Don't compromise your professional image with leggings, warm-up pants, skintight styles, or overalls. Look instead for classic back-zip pants or fly-front, pleated styles with a conventional waistband and straight or slightly tapered legs. The vertical design lines—pleats, creases, angled side pockets—add up to a slimmer silhouette and a more tailored, business-like appearance.

before&now

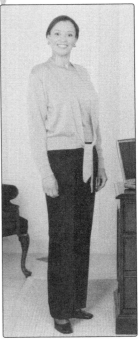

before This baseline business casual is too loose fitting and shapeless. She also needs the polish of makeup. **now** Smooth and trim, this outfit offers comfort without being misshapen or sloppy. A matching sweater set is versatile. Slim trousers are often more professional than a flowing skirt. Makeup is the accessory that pulls it all together.

before Cropped tops never work. There isn't a single legitimate business environment where this adds any advantage. It only subtracts from good-quality work and diminishes a woman's professional perception. Jeans can be too seductive if a woman has a good figure, or sloppy and unattractive if they are a bad fit. **before** Sheer fabric and inappropriately strappy sandals paired with an unsophisticated hairstyle and no makeup relegate her to lesser jobs and fewer career opportunities. **now** Smooth and chic, this is a business casual combination that enhances her career credentials. Smooth hair, a crisp white blouse, and well-fitted trousers with closed-toe shoes transform her appearance.

Pants in neutral solid colors are the most versatile and professional. Save bright colors and patterns for coordinating tops that will draw a viewer's attention up toward your face. Classic khaki is the number one color choice for baseline business casual. But black, gray, navy, burgundy, taupe, brown, or camel are equally appropriate. A subtle glen plaid or narrow vertical stripe can also look fine at the office.

Very casual pants usually are made from a cotton or cotton-blend fabric. The cotton absorbs body moisture and lets air circulate through the garment. Adding up to 45 percent synthetic fiber will prevent wrinkling and add durability without sacrificing comfort. But don't believe a care label that says "permanent press." To look crisp enough for the office, nearly every pair of pants needs some intimate contact with the bottom of an iron.

- Twill is a very crisp fabric originally developed for military uniforms and known for its durability. Recognize twill by the subtle diagonal ridges on the fabric's right side. Some twills are brushed to create a slightly fuzzy surface and a softer hand or drape.
- Chino is another firm, durable fabric, woven with longer "float" threads on the surface for a slightly glossy look on the right side.
- Corduroy is distinctive for its lengthwise ribs of plush threads called wales. The wider the wales, the sportier the corduroy. Pinwale corduroy (twelve or more ribs per inch) is most common for cool-weather pants or skirts. Jumbo corduroy (three to four ribs per inch) is usually reserved for jackets and outerwear. The fuzzy surface (nap) creates a distinctive shading. Examine a corduroy garment to be sure all pieces are cut in the same direction of the nap and therefore appear the same color. Corduroy should be pressed from the wrong side to remove wrinkles without crushing the surface ribs.

Test the quality of these fabrics before you purchase. Rub an inconspicuous area of the garment vigorously between your hands. Check for a fine white powdery substance called "sizing" that is used on poor-quality cotton fabrics to make them feel more full-bodied and durable. After washing, the sizing disappears, leaving the garment limp and lifeless. If there is no white powder, there's no sizing, and you can expect the fabric to hold its body after laundering.

Squeeze the fabric tightly for a few seconds, then release and see how readily the resulting wrinkles begin to disappear. That is your best indication of how the garment will wrinkle in wearing and whether it will form "smile" lines across the front after you sit.

Pants for work should meet demanding standards of fit—not just be "big enough to go around." The same body may fit into a size six from one manufacturer, but require a size ten in another brand. Before you buy, "test-sit" in pants to check fit and comfort:

- Choose pants to fit your hips, then have the waist made smaller if necessary. You should be able to pinch an inch of loose fabric at the hip line, as an absolute minimum. Be sure any pleats fall straight and lay close to the body, never spread apart.
- The rise (crotch-to-waist measurement) should be comfortable, neither too short nor hanging too low. A too-long rise can be altered from the waistband, but not easily. A too-short rise usually can't be corrected.
- The pants should fall straight down from the buttocks in back and the tummy in front. Fitting too snug below either area simply accentuates the bulge above. Buy a size larger if necessary for best fit.
- Look for telltale wrinkles radiating from the crotch point in front. They signal that the pants are too tight in the upper thigh. Try a larger size to correct the problem.
- Droopy or baggy fabric below the seat is another clue to poor fit. Try correcting the problem by pulling the pants up at the center back waist. If that works, the problem can be permanently solved by removing the waistband and sewing it on lower in the back.
- Most cotton fabrics will shrink lengthwise. If you plan to launder your casual pants, wash them twice before marking the final hem length at the point where it touches the top of your shoe.
- A 1" cuff makes pants look more finished and keeps the legs hanging more gracefully. Very petite women, however, will look taller in pants that are not cuffed.

When you find a brand of pants that meets your personal fit standards, you may want to purchase several pairs. At least make note of the brand name for future reference.

Don't ruin a casual pants look with the wrong accessories. Tennis shoes, clogs, or sandals just don't work for business. Dark leather loafers or flats are the safest choice. Add a quality leather, canvas, or braided belt to cover the waistband.

Top your tailored casual bottoms with an equally smart casual top. A turtleneck can be worn with unconstructed jackets, or a vest, cardigan sweater, casual scarf, interesting necklace, or sporty pin. A solid-colored, fitted, T-shirt can work, but not if it is imprinted with a logo or slogan.

Solid colors appear the most businesslike, but narrow stripes are also acceptable. The color range is wide open, except for garish neon shades or metallics. Choose the colors that spotlight your personal coloring and fit the time of the year.

Because knit shirts can cost from $5 to $75, it is important to understand the differences in quality. The most important quality consideration is fabric. All-cotton knits are the softest and coolest but will shrink with the initial washing and drying; cotton-polyester blend knits shrink less, retain shape better, and are still reasonably cool. Blended knits, however, are more likely to develop "pills"—those annoying little balls of fuzz in areas of abrasion.

A jersey (or single knit) is made from a single layer of interlocking thread loops. Jersey has good side-to-side stretch, but minimal lengthwise give. Jersey is typically a thinner knit, and the hem edge can roll up to the right side after washing.

Recognize jersey by its pattern of slight lengthwise ridges on the right side and crosswise ridges on the back. Most knit stripes are jerseys. After washing, the stripes may skew, causing the garment to twist around your body.

Ribbed knits show a pronounced lengthwise ridge on both sides of the fabric and have great crosswise stretch. Rib knits tend to fit very close to the body, so only the firmest rib fabrics are suitable for businesswear and then only in gently fitted styles.

Interlock knits are made from two layers of thread loops, actually interlocked from one layer to the other. This creates a more full-bodied and opaque fabric with a softer stretch in both directions and no curling or twisting. An interlock looks exactly the same on the front and back sides. Very high-quality striped knits are of interlock construction.

Lacy pointelle knits and the waffle texture borrowed from long underwear, plus velour and knit terry are all inappropriate in even the most casual office setting.

Excellent fit is a must in knit tops for work. Oversized looks are sloppy, and too snug looks are suggestive. Find a size that tucks smoothly into your pants or skirt, but blouses just slightly above the waistline and doesn't hug your ribcage. A style with a small shoulder pad creates a more authoritative look and balances figure flaws as well. You can purchase foam shoulder pads in most clothing stores, if the top doesn't have them. Be sure body and sleeve lengths are adequate to allow for the inevitable lengthwise shrinkage when the garment is washed.

Knit shirts demand properly fitted undergarments. Select a bra with smooth fabric cups rather than a lacy pattern that could show an imprint through soft knit fabric. Be sure the band and straps fit loosely enough, rather than pressing into your flesh and creating unsightly lumps and bumps. Buy a cup size full enough to avoid "spill-over" at the center front or armhole.

Shirts sewn from woven fabrics are another baseline casual alternative.

- All-cotton shirts take a crisper press, but wrinkle more in wearing. Polyester-cotton blends are softer, and somewhat less wrinkle-prone.
- White and pastel or darker solids are traditional; a stripe of one color on white is updated.
- Multicolored stripes or plaids are the most casual (think madras). The best-quality plaids are actually woven into the fabric, creating a fabric that looks the same on both sides. An obviously different wrong side is an indication of a cheaper printed plaid.
- Avoid floral prints or pictures of animals, scenes, or the like. Save sheer, see-through, or lacy fabrics for your private time.
- Tailored styling with a front placket and button-down collar looks right anytime. Roll the sleeves for hot summer weather, or substitute a camp shirt with an open neckline and fuller-cut short sleeve.
- Avoid tank tops, sleeveless shells, and camisoles except possibly as a color layer under a more traditional shirt. Always avoid tube tops.
- Proper fit is key. Go roomy enough to fit comfortably, but trim enough to avoid looking sloppy and to tuck into pants or skirt without undue bulk.

You can use your head—quite literally—to finish off an effective casual look. Be sure your hair is well-cut, freshly washed, and styled. Keep makeup light and fresh, but don't be tempted into skipping it altogether. A pair of simple hoop or pearl earrings (just one earring per ear, please) adds polish without looking overstated.

A Suggested Baseline Casual Wardrobe for Women

Because we recommend this category for only the most casual occasions, a limited selection of these items should be adequate for most businesswomen's needs. If the environment is a rustic resort in the summer, add above-the-knee cotton shorts in khaki or black. If baseline business casual is a part of your wardrobe every day, increase the suggested numbers accordingly.

- Pants (suggested number: 2)
  - *Khaki, black, or olive cotton twill trousers*

- Skirt (suggested number: 1)
  - *Traditional blue denim skirt*

- Tops (suggested number: 5)
  - *Solid red, black, olive, or white cotton tops*
  - *Solid white, red, or black cotton-blend camp shirt (button front)*
  - *Red/black/olive combination tartan plaid, long-sleeved shirt*
  - *Solid red, black, olive, or white long-sleeved cotton turtleneck*

- Sweaters (suggested number: 1)
  - *Black cardigan sweater*
  - *Twin set in bright color*

- Belts (suggested number: 1)
  - *Black leather with gold or sterling buckle*

- Shoes (Suggested number: 1 pair)
  - *Black leather, closed-toe slip-on with rubber sole*

By wearing the tops alone or layered in pairs, you can create at least eighteen combinations in all from just these seven pieces: khaki pants, black pants, red T-shirt, black camp shirt, white turtleneck, black cardigan, and a denim skirt:

1. Khaki pants/red T-shirt
2. Khaki pants/black camp shirt

3. Khaki pants/white turtleneck
4. Khaki pants/white turtleneck/black cardigan
5. Khaki pants/red T-shirt/black cardigan
6. Khaki pants/black camp shirt/black cardigan
7. Black pants/white turtleneck
8. Black pants/white turtleneck/black camp shirt
9. Black pants/white turtleneck/black cardigan
10. Black pants/red T-shirt
11. Black pants/black camp shirt
12. Black pants/red T-shirt/black cardigan
13. Black pants/ black camp shirt/black cardigan
14. Denim skirt/red T-shirt
15. Denim skirt/white turtleneck
16. Denim skirt/black camp shirt
17. Denim skirt/black camp shirt/black cardigan
18. Denim skirt/white turtleneck/black cardigan

The key to tying these combinations together is to use accessories—neckpieces, belts, and jewelry—in these same colors.

chapter nine

mainstream casual dress

> Businesses had to find low-cost ways to motivate employees, and casual dress becomes a kind of free benefit.
>
> Alan Cohen, researcher on business casual
> and professor, Babson College

true to its name, this is the category into which the majority of managers and staff seem to settle for casual dressing. Nearly as relaxed and comfortable as baseline, mainstream adds a certain polish that clarifies its "down-to-business" attitude.

Mainstream is an appropriate choice for nearly everyone in more traditional companies and for high-visibility individuals even in very casual fields. The employees of most ad agencies, where occasionally someone dresses like a duck or in some other zany costume to stimulate creativity, still select mainstream casual for office attire.

One of our clients chose his new career in part because it allowed him to dress this way. "I've been a lab-coated scientist and an Armani-suited broker," he explains, "but my career move into suburban real estate leasing lets me dress the way I feel most comfortable. I truly believe I'm most effective when I feel good, and dressing casually gives me that feeling. Of course, I still have a closet full of suits, and I wear one when I negotiate a contract. But most of my customers are retailers, regular shirt-sleeved kinds of people. They relate well to a relaxed look. As an added bonus, this more flexible professional style lets me wear the colors that make me look the most healthy and likable. I'm no longer limited to dark suits and white shirts. I don't follow fashion trends, but stick with the choices I know are flattering."

"The rulers of corporate and political America wear suits—always have, always will."

John T. Molloy, author of *Dress for Success*

Mainstream Casual Dress for Men

Mainstream casual contains a wide range of choices and countless ways of combining those choices into ensembles that are either more or less casual. Occasionally all those choices can seem overwhelming to a traditional dark-suit-white-shirt-red-tie man. A favorite ad of ours shows a befuddled man in boxer shorts. The caption proclaims loudly, "I'll wear whatever I want to wear!" Then, in smaller print, follow the words: "Honey, what do I want to wear?"

Part of the problem is that the last major change in menswear, the leisure suit, was an ensemble. Everything pretty much came together. The jacket and trousers matched, and all that was necessary was adding a belt and a shirt. Today the look is harder to manage because it can't be purchased as a total unit. Corporate casual requires the wearer to coordinate and accessorize separate pieces and make the look work.

"With all due respect to Casual Fridays, there are still four other days in the week and a lot of men still wearing suits."

James Leddy, vice president, Corbin Ltd.

A few men try to sidestep the entire issue by continuing to dress traditionally when their firms embrace a casual dress code. Dressing up for an important meeting or client call is just smart business. But as some of our clients have been dismayed to learn, overdressing on a daily basis when the rest of the company is in mainstream casual invites ridicule.

Observe your peers and supervisors. Pay attention to the way your various clients dress. Then make appropriate choices for yourself from among these mainstream options.

Trousers

This look begins with upgraded trousers in a range of neutral colors. These characteristics define a more formal, mainstream pants style:

- Seams pressed open, or serged together, no topstitching
- Front pockets that are on the seams
- Back double-welt pocket
- No topstitching on belt loops or waistband
- Center back seam in waistband
- Turned-up and invisibly stitched hem, preferably with cuffs
- Pleated or flat-front styles are both appropriate; the two ebb and flow in fashion focus, although most men prefer pleats for comfort

Fabric choice also helps determine a garment's suitability for mainstream casual. The cotton-blend twill described in the baseline group will still work here, but denim won't. Here are some additional fabrics to consider:

- Gabardine is woven with fine diagonal ridges on the surface. A blend of polyester-wool or polyester-rayon can closely mimic the richness of 100 percent wool at a more affordable price, but all-polyester gabardine looks cheap and stiff. Beware of overpressing, which creates shiny areas around seams and hems.
- Microfiber is a manufactured fabric that is soft, very durable, drapes well, and can often be laundered at home.
- Flannel, with its lightly brushed surface, is available in wool or blends of wool with nylon or polyester. In both solids and muted plaids, wool flannel is a good cool-weather basic, but only if cold weather in your area lasts for six months or more.

More-tailored trousers require a more exacting fit than their very casual counterparts:

- Wear pants at your natural waistline, not slung under a full tummy.
- Keep pants loose enough for pleats to lie flat, not pull open.
- Pockets should never pull or gap, showing the lining fabric.
- Correct bagginess in the seat by taking in the center back seam or inseam and lowering the waistband.
- A plain hem should just break over the shoe and angle downward about ¾" to the back.
- Cuffed pants should not be hemmed on an angle but should just skim the shoe in front.

Although solid colors are most widely used for casual trousers, a subtle check or very subtle plaid, especially in black and white, is an appropriate way to add a touch of fashion interest.

Shirts

The dress-down phenomenon has stimulated manufacturers to expand their range of crossover shirts. Traditional business shirt styling sewn from casual fabrics can be dressed up or down by the other pieces with which it is coordinated.

The original crossover shirt is the oxford cloth button-down, named for its Oxford, England, origins. The style is said to be an evolution of the authentic English polo shirt, on which the collar points were buttoned down to keep them out of the athlete's face. Oxford cloth is a basket-weave fabric. Pairs of lengthwise threads intersect with pairs of crosswise threads to create a fabric that is soft and comfortable, with a slightly textured surface. Using colored threads in one direction and white threads in the other creates pastel colors and stripes with a subtle, almost frosted appearance.

Unlike the collars of more formal business shirts, the button-down collar is lightly interfaced and meant to roll softly into place without excessive starch. It works equally well with or without a tie. Even these relaxed business shirts should only be long-sleeved.

Other collar options for mainstream casual include straight collars worn unbuttoned and banded necklines with no collar at all. Other fabric choices include "pseudo-solids"—fabrics that look solid at first glance, but actually incorporate a small, subtle pattern. This range includes:

- Tone-on-tone—the weave creates the illusion of shiny and matte areas forming a pattern in the fabric
- Micro-check—a gingham-style or houndstooth pattern as small as $1/16"$
- Micro-plaid—very tiny plaid designs, usually in monochromatic colors
- Tonal stripes—narrow stripes in shades of one color, perhaps mixed with white
- Mini-herringbone—the classic zigzag pattern in miniature scale and subtle colors
- Subtle tattersall—vertical and horizontal stripes that form tiny squares on a lighter background
- End-on-end—irregularly colored yarns (a single color mixed with white) both lengthwise and crosswise create a heather look

With so many more color options than in traditional business shirts, be sure to choose the ones that flatter your personal coloring for a healthy vibrant look. Review the color information in Chapter 3 for details. Men with warm coloring look healthiest in yellow-based colors such as teal blue, jade green, rusty reds, gold, and olive. Clear bright blue, hunter green, burgundy, and true red are good choices for men with cool coloring.

Instead of a jacket, a pullover sweater worn over a shirt creates a very relaxed feeling. That same sweater or a sweater vest worn as a layering piece under a jacket adds a spark of fashion interest, color, and texture. A plain fine-gauge knit is a dressier look, and cables and other knit-in designs are more relaxed but still appropriate. Bold multicolor patterns require more fashion savvy to coordinate with other pieces. Coogi, the Australian knit sweater line, and Ralph Lauren are higher-price choices. Most stores offer private label brands, which are usually an excellent value. Nordic ski patterns and Irish fisherman knits are off-work, sportswear choices, not for the office.

Wool and wool blends are the traditional choices for sweaters. Cotton sweaters are a season-spanning alternative, but the rib at the sleeves and hemline can easily stretch out of shape unless it is reinforced with elastic threads. Look at it before purchasing a sweater.

Although many nice sweaters are simply cut from knit fabric and sewn together, the best are "fully fashioned"—shaped in the knitting process for a more graceful look and fit. The rib trim should be knit right onto the edge of the hem, sleeve, or neckline, with no visible seam.

Choose the neckline that is best for your facial shape. Crew neckline is more flattering for a man with a long neck or very thin face. A V-neck appears to lengthen a short, thick neck or round face.

Jackets

A sportcoat or blazer is the ideal complement for a mainstream casual outfit and can often cross the blurred line into executive casual as well. What is the difference between the two?

- A solid-color fabric in a heavier weight defines the blazer.
- A patterned fabric, most often a tweed, plus horn buttons defines a sportcoat.

The blazer is a must-have in any man's wardrobe. Navy coordinates easily with trousers in gray, khaki, or taupe. A camel or golden tan blazer pairs well with navy or gray trousers for a classic combo.

A tweed sportcoat adds versatility to a wardrobe. The accent colors in the fabric design suggest colors for coordinating trousers, shirts, and ties. Wear your tweed jacket for a range of casual combinations.

- Dress down with khaki cotton pants and a denim or chambray shirt.
- Dress up with dressier trousers, a button-down shirt, and a casual tie.

Ties

A necktie, though optional with many mainstream combinations, is an obvious way to upgrade a casual look for a more important business event. Don't pair a dressy pin-dot or solid silk tie with casual clothing. Opt for a more casual geometric, a club tie, or a plaid.

- A geometric design, made up of various shapes and colors, looks most casual in larger motifs and fashion colors and more formal in a smaller motif. Geometric designs are a great device for linking solid-color shirts, trousers, and blazers into coordinated ensembles.

- In a textured design the pattern and colors are very subtle and almost look like one color from a distance. Up close, there is both color variation and a raised design.
- A club design features small repeating motifs woven into the fabric. The motifs usually represent some sporting theme—hunting horns, game birds, and so on. Sometimes the motifs are combined with a stripe for added interest.
- A plaid design is a good choice for enhancing color coordination. The bars of the plaid will be positioned diagonally on the tie. Check for a balanced placement before you buy. Sporty plaid ties are typically featured in wool challis for winter, cotton or linen for summer. Mainstream casual is not where old ties go to die. Do not attempt to substitute oversize splashy prints, a full-size fish motif, your child's artwork, or any old, soiled, or wrinkled tie demoted from your basic business wardrobe.

left A dark jacket and trousers without a tie is a comfortable mainstream business casual look.

right A midcolor sports jacket, pressed shirt, and no tie works well because the grooming and accessories support this relaxed, professional look.

A Suggested Mainstream Casual Wardrobe for Men

This coordinated grouping should cover your needs for casual days. Increase the quantities if mainstream casual is your standard business attire all week.

- Trousers (suggested number: 3)
  - *Gray or black pants in a dressier wool fabric or microfiber*
  - *Khaki, olive, or black pants in a cotton twill*

- Jacket (suggested number: 1)
  - *Navy blazer*
  - *Gray tweed or earth-tone tweed sportcoat*

- Shirts and tops (suggested number: 4)
  - *White, cream, light blue button-down oxford shirt*
  - *Black/white/olive striped oxford shirt*
  - *Gray, taupe, or olive fine-gauge turtleneck*
  - *White, cream, blue (all ranges), green (hunter, moss, olive), rust, solid polo-style shirt*
  - *Burgundy/blue olive/brown/rust patterned polo shirt*

- Ties (suggested number: 4)
  - *Geometric ties in cream/black/gray/white/burgundy/olive combinations*
  - *Black, gray, or taupe textured ties*

- Sweaters (suggested number: 2)
  - *Solid navy or black crew-neck sweater to coordinate with trousers*
  - *Crew- or V-neck sweater in multiple colors to coordinate with trousers*

- Belts (suggested number: 2)
  - *Black or brown leather belt*

- Shoes (suggested number: 1 pair)
  - *Brown or black leather, woven loafers*

Mainstream Casual Dress for Women

Businesswomen we work with feel more confident about maintaining their visual credibility and authority wearing mainstream casual clothing even when they could wear baseline. The key elements that differentiate this look from baseline casual include:

- More upscale fabrics with more structure
- Addition of a third-layer garment—either a jacket or a cardigan sweater—to project authority

The third-layer garment also builds more mix-and-match options into a mainstream casual wardrobe, allowing women to create a variety of outfits from relatively few pieces. Certain tops from the baseline casual category also can work into mainstream combinations, and pieces from the executive casual level can be "dressed down" to fit here as well.

Pants/Skirts

Layer number one—the bottom garment—can be either pants or a skirt. For a professional look and added wardrobe versatility, select bottoms in neutral solids. Of course, certain bottom styles have a more businesslike presence than others.

- Pants need to be tailored, with a fitted waistline and straight or slightly boot cut legs.
- Side seam, slightly angled pockets, or no pockets are a more polished look than topstitched patch pockets.
- A partially elasticized waist gives flexible fit but maintains a tailored appearance. Fully elasticized pull-on pants are too sporty and often look bulky and unattractive as well.
- Fly-front trousers and basic back-zip styling are equally appropriate.
- Avoid pants with a side zipper.
- Cuffs are perfectly acceptable, but optional.
- Avoid any gimmicky styles, such as very narrow or overly wide legs, excessive embroidery, or metallic trim.
- Pants for business must fit perfectly. See the fit guidelines in Chapter 8 (Baseline Casual Dress) for details.

A wide variety of skirt styles are appropriate for mainstream casual wear. Some examples include:

- A slim skirt that falls straight from the hip or tapers slightly, knee-length or longer
- Trouser styling with fly-front zipper, front pleats, and angled side pockets
- A slightly gathered skirt, provided the fabric is lightweight and the length not too short

Styles to avoid include:

- Anything much shorter than 3" above the knee
- Revealing slits, regardless of the skirt's length
- Gathered tiers or flounces—too costume-like
- Sarong styles, especially in tropical prints

Fabric choice also helps determine a garment's suitability for mainstream casual. The cotton-blend twill and chinos described in the baseline group can still work here, but denim won't. Also consider these fabric options:

- Gabardine is a rich-looking woven fabric with fine diagonal ridges on the surface. All-polyester gabardine often looks cheap; polyester-wool or polyester-rayon blends look richer. Many blended gabs can be gently washed, but beware of too much pressing, which creates shiny areas around seams and hems.
- Linen-look fabrics have a pebbly surface texture and crisp appearance. Pure linen wrinkles terribly and isn't a good choice for casual career wear. Blends of linen-cotton, linen-polyester, rayon-cotton, or rayon-polyester create a linen-like appearance without the excessive wrinkling or the fancy price tag. Linen is usually limited to warm-weather wear.
- Flannel is a plain-woven fabric with a lightly brushed surface, available in wool or blends of wool with nylon or polyester. Flannel often is available in both solids and plaids and is a good basic for cool-weather months if your cool weather spans at least six months.

Tops

Layer number two—the top—can be in either a knit or woven fabric. Solid colors provide maximum versatility and coordination, but subtle stripes, plaids, or artistic or understated animal prints can add appealing visual interest. The closer to your face a garment is worn, the more important it is that you choose colors that are flattering to your unique personal coloring, warm or cool.

Like their layer number-one counterparts, certain tops have a more businesslike mood than others.

- A tailored shirt in solid is the surest bet. Stripes and subtle patterns can work, too. Look for details such as a front button placket, topstitching, and a collar on a band. Contrasting white collars look fresh.
- Blouses are more softly styled than shirts. Design features may include soft gathers, decorative tucks, rounded collars, and slightly fuller sleeves. Avoid excessively frilly details such as ruffles or lacy collars.
- A shell is similar to a blouse, but more streamlined in styling. Long or short sleeves are usually straight and without cuffs, and the round neckline has a binding or narrow band instead of a collar. A simple shell lets the third-layer garment become the center of attention.
- An upscale T-shirt or fine-gauge sweater really is a shell made from knit fabric. These comfortable, easy-to-wear garments convey a much more professional message than their boxy, rib-trimmed sportswear cousins.
- Turtlenecks from the baseline casual category can function as mainstream tops as well.
- More revealing styles such as tank tops or ribbed knit shells are acceptable only if the third-layer garment, which should cover the arms completely, is worn at all times.
- Halters, camisoles, and cropped (above the waistline) tops simply don't belong at the office.

Fabric choices contribute to making these top styles more dressy or casual. Cotton or poly-cotton blends look more formal in smooth broadcloth or more relaxed in an oxford cloth. Solid colors appear more formal than stripes, and plaids are the most casual. Narrow bands in one or two colors create a more formal stripe or plaid than wide bars of multiple colors.

- Sandwashed silk and its synthetic look-alikes create a feeling of relaxed elegance, providing the garment quality is high. Synthetic silk (usually microfiber, polyester, acetate, nylon, or a blend of these) come in a wide range of qualities. The best are nearly as lustrous and fluid as the real thing. Cheap imitations feel stiff rather than soft and have a telltale chemical sheen.
- Cotton and cotton-blend jersey and interlock are more casual than fine-gauge sweater knits.

- Wool and acrylic sweaters are only for cold weather, whereas light-weight cotton and synthetic blends can usually be worn year-round.

Skip any fabric with see-through potential (voile, chiffon, georgette, or lace) or anything with excessive shine, such as satin.

Jackets

Layer number three—the jacket—is the element that pulls casual pieces together into a polished business appearance. Any skirt-top or pant-top combination needs a third layer to convey a strong message of professionalism and authority.

The most obvious third layer is a jacket. Traditional jacket styling is the first choice, but some sportier jacket styles that wouldn't work for conventional business attire also may be right at home in mainstream casual. A bright jacket with snaps instead of buttons in a good-quality fabric can be a fresh alternative. A blazer in solid or tweed can dress up even the most casual underlayers. Cardigan styling—with a zipper or buttons—looks relaxed and comfortable.

Easy-fitting unlined jackets with pushup sleeves are an ideal casual look. But choose only the highest-quality knits and other unlined fabrics, as there is no lining to help the garment retain its shape and resist wrinkling. Shorter waist-length or bomber-style jackets are good choices for women who have no major figure challenges below the waist.

Some very casual jackets simply don't belong in a career wardrobe even on casual day. Don't wear these in the office:

- Zip-front hooded sweatshirts
- Nylon parkas or windbreakers
- Satiny sports team jackets
- Denim jean jackets
- Any jacket with a product slogan or logo

Jackets that belong to business suits often are too dressy to mix with mainstream casual garments. If you're uncertain about a particular piece, ask yourself whether the jacket would look silly with the sleeves pushed up

left Pants for mainstream business casual should be finished with a jacket or an additional third piece. This is a more classic, dressy trouser suit because of the traditional jacket styling and matching color.

center This is a more casual mainstream look. The jacket is cotton and has snaps rather than buttons. But paired with black pants and closed-toe shoes, it works well.

right Mainstream business casual allows for more color, flair, and styling. Matching the striped collar with a striped top is a lively, pulled-together look.

or the cuffs rolled back. If it can't be "loosened up" that way, it probably can't look casual.

A sweater jacket is another third-layer option. An ancient fisherman-knit cable sweater won't make the grade. But a flat-knit cardigan in a quality wool blend could work beautifully, especially one without a hip-hugging bottom band. Or look for a sweater with style details that mimic a blazer or bomber jacket.

A crew neck or V-neck pullover sweater can also be a third layer, worn over a turtleneck or collared shirt, when you prefer to look less authoritative.

A vest is yet another third-layer option for casual dressing. It is often referred to as a jacket without sleeves. As a more relaxed jacket alternative, a vest can individualize a look and link solid-color tops and bottoms into coordinated ensembles. Some vests can do double duty as a second-layer blouse under another jacket. Vests can be fitted waist-length styles or longer and more loosely cut. They can be knit or woven, button-up, or pullover, in solid colors, plaids, prints, or embroidered designs. But the overall effect should be tailored or elegant rather than funky, ethnic, or outdoorsy. Some second-layer shirts can double as third-layer pieces, worn bloused and belted over a polo shirt or fine-gauge sweater.

Even a scarf can be a third-layer piece. Picture a black twill skirt and cream turtleneck. Ho-hum. But add an animal print scarf in shades of black, brown, cream, and charcoal—instant ensemble.

One major advantage of planning a casual business wardrobe around this three-layer concept is the versatility and mix-and-match potential it offers. This sample wardrobe—with selections for women with warm and cool coloring—shows how just fifteen well-chosen items can yield at least thirty outfits in varying degrees of casualness. That's over six months of Fridays without repeating an outfit!

A Suggested Mainstream Casual Wardrobe for Women

Because we recommend this category for many casual occasions, the number of items can be adjusted upward. If mainstream business casual is a part of your wardrobe every day, increase the suggested number significantly.

- Skirts (suggested number: 2)
  - *Black, taupe, olive, or brown slim or slightly gathered skirt*

- Knit dress (suggested number: 1)
  - *Black, olive, or red two-piece casual knit dress*

- Trousers (suggested number: 2)
  - *Solid black, olive, taupe, or brown tailored trousers*

- Jackets (suggested number: 2)
  - *Black/white tweed, or earth-tone tweed blazer or jacket*

- Sweater jacket (suggested number: 1)
  - *Black, red, or taupe cardigan sweater jacket*
- Tops (suggested number: 4)
  - *Solid red, black, olive, or white long-sleeved cotton turtleneck*
  - *Solid red, black, olive, or white fine-gauge mock turtleneck*
  - *Red/black/olive combination long-sleeved print blouse*
  - *Solid white, red, black, or olive camp shirt (button front)*
  - *Solid red, black, olive, white cotton-knit polo shirt*

- Accessories (suggested number of each: 2)
  - *Black or brown leather belt*
  - *Black/white/taupe/red patterned scarves*

- Shoes (suggested number: 1 pair)
  - *Black or brown leather loafers*

By wearing the tops alone or layered in pairs, you can create at least thirty combinations in all from just fifteen pieces. Black, white, red, and taupe can mix and match in nearly any combination.

Mainstream business casual is safe, affordable, and coordinated enough for most business environments that permit casual attire. Whether at meetings, retreats, training, in front of customers who are mirroring the same attire, on the airplane, or at a casual dinner, this is what the majority of corporate America is wearing to dress down.

chapter ten

executive casual dress

Luxury need not have a price—comfort itself is a luxury.

Geoffrey Beene

executive casual describes the very upper crust of casual clothing, soft and elegantly tailored in luxurious fabrics. It describes quality clothing on par with your classic business wardrobe, but more relaxed in mood, and coordinated with a personal flair that traditional business attire often doesn't permit.

This is the logical look for business owners and senior management. If you own a business or are in a leadership position in your firm, make sure you set the tone for casual dress. The upper-level management executive needs a look that supports the concept of dressing down, but that also commands the respect of his or her employees and the firm's clients or customers.

In conservative fields such as banking, accounting, and law, the credibility of executive casual is the only standard for anyone with client contact. It also is the most authoritative casual choice for high-visibility roles in more relaxed professions. Creative fields such as entertainment and advertising may embrace executive casual as their basic business attire.

The elegance of executive casual doesn't come cheaply, so focus on quality rather than quantity. It is less important to have an extensive wardrobe than it is to have each piece convey a powerful message. A few key items can coordinate a variety of looks and help you project a positive visual image.

Executive Casual Dress for Men

A man's executive casual wardrobe is made up of separates—trousers, shirts, and blazers or sportcoats—defined by just a few common characteristics:

- Contemporary, but classic, styling
- Top-quality fabrics—natural fibers and upscale microfibers
- Exceptional construction and tailoring

Trousers

Trouser styling can be traditional or follow fashion cycles. Flat-front designs and pleated styles are both appropriate. Successful agents know that the three absolutes in real estate are location, location, and location. Similarly, the three absolutes in building a quality wardrobe are fabric, fabric, and fabric. Choosing garments in excellent fabrics sends a clear message that you won't compromise on value. Top-quality fabrics for trousers include the following:

- Pure wool gabardine is a superstar for its shape retention and long wear. Gabardine's flat surface and solid colors showcase important details such as pleats and creases. Because wool breathes, lightweight gabs are comfortable year-round in many climates, at least three seasons in nearly every area of the country.
- The term worsted describes smooth-surface wool fabrics in solids and very subtle patterns typical of menswear looks. Worsteds perform very much like lightweight gabardine.
- Flannel is a slightly thicker wool fabric with a lightly brushed surface. Often made in heathered colors, it is limited seasonally because it only works well in cold weather.
- Microfiber is not actually a fiber at all, but a process for making virtually any synthetic, including polyester, nylon, acrylic, and rayon. By making the individual fibers very, very small—about half the diameter of the finest silk—manufacturers can create almost indestructible fabrics that drape beautifully, breathe, and absorb body moisture. Microfiber trousers are virtually wrinkle-proof, hold a crease beautifully, and yet are not stiff.

Shirts

Shirts for executive casual share many characteristics with fine dress shirts, but usually with a fashion "twist" in color or detail:

- Long sleeves always; ¼" to ½" should show beyond the jacket sleeve.
- Barrel (button-over) cuffs with a buttoned sleeve placket; French cuffs are too dressy.
- Choice of traditional or updated collar styles:
  - *A pin or tab collar looks fresh and sharp.*
  - *A rounded collar, especially white on a colored shirt, is a crisp option.*
  - *White and pale blue are the obvious color choices, along with less traditional pink, yellow, or deeper blue.*
  - *Narrow, evenly spaced stripes or plaids of one color on white are an alternative.*
  - *Banded collar shirts in white work well, too.*

The button-down is not a preferred option for the elegance of executive casual. Also, putting monogrammed initials on any shirt, straight collar or button, is dated and could be perceived as pretentious.

Some men prefer the relaxed look and feel of a luxury turtleneck in their executive casual wardrobe. A discount-store cotton pullover will look out of place with fine trousers and jackets, so shop carefully for pima cotton knits, cotton-silk, and wool-silk blends or elegant cashmere. The more updated version of the turtleneck features fine ribs and a shorter neck.

Jackets

A blazer or sportcoat is a must to complete this executive look. Traditional navy or camel single-breasted blazers from the mainstream category can function here, or you may choose to add another jacket featuring one or more of these sophisticated elements:

- *Double-breasted shaping.* The angular lines of a double-breasted blazer or sportcoat create a polished, authoritative appearance. Many men with shorter legs or fuller bodies are concerned about looking heavier wearing a double-breasted style. Depending on how a man's weight is distributed, double-breasted may not be a good option.

A jacket with six buttons—two that actually button—will shorten the silhouette. But a six-button jacket in which only the single bottom button closes can visually elongate the body as the viewer's eye follows the longer expanse of diagonal lapel. The elongating effect of a six-to-one jacket is greatest in a tweedy fabric with color-blended horn buttons. The abrupt color contrast of brass buttons on a solid-colored blazer draws attention away from the long lapel line. However, if a man carries much of his weight in his midsection, single-breasted is the better choice.

▪ *Interesting fabrics.* A silk-blend tweed or small check has a luxurious look. "Raw" silk fiber, as it comes directly from the cocoon, makes a fabric similar in weight to linen suiting. Advantages of silk suiting include a rich appearance and the ability to lose wrinkles. On the minus side, silk is relatively fragile and subject to wear in areas of abrasion. Wool tweeds should be fine in texture and subtle in color. Coarse tweeds, leather buttons, and elbow patches belong in the country, not in the office. The pebbly surface of a worsted wool crepe gives a rich look to a blazer. A fine herringbone weave is yet another sophisticated option. Camel hair and cashmere blazers are luxurious, but more fragile.

▪ *Nontraditional colors.* A black blazer is a smart wardrobe addition, creating a sophisticated pairing with trousers in gray, tan, celery, putty, or taupe. A very handsome shade of dark hunter green can be equally versatile in a blazer, but don't confuse this color with the brighter green you might see at a St. Patrick's Day party or on the winning golfer at the Masters.

A casual blazer or sportcoat should meet the same exacting fit standards as a suit jacket. Try on the jacket with a business shirt and trousers, plus the same paraphernalia you usually carry in your pockets. Refer to Chapter 3 for fit and alteration information.

Ties

The executive casual look is usually finished with a necktie, unless of course a turtleneck or banded neck is replacing the traditional collared business shirt. The casual elegance of silk in a geometric, woven, club, or

striped motif makes a good balance with clothing in this category.

Pair a high-contrast tie fabric with a dark jacket and pants and light shirt. Select a muted tie pattern to wear with a subdued jacket/pant/shirt combination. Use the colors in the tie pattern to link the shirt, trouser, and jacket colors into a coordinated ensemble:

- A burgundy tie with a black-and-gray geometric print would blend well with black-and-white subtle plaid trousers, a black blazer, and white shirt. The burgundy adds interest.
- With khaki trousers, blue shirt, and navy blazer, add a navy tie with a small design in olive, light blue, and red.

Match the light neutrals with your tie and shirt. With a white shirt, a tie with cream in the pattern will look tired and dingy. Find a tie with white accents instead. With a cream or ecru shirt, wear a tie with ivory touches instead of bright white.

When you can duplicate your hair color within the pattern of your tie, the look is especially harmonious and individualized:

- For a red-haired man, look for ties that include rust or reddish-brown shades.
- Blond men look good in ties with some tan, gold, or camel accents.
- Dark-haired men are flattered by ties that include a touch of black.

Because of the significant investment in purchasing executive casual items, the suggested number of items is minimal. However, if you have the means and the opportunities, adjust these suggested numbers accordingly.

A Suggested Executive Casual Wardrobe for Men

- Trousers (suggested number: 2)
  - *Putty, taupe, or dark olive microfiber, flat-front or pleated trousers*

- Jackets (suggested number: 1)
  - *Earth-tone tweed, single-breasted, silk-blend sportcoat*

- Shirts and tops (suggested number: 2)
  - *Putty, taupe, or dark olive fine-gauge Merino wool mock turtleneck*
  - *White/olive stripe rounded-collar shirt*
  - *Solid black wool vest*

- Ties (suggested number: 2)
  - *Earth-tone combination geometric tie*
  - *Earth-tone combination textured tie*

- Belts (suggested number: 1)
  - *Deep brown leather belt*

- Shoes (suggested number: 1 pair)
  - *Dark brown exceptional-quality woven leather loafers*

This is the most formal of executive business casual—the classic blazer without metal buttons paired with gray wool trousers, a white shirt, 100 percent silk tie, and a linen handkerchief in the pocket. Updated eyeglasses and beautifully styled hair put him in the boardroom or on any senior team.

Executive Casual Dress for Women

Executive casual dress for women demands clothing on a quality par with a boardroom-level business wardrobe but more relaxed in mood. In fact, by blending in just a few well-chosen executive casual items, many professional women can fairly easily extend their current boardroom wardrobes into executive casual.

Executive casual lends credibility in conservative businesses, such as the legal and financial fields. It also is the most authoritative casual choice for upper-level or high-visibility women in more relaxed professions. Many women in creative fields, such as entertainment and advertising, adopt executive casual—spiced up with their own signature touches—as their basic business attire. High-volume real estate agents live in such clothes. Every woman should have at least one selection from this category, if only for the day that an important meeting or presentation falls on casual day—yours or the client's.

The defining characteristics of an executive casual wardrobe are:

- Comfortable, but updated, classic styling
- Exceptional fabrics
- Exquisite construction and fit

All that elegance can carry a hefty price tag. But you don't need too many pieces—just the right ones. A few key items can mix into a multitude of looks, each one making a positive visual statement about your ability and your attitude.

For example, one of our clients had to take several deep, relaxing breaths before writing a $900 check for a black microfiber pantsuit with a matching skirt. A month later she called to say it was the best clothing investment she'd ever made. She takes the suit on her frequent business trips, and finds she can wear it countless ways, up and down the formal-to-casual continuum:

- As a skirted suit
- As a pantsuit
- As a tailored jacket with other skirts
- As a relaxed jacket, sleeves pushed up, over other pants
- As basic pants with a sweater set
- As a basic skirt with other jackets
- As a cocktail suit, with five strands of pearls and buttoned up without a blouse

She reports wearing at least two pieces of the trio several times each week. In microfiber, which is not restricted by weather, her purchase can easily yield 100 or more wearings in the first year alone.

The moral is the same whether your budget can manage $200 for a suit or stretch for a $900 ensemble or accommodate even pricier clothing: Learn to judge the true value of clothing purchases by more than just the number on the price tag.

The components of an executive casual wardrobe are basic pieces—pants, skirts, blouses, and jackets—made special by their fabric, styling, and detailing.

Pants

All pants in this category fit the general description "tailored," but express that term in a variety of subtly different ways:

- Waistlines can feature a conventional waistband, a narrow binding, or simply a raised edge.
- An elasticized section in a waistband gives flexible fit, especially for figures that require more comfort.
- Unpleated fronts show off firm, flat tummies, whereas soft pleats can hide a multitude of sins.
- Heavier gabardine looks best in straight leg shapes.
- Slightly fuller leg styles fall gracefully in softer fabrics.
- Cuffs weight the lower edge to help the leg fall most smoothly.
- Interesting details such as double welt pockets or innovative closures imply quality clothing.
- Trousers are usually fully lined.

Look for these "dress-to-impress" pants in a variety of beautiful fabrics:

- Pure wool gabardine holds its shape well and wears for years. Its flat surface and solid colors showcase crisp details such as pleats, creases, and topstitching. Lightweight gabardine lets air circulate and body moisture evaporate, making it comfortable year-round in many climates.
- The term worsted describes fine-quality wool fabrics in very subtle plaids and stripes typical of menswear looks. Worsted stripe trousers can make short legs appear longer. Worsteds perform very much like gabardine.
- Wool crepe has a pebbly surface texture that absorbs light for exceptionally rich-looking color. Crepe works to its best advantage in softer

style details and requires a lining to prevent bagging in the knees. Its looser weave makes crepe very wearable even in warmer weather.

- Though pure linen is simply too wrinkle-prone for career trousers, innovative fiber blending can overcome the problem. Adding about 20 percent polyester to 80 percent linen creates a virtually wrinkle-free fabric with the rich luster of natural linen. Blending roughly equal amounts of linen and viscose makes a more matte finish fabric that retains the traditional fine surface wrinkles while holding the garment's shape and withstanding any deep-set creases.

- The silk fiber, as it comes directly from the cocoon, can be woven into rich-looking canvas and hopsack fabrics, similar in weight to linen suiting. (This is a completely different fabric group from the lightweight blouse fabrics most women associate with the term silk.) Wrinkles hang out quickly from silk suiting—a special plus for travel. On the minus side, silk is relatively fragile and subject to wear along edges or in areas where the fabric rubs against itself.

- Microfiber is created through a process for making virtually any synthetic, including polyester, nylon, acrylic, and rayon. By making the individual fibers very, very small—about half the diameter of the finest silk—manufacturers can create almost indestructible suiting fabrics that drape beautifully, breathe, and absorb body moisture. Microfiber suits are virtually wrinkle-proof, yet they never look stiff.

before&now

before A floral-patterned dress, in flimsy fabric, with a worn-out sweater is not an effective business casual outfit. Her hair needs a cut and makeup will bring out her eyes and smile. **now** A striking pantsuit with a shaped jacket finished with pearls is an elegant look for business casual. The white top adds punch to the whiteness of her teeth. Her hair and makeup are smooth and sophisticated.

Jackets

Some women express concern about looking heavier when wearing a double-breasted style. While it is true that the parallel rows of metal buttons can draw the viewer's eye in a horizontal direction, slight design variations can make a double-breasted blazer flattering, depending on how a woman's weight is distributed.

- Straight-cut jackets with little or no waistline shaping are the best bet for straight figures.
- Jackets with princess seams or darts to shape a curved waist flatter hourglass figures.
- Contrasting color buttons emphasize their horizontal placement. Consider changing to color-matching buttons.
- The lower the topmost working button is placed—on the jacket and therefore on your body—the more elongating and slenderizing the lapel line.
- Peaked lapels lengthen the total look more than a traditional or rounded lapel.

For the tallest, trimmest silhouette, pair a double-breasted blazer with pants in the same color. For variation, select a similar color value, not dramatically lighter or darker. A double-breasted blazer should be buttoned when you are standing, but usually needs to be unbuttoned for you to sit comfortably.

Other jacket styles, many of them from the suits in your basic business wardrobe, can combine with upscale trousers for an executive casual look. Check your closet for single-breasted jackets, shawl-collared blazers, no-lapel cardigan styles, short Chanel-style jackets, or shaped, belted jackets that you can mix and match.

Tip: Minimize wrinkles in natural fiber pants and skirts. Each time you sit, rearrange the folds that form across your lap into a single deep pleat across your tummy. Eliminate baggy knees by grasping the pants legs at midthigh and lifting slightly as you sit. Always remove your jacket when entering a car, and lay it flat or hang it up. When flying, look for an overhead compartment or hanging area for your jacket.

Skirts and Shirts

The skirts from those same suits may also have a second life in executive casual. Pair slim or softly pleated skirt styles with a sweater-knit jacket or cardigan for a new spin on relaxed elegance. Sweaters for this category should be high-quality wool, cashmere, cotton, or silk blends with a smooth surface and firm enough to retain shape well.

Shirts, blouses, and tops for this category continue the theme of top-of-the-line quality and casual elegance. Here are some of the best options:

- Cotton shirts or blouses in pima or Sea Island cotton have a beautifully soft hand and subtle sheen. Specially cultivated plants grow the extra-long cotton fibers for this luxurious fabric. Professional laundering and pressing will give these garments the most polished appearance.
- Handkerchief linen—a lightweight fabric made from natural flax fibers—is another elegant option. Linen's tendency to wrinkle is less of a problem in blouses than in pants and skirts. Professional laundering optimizes the look.
- Silk broadcloth also makes rich-looking shirts, especially in woven stripes or small check patterns. Other silk fabrics such as crêpe de Chine, charmeuse, or jacquard work only in versions that are not too soft or shiny for the personality of executive casual dressing.
- A silk or wool lightweight sweater shell is a comfortable alternative. A jewel or mock-turtle neckline works well with a variety of jacket styles. Look for a firm knit that holds its shape well and doesn't cling to the body.

The colors of executive casual typically are the classic neutrals. A high-contrast combination of light and dark color values communicates the most authoritative message. A woman with cool coloring might develop a coordinated grouping in black/white/red or navy/burgundy/off-white. A warm-toned woman could build a collection of pieces in dark brown or black/warm red/ivory or teal/rust/cream. Black is considered to be a basic for both warm and cool skin tones, but a woman in the warm category needs to add an accent of softer or brighter color near the face.

Here is a real-life example of adapting an existing business wardrobe to meet an executive casual dress code one day per week.

From current wardrobe:

- Black wool crepe longer jacket
- Matching black slim skirt
- Black/ivory plaid fitted jacket
- Ivory midcalf slim skirt
- Black silk fine-gauge sweater

Additions:

- Black wool trousers (same brand and fabric as existing suit)
- Black wool cardigan sweater with ivory bands at front and sleeve
- Ivory long-sleeved silk T-shirt

Consider the combinations for these executive casual items:

- Black pants, black silk sweater, black jacket
- Black pants, ivory tee, black jacket
- Black pants, black silk sweater, banded cardigan
- Black pant, ivory tee, banded cardigan
- Black skirts, black silk sweater, banded cardigan
- Black skirt, ivory tee, banded cardigan
- Ivory skirt, ivory tee, banded cardigan
- Ivory skirt, black silk sweater, banded cardigan

All the necessary accessories—belts and low-heeled pumps in black and taupe, black purse, and gold earrings—are usually already in most women's business wardrobes.

Unlike men, who can't break apart their business suits to create separates, women generally have this option, and it works especially well for executive business casual.

chapter eleven

the plus-size professional

> Personal style is being able to say no. No one who we think of as a person of great personal style was a fashion victim. They are people who are very aware of their bodies, their features, and what works.
>
> Michael Kors

if you are a plus-size professional, you join two-thirds of American adults. In fact, the most popular size in the United States for women is size 14. Yet well-made, flattering plus-size garments are not always easy to find. This chapter is directed to both men and women with an online resource guide at the end. Although there needs to be more selection and availability, clothing manufacturers are doing a better job of addressing this business population that constitutes more than $18 billion in sales.

The plus-size professional has two choices when it comes to wardrobe and image—lose weight and make clothing shopping easier, or accept your body proportions and commit to dressing well. We can help you with the second choice.

Both men and women in plus-sizes can radiate a confident, attractive, and powerful presence with carefully selected, well-cut clothes. Generally, it takes more shopping time, more money, and more alterations to find the right garments; but the self-assurance and confidence gained is well worth the investment.

Residing to the right of center of the bell curve in size or weight means that there are fewer choices. As mentioned before, clothing manufacturers don't offer this market the full range and style of other sizes. However, when plus-size professionals spend the requisite time and money to create a thoughtful, well-designed business wardrobe, they get added leverage because no one is more spectacular than a stylishly attired plus-size man or woman who carries himself or herself with grace, confidence, and elegance. Personal impact is truly about the whole package, not just a set of measurements.

One important fact to consider is that all of us are seen from a 360-degree viewpoint. This means that looking in a store mirror provides only a 90-degree perspective. We need a full-length, three-way mirror to determine how the other 270-degree view looks. Be sure to sit down in any purchase in front of a mirror before making a decision. All of us expand when seated, and it is important to determine if our potential purchase will be both comfortable and attractive. At home, be sure to have a full-length mirror with a hand-held mirror close by. Always do a thirty-second, 360-degree detail check before leaving the house.

We are going to consider four areas of wardrobe development for the plus-size professional and make recommendations for both men and women.

1. *Body type and fit.* Body types vary greatly, so finding your best styles and sticking with them will make the most sense. The goal is to create length and visually stretch out your proportions.
2. *Color.* Color doesn't cost anything extra and adds so much. While black is a basic for women and navy is a basic for men, draw focus to the face with a colorful top or scarf or an interesting necktie. This puts the emphasis above the shoulders.
3. *Fabric.* Fabric will be the single, most important area to consider in terms of investment. Fabric constitutes about two-thirds of the cost of a garment. The right fabric will skim, slim, and last for years.
4. *Accessories.* Jewelry, interesting buttons, gold chains as part of a garment, collar pins, and all the other wardrobe details add interest and impact. They provide your personal style and individual signature.

Body Type

All of us carry our weight in different areas. Each plus-size body is unique in weight distribution. Some bodies are top-heavy, some are bottom heavy, and others carry weight right in the middle. Knowing exactly where your challenges are makes it easier to zero in on the right styles, details, and colors, and invest well.

Arms

If you are a plus-size woman, chances are that heavy upper arms are the number one figure challenge that you will want to conceal. Steer clear of sleeveless styles, unless you are sure that your jacket or sweater won't come off during the day, if you feel your arms are a problem area.

Consider the following styles as excellent choices for women's business tops or blouses:

- Long-sleeved tops or those that end above the elbow
- Tops with sleeves that taper to the wrist
- Raglan or dolman sleeves that are seamed off the shoulder
- Tops with vertical lines, like seams or a long, thin lapel
- Simplicity around the neckline
- Modest V-necks or lower-cut crew necks, but not high-cut crew necks (V-necks are especially good because they visually lengthen the neck.)

Consider the following styles as excellent choices for men's shirts:

- Long-sleeved business shirts, even rolled up, will be the most flattering
- Polo shirts long enough to tuck in neatly, with arm holes that are cut generously for all-day comfort
- Custom shirts for the best fit and investment

Midsection

The stomach area is actually easier to camouflage than heavy upper arms. Jackets and tops can skim across larger proportions and move the eye either up or down, and away from the middle.

left Low-cut tops are not professional, regardless of a person's stature or looks. Cleavage distracts and detracts from the overall image a professional woman wants to convey.

right Sharp, crisp, and nicely styled, this top and jacket are relaxed and professional. Her hair is nicely cut and foundation, lipstick, and mascara finish her look.

These are the recommended styles for women:

- Long, trim, third-piece items like tunics, cardigans, jackets, and shirts in heavier fabrics stay on the outside of trousers and skirts. The second piece includes tops or blouses, which can be tucked in so the third piece can provide the slimming.
- When any hem is worn outside, it must be finished and neat. A single vent in the back is attractive and comfortable.
- Jackets and tops that nip and taper slightly inward at the waist produce a shapelier silhouette.
- Jackets and coats that are longer, single-breasted, and have one, two, or three buttons can help hide midsection figure challenges.
- Sheath dresses that skim but aren't tight on the body, worn with a third piece, are comfortable and flattering. A shorter skirt with a longer tunic or jacket is a great combination.

- Moderate shoulder pads balance a challenging tummy area.
- Narrower pants with very little pleating, as opposed to styling with voluminous fabric, create a sleeker look.

These are the recommended styles for men:

- Single-breasted jackets with a two- or three-button close will hide a large stomach.
- A little more shoulder padding balances the physique.
- Single-vented jackets are the most flattering, as opposed to double-vented or no-vent jackets.

left Anything too tight will always add pounds. The jacket and the trousers are too small.

center This suit is too large and looks misshapen and bulky. The jacket needs tailoring and the sleeves need shortening.

right Well-tailored and elegant, a dark, worsted wool suit with a coordinated tie and a crisp white shirt are attractive and slenderizing.

- Classic jacket styles that are close to the body are the most flattering.
- The trouser waistband should rest just below the navel. Nothing will add more to a man's midsection than a waistband that is too small, forcing the stomach to hang over the top of the trousers.

Bottom Heavy

Large hips, derrières, and thighs can be challenging for women and men in selecting the right choices. The good news is that we spend most of our business day seated, so our bottom half is more camouflaged than our top half. These are suggestions for both genders to slenderize from the waist down.

For women:

- A-line or gently gathered skirts, but nothing voluminous
- Slightly lower-rising skirts and trousers to elongate the torso
- Straight-leg, flat-front trousers that have enough fabric in the rise to be comfortable when seated
- The hemline is very important—generally right below the knee is the most flattering, but if you have shapely legs, go for midknee to even above the knee

For men:

- Straight-edge pockets that lay flat and don't bulge
- A trouser length that drapes slightly on the top of the shoe
- Cuffs for nice detail and added weight at the bottom of the trouser for a trimmer fit

Color

Let's face it—solid, dark, muted colors, especially from the waist down, are the most flattering for the plus-size professional because they tend to recede. Psychological research and just simple observation confirm it. But adding bright color in strategic places is essential. It provides energy, interest, and style.

Choose colors for each clothing piece with careful attention to the figure areas that you wish to emphasize or de-emphasize. Color will guide attention where it is wanted and divert attention from where it is not wanted. Using the monochromatic approach, the same color from top to toe (or knee), is also very elegant. Monochromatic ensembles have the most slenderizing effect of all. Wearing the same shade from top to bottom, including women's hosiery or men's socks and then matching shoes to the hem, lengthens and thus slims.

The monochromatic look does not equal monotony. Create subtle interest within a single shade by pairing pieces with contrasting textures and fabrics. If the shades are precisely matched, the effect will be rich and interesting. One striking accessory, like a beautiful tie or necklace, will add interest as well.

A plus-size man will be more flattered in a suit than a sports jacket and contrasting trousers. A plus-size woman will be more flattered in a matching trouser or skirted suit than in contrasting separates. The following are ways to think about color as accent, interest, and a slenderizing technique.

For women:

- Black, brown, gray, olive, navy, hunter green, and dark cranberry work well for jackets, skirts, and trousers but not with a large print or pattern. Solid colors mix and match the best and are the most slimming. However, a subtle print or tone-on-tone can work beautifully.
- Monochromatic/tone-on-tone is flattering in all colors, but especially in black, blues, browns, grays, and heather.
- Matching buttons on a women's jacket, rather than contrasting gold metal buttons, keep the eye moving.
- Cobalt, red, turquoise, emerald green, and a subtle animal print are especially beautiful accent colors.

For men:

- Consider a navy, charcoal, olive, or medium blue suit when the occasion calls for it. It will be the most powerful, slimming, and attractive of all business choices.
- The navy blazer with minimal detailing is the best choice for a sports jacket.
- Select solids, pinstripes, or anything with a faint pattern.

- Avoid brass and metal buttons. Select garments with matching buttons.
- Black is perfect for a tuxedo, but dark charcoal or navy is more flattering for daytime wear.

Fabric

If you are an individual who cools off through excessive perspiring, consider wearing lightweight to medium-weight fabrics year-round. These fabrics will allow your skin to breathe. Overheated offices are a problem, but by adding lighter layers that you can remove, you will have warmth when you need it, and comfort if you begin to perspire.

Most of the garments sold in the United States are manufactured outside of the country. This means that a substantial portion of what you pay for in a garment is for the fabric. For the plus-size professional, this is money extremely well spent. Quality fabrics will drape more attractively and alter much easier. The same color in two fabrics of very different qualities won't even resemble each other in appearance, fit, or durability.

The idea is to add crispness without adding bulk. A common misconception regarding plus-size attire is that flimsy fabrics are most flattering. Lighter fabrics, such as microfiber and fine-gauge acrylics, have a tendency to cling in an unflattering manner. Consider crisper fabrics, such as a lightweight wool gabardine, which will still drape nicely to skim, smooth, and conceal. Avoid bulky fabrics such as tweed, thick linen, or heavy wool, which add both weight and inches.

For women:

- Soft, drape-friendly fabrics: A quality matte jersey, tensel, rayon with Lycra, 100 percent light- to medium-weight wool, wool-blends, cotton with no more than 30 percent of a synthetic blend, heavier gauge silk, and other quality synthetic fabrics that look, drape, and perform like natural fibers.
- Avoid any fabric with a distinct shine to it. It adds pounds. Matte finishes are much more attractive.
- Heavier weight crepes can be a very attractive finish for wool jackets, trousers, and skirts.

left Tight trousers in a large print draw the eye to an area that she wants to camouflage, not emphasize. The low-cut top is too revealing, her hair is too flat, and makeup will add sparkle and sophistication.

center Tightness in any garment always adds pounds and is distracting. When seated, this dress becomes even more uncomfortable and ill-fitting.

right From top to toe, this is a fresh, slimming look. Her hair is well cut, makeup accents her eyes and cheeks, and her dark matching suit is classic and trim. Her necklace is more elongating, and the toned hosiery and shoes create a beautiful, finished look.

■ Knits can be elegant if they are heavier in gauge, include a longer jacket or tunic, and are extremely well fitting. They require additional undergarments; without them, they can be a disaster.

For men:

■ Select light- to medium-weight fabric for all suits—Super 120s, Super 100s, tropical-weight wools, and medium-weight worsted wool are great choices.

- Select a heavier weight fabric for shirts to camouflage any body hair and weight. Have them professionally laundered for the best finish.
- Heavier weight cotton and cotton blends are good choices for casual polo-style shirts.
- While technology has produced some remarkable fabrics, most microfiber is not the best choice for trousers and other wardrobe pieces for the large man. It is usually too flimsy and clinging. Tighter woven fabrics will work much better.

Accessories

When we had the opportunity to meet Oprah and be on her show, she showed us a roomful of beautiful shoes in a size eight. She laughed and said, "This is the only size that stays constant for me!" The value of accessories, with the exception of belts, is that we don't have to worry about fitting into them. They always fit. More than that, they last for years, travel from outfit to outfit, and add our personal signature to what we wear.

For women:

- Hair, makeup, and extra attention to grooming are essential and worth every dollar you invest. The wrong haircut will add ten to fifteen pounds to your look. The right one will subtract the same amount. Schedule a cut every six to eight weeks and color as often as needed. Makeup will slim down a full face and bring out beautiful eyes or attractive lips. Invest in a makeup consultation and use the products every morning. Nails and hands should be especially well taken care of. During the summer, it is especially important that feet are maintained either at home or with professional pedicures. Toenail polish should be chip-free and any calluses or rough skin should be buffed away. Sheer polish or a French manicure is the most fresh and attractive look for both fingers and toes.
- Jewelry should be one larger, chunkier piece that draws attention to the right places. Avoid small-scale pieces. Select a dramatic gold bracelet for nice wrists and well-manicured nails, a semiprecious stone necklace or pearls for a nicely defined neck, or sterling silver earrings to show off makeup or hair.

- Leather belts with gold or silver accents will work well on a figure with a defined waist. They are most flattering with a tunic or jacket over them.
- Scarves can tie a look together, but they need to be in silk and well knotted so they stay in place all day.
- Hosiery toned to the hemline is very slimming. A sheer denier is dressier; opaque is more casual looking. Trouser socks should match the hemline as well.
- Shoes should not be fragile; stay away from stiletto heels or thin, strappy sandals. If comfortable, wear at least a 2" heel to elongate the calf muscle and add overall height.
- Carry a moderately sized handbag or briefcase. Too small will look out of proportion and too large is bulky and adds unnecessary weight to an ensemble.

For men:

- Hair and grooming are essential. Most men need a haircut every three to four weeks. Hair color is optional; a salon will provide the most natural results. However, there are many hair color products that work well at home but may require that you have someone at home apply them.
- Facial hair is a risk. It can look grubby and add weight to the face. A clean-shaven look will be more attractive and slim down a full face.
- Nails need special attention. Regular maintenance is important. Consider a weekly or bimonthly manicure either professionally or at home.
- Belts should be leather—woven, for business casual, smooth or crocodile for traditional business. Purchase the right waist size so you won't be on the last notch. Keep the buckle gold or silver in a conservative style.
- Shoes should be leather with a well-constructed sole. Either slip-ons or tie will work, but make sure they balance your overall proportion. Most thin, Italian-made shoes will look too fragile.
- If you wear traditional business dress, neckties should be your signature accessory. Select 100 percent silk, with one color matching your hair color.

- Select the highest-quality watch you can afford, but take extra time to shop for it. The investment can only be justified if you truly enjoy your watch. As a long-term investment, it adds value to everything you wear.
- Select a medium-scale leather wallet. The jumbo size just begs to be overstuffed.

Final Tips

Select clothing that fits and disregard the label. Sizing varies significantly between manufacturers. Wearing anything that is too tight only adds pounds. Invest in alterations. It will give you a custom look. For women especially, invest in well-fitting, high-quality undergarments. Everything will fit much better with the correct foundations.

The Winning Combination

A flattering, high-quality wardrobe for the plus-size professional is only one part of a strong, polished presence. Adding in confidence, charisma, and energy creates the winning combination. Few persons are as magnetic as plus-size professionals who carry themselves with poise, style, and flair.

Resource List for the Plus-Size Professional

The following are excellent merchants who offer extended sizes.

Women's Clothing
Bacca, Inc.—Offers contemporary styles in baseline casual, as well as helpful hints; Plus sizes 14-24W. *www.bacca.com*

Catherines—Plus, petite plus, and extended sizes, up to 34W. *http://catherines.charmingshoppes.com*

Elisabeth.com—Liz Claiborne's plus-size collection features mostly business casual and sports items. *www.elisabeth.com*

J. Jill—Comfortable clothing for business casual and some traditional dress in sizes 14W to 28W. Items are shown on and off models with suggested accessories. *www.jjill.com*

Kiyonna—Sophisticated pieces exclusively in plus sizes from 14 to 5X. *www.kiyonna.com*

Lane Bryant.com—Moderately priced fashion for business casual in sizes 14 to 44. *www.lbcatalog.com*

Merci Woman—An upscale boutique presenting an elegant array of styles for the full-figured woman from casual to business to special occasion dressing. *www.merciwoman.com*

Nordstrom—The upscale department store offers extended sizes for both men and women. Check out the plus-size designers—Emme, Exclusively Misook, Ralph Lauren, Vikki Vi, and Liz Claiborne. *www.nordstrom.com*

Statuesque—Features quality business and fashion shoes in sizes 9½ to 13, AA to WW. *www.statuesque.com*

Ulla Popken—European designer specializing in well-made clothes in plus sizes 12 to 34. Casual suits. *www.ullapopken.com*

Men's Clothing

Mark Shale Menswear—The upscale menswear department caters to the larger man for both business casual and especially for traditional attire. They offer made-to-measure shirts and suits as well. *www.markshale.com*

Paul Frederick Shirt & Co.—Their online catalog has a great selection of well-made shirts for men in extended sizes. *www.paulfrederick.com*

Rochester Big and Tall—Clothing for the big and tall man since 1907. Offers business casual and traditional wear as well as shoe sizes up to 18. *www.rochesterbigandtall.com*

Tall.com—The most extensive selection of online suits from Ralph Lauren, to Palm Beach, to Zino (Italian) and other Italian brands. Casual wear as well. Sizes from 36 portly up to 60XL. *www.tall.com*

Tovi—Casual items that are well priced for 7XL to 10XL, including men's underwear. *www.tovi-largesizeclothing.com*

part four

professional presence

chapter twelve

nonverbal communication

> If you think you have power, then you have it. If you don't think you have it, then even if you've got it, you don't have it.
>
> Herb Cohen, author of *You Can Negotiate Anything*

we can easily recognize an assured, confident presence in others, but it is harder to identify and assess our own. What is it that makes one person inspire respect and confidence, and another generate a vote of "no-confidence"?

An assured professional presence is really an entire set of behaviors and attitudes that say clearly to others, "I am important—and so are you." That self-assured demeanor is developed in two closely related ways—internally and externally.

Internal self-assurance flows from a sincere belief in your own worth and abilities. Each of us has a wealth of accomplishments that can generate that confidence. But even the most successful people occasionally focus instead on their shortfalls and missteps, so confidence sometimes plummets.

Counter your negative self-talk by keeping a "Good job" file and reviewing it frequently. Into the file, put every bit of tangible praise you receive:

- A stellar performance review
- Newspaper clippings about your achievements

- A note from a satisfied client
- Your grade sheet from that night school graduate course
- The trade journal article published under your byline
- An "I love you" drawing from a child

The file will fill up faster than you expect. Anytime your belief in yourself falters, pull out the file and reaffirm your successes and triumphs. The effect is surprisingly powerful.

Greater self-confidence can also be generated by external behaviors. Most of us believe that we behave in certain ways because of how we feel. Experts, however, believe the reverse is true—we actually feel the way we do because of our behavior.

William James, considered by some to be one of the fathers of modern psychology, writes: "Action seems to follow feeling, but really action and feeling go together. By regulating the action, which is under more direct control of the will, we can indirectly regulate the feeling." In other words, we can't feel supremely self-assured just by making up our minds to do so, but we can assume the actions of a confident person and our feelings can quickly catch up with the behavior. As others "read" confidence from our behavior, they treat us with greater respect and boost our self-esteem even further.

Exactly what behaviors convey that assurance and poise? In the first few moments of an interaction, we telegraph dozens of messages through our posture, facial expressions, eye contact, handshake, and gestures. Orchestrate those elements to maximize your impact.

"The eye's optic nerves contain eighteen times as many neurons as the cochlear nerves of the ear, suggesting that around eighteen times more information flows along them."

David Lewis, author of *The Secret Language of Success*

Posture

Good posture identifies you instantly as someone with something to contribute. Powerful posture is squared, direct, and erect, but not rigid or tense. It has to do with alignment, more than throwing out the chest. Try this: Move your rib cage up 2". Notice how your shoulders, tummy, chest, head, and chin go into the correct alignment. You'll not only look more authoritative, but you'll literally feel increased energy as more oxygen enters your system.

"Sternum up, shoulder blades down."

Karin Stephan, master yoga instructor

Support your own weight, rather than leaning against a wall, doorway, or reception desk. Men look most balanced with feet parallel about 10" to 12" apart. Women create a more graceful look with one foot slightly forward, angled but not "posed."

Hands look natural hanging relaxed at the sides of the body. Standing with one hand in a pocket looks casual and comfortable, but both hands in pockets might be too informal. Avoid the "fig leaf" pose or arms folded across the chest; both can imply defensiveness. If you are holding samples, papers, or a briefcase, try to keep your right hand free for handshaking.

"I've found that people don't trust you as much if they can't see your hands . . . so keeping both hands in your pockets is not only too informal but may also be interpreted as untrustworthy."

Jane Wilger, president, Wilger Image Development

Walk with that same erect stance and a strong, purposeful, but unhurried, stride. A short person may need to consciously lengthen his or her stride to avoid the childlike appearance of running to keep up with a taller companion.

Seated posture is equally important. Slumping into a chair never looks good, but leaning back a bit can communicate a relaxed, confident attitude. Sitting forward in a chair, and leaning forward as well, signals attentiveness and an eagerness to engage in interaction.

Avoid a very restricted, symmetrical position with feet together straight ahead and hands clasped in your lap. Try sitting slightly off-center, with legs crossed knee-on-knees or ankle-on-ankle and hands relaxed in your lap or on the chair arms. Of course, women need to take skirt length into consideration and generally cross their legs more carefully than men. Women also need to be conscious of keeping their heads up, not tilted to one side.

Eye Contact

Solid eye contact instantly conveys the twin messages, "I am important—and so are you." Lack of eye contact communicates an array of negative messages:

- Lack of confidence
- Lack of interest in the individual or the information presented
- Dishonesty
- Unfavorable response to the message you're hearing
- Disregard or dislike for the other person
- Less intelligence

In fact, withholding eye contact can very successfully express negative messages that you may not want to verbalize.

Seminar participants repeatedly ask us how many seconds of continuous eye contact they should maintain. Think about that for a minute. The purpose of eye contact is to make a connection with the other person. How attentive and connected can you possibly be if your brain is busy counting "one—Mississippi—two—Mississippi—three . . ."?

Don't worry about the number of seconds; concentrate instead on maintaining eye contact most of the time. Note the color of the other person's eyes. In workshops, we ask pairs of participants to role-play a greeting handled the usual way, with initial eye contact, a break, and then eye contact again for the handshake. We then have them repeat the role-play, sustaining eye contact throughout. The verdict is unanimous: Unbroken eye contact looks and feels both more confident and more personal.

Another opportunity to show assurance through improved eye contact occurs when you are introduced to several people at once. Most people make eye contact with the second person while still shaking hands with the first and continue that pattern throughout the introductions. No wonder they can't remember the names and faces. Try slowing the process down. Maintain eye contact through your handshake with Mr. A., and then move your hand and eye contact simultaneously to Ms. B. The introducer will usually slow to your pace, and each person you meet will feel important and acknowledged.

When seated, locking your gaze to another's eyes for a long period can feel uncomfortable for both people. Break up a "laser-gaze" with one or more of these methods:

- Look at the person's lips, paying close attention to what they are saying.
- Direct your attention, and your companion's, toward something else—an office accessory, a product sample, a document, or whatever.
- Drop your eyes as you take an occasional written note of an important point.

Don't drop your gaze for no apparent reason, or let your eyes flit around the room uncontrolled. The ability to hold eye contact, especially when hearing a message of refusal or criticism, conveys assurance more clearly than any other single behavior.

"The eye obeys exactly the action of the mind."

—Ralph Waldo Emerson

When your conversation partner avoids eye contact with you, ask yourself why. Is he bored or uncomfortable with the conversation? Has someone else entered the room that she needs to speak to? Immediately stop telling and start asking. The secret of a savvy conversationalist is the ability to be a better listener than talker. Introducing a question can engage him in discussion and/or clarify his reaction. Either way, the conversation is back on track.

Strong eye contact is a learned skill. It pays to practice continuously in low-risk situations. Make eye contact, smile, and greet strangers at the grocery store, the bank, and in your office building. Make a point to sustain eye contact and really connect with each person. You'll not only develop this important skill, but you'll also be safer. Personal safety experts say you're less likely to be mugged if you appear in control and confident.

"One study found that job applicants who engage in more eye contact are seen as more alert, dependable, confident, and responsible. In another study only applicants who used an above-average amount of eye contact (accompanied by a high-energy level, speech fluency, and voice modulation) were invited back for a second interview."

—Connie Brown Glaser and Barbara Steinberg Smalley, authors of *More Power to You!*

Handshake

The handshake is usually the only physical contact permitted in business situations, so it's an invaluable opportunity to set a cordial tone for interaction. If your handshake is firm and direct, warm and friendly, you're immediately off to a positive start.

In ancient times, handshakes were gestures of peace. Originally the clasp was made on the forearm to ensure that no weapon was hidden in the sleeve. Over time, the greeting evolved to its modern form:

- Keep your hands clean and void of perspiration. Keep a handkerchief in your pocket or carry alcohol-based hand wipes in your car or office.
- Extend your right hand, thumb up and fingers together.
- Slide forward until the web between your thumb and forefinger meets the web of your companion.
- Squeeze firmly, match pressure, shake in a short one, two, three rhythm, then release.

Accompanied by eye contact and a smile, the entire process seems relatively straightforward and simple. Yet nearly everyone has experienced each of these hapless handshakes:

- *The dead fish*—a limp, clammy handshake is an instant turnoff, expressing lack of purpose, confidence, enthusiasm, and nearly everything else that is valued in business. In this event, resist the urge to pull your hand away in disgust. But vow never to give a limp handshake yourself. An obvious exception exists for those who are disabled, elderly, or who suffer from arthritis.
- *The bone crusher*—an overly firm grip implies that the giver is trying to intimidate, perhaps overcompensating for some insecurity. Protect yourself from pain by returning the grip as firmly as possible.
- *The finger-only shake*—a candid admission that a person is uncomfortable shaking hands or unfamiliar with the mechanics of a good handshake. You may be able to improve the moment by keeping your own hand open a moment longer to achieve at least a partial web-to-web position.

- *The sandwich*—a two-handed shake appears condescending, especially if the recipient's hand is turned to a horizontal position. A vertical sandwich is appropriate to express genuine affection or sympathy for a personal loss, but not in normal business interaction.
- *The pump*—a repeated, vigorous up-and-down motion seems artificially enthusiastic.

Though confusion is diminishing, some men are still uncertain about shaking hands with women. Don't wait for a woman to extend her hand. Offering yours first clearly says that you regard her as a professional equal.

Of course, if a man fails to offer his hand, the woman can initiate a handshake herself. The ritual is too important a business custom to be omitted. Women should readily shake hands with one another as well. If you are uncertain about your handshake, solicit feedback from a colleague.

Facial Expressions

Our faces communicate far more clearly and more honestly than our words. When the spoken and unspoken messages are congruent, communication is comfortable. When nonverbal signals contradict the words spoken, a savvy listener will believe the nonverbal every time.

"The most powerful initial entrance deals with four essential areas: posture, the effective use of personal space, eye contact, and the smile. There should be good use of your personal bubble, meaning the space you claim around you. Good posture allows you to naturally claim your space. The ribs should be pulled up, the knees should be straight but not locked. The way in which the hand extends away from the body can show confidence or hesitancy. Establishing eye contact immediately and smiling authentically gives others the sense that you are genuinely interested in them and the relationship to follow."

Lynne Marks, president, London Image Institute

The most appealing, congenial facial expression is a sincere smile. A genuine smile never looks pasted on, but blossoms across the entire face, including the eyes and cheeks as well as the mouth. As simple as it sounds, the smile is a vastly underused business tool. When you smile, you immediately feel more confident and upbeat. Your colleague automatically smiles in return and generates her own positive feelings, too. What better way to communicate the message, "I am important—and so are you"?

Work to keep your facial expressions synchronized with your verbal message so listeners know what to believe. Smile if the news is positive, but avoid nervous grins when your message is negative or the response uncertain. When external factors affect your facial expressions, explain the situation to your companions. "I have a sinus headache, but I still want to hear your proposal" can reassure associates that your frown and forehead massage aren't a response to their conversation.

Gestures

Gestures add to the impact of our spoken words—for better or for worse. Certain gestures have fairly standard negative meanings:

Gesture	Connotation
Drumming fingers	Impatience, boredom
Twisting a ring	Nervousness
Bouncing a foot	Nervousness, impatience
Excessive head nodding	Lack of confidence, overeager to please

"He that has eyes to see and ears to hear may convince himself that no mortal can keep a secret. If his lips are silent, he chatters with his fingertips; betrayal oozes out of him at every pore."

Sigmund Freud

Speaking with a hand near or covering your mouth suggests that you are telling a falsehood. Massaging your temples, forehead, or the bridge of your nose communicates stress, discouragement, or exhaustion.

In many cases, these negative gestures are used unconsciously to release nervous tension and relieve stress. They can be as calming to adults as thumb sucking is to children. Rather than consciously trying to stop using them, plan to adopt other more effective gestures in their place.

Use your hands to paint a picture of your message. Spread your hands apart as you mention expansion. Clasp your hands together when you talk about unification. Draw stair steps in the air to illustrate an upward trend in revenues or profits. Make a fist to illustrate determination. Emphasize your verbal approval of an idea with a hearty "thumbs-up." These physical movements can dissipate your tension in a positive way, and they actually help convey your message to listeners who are more visually oriented.

Keep any gesture smooth and flowing, rather than sudden and jarring. Broader gestures look more confident than tight, tiny ones. The very act of taking up more space implies comfort with yourself and your surroundings. Of course, it is possible to gesture too wildly and look like laundry flapping in the wind.

One classic at-rest gesture that implies poise and confidence is the "steeple"—hands together with the fingers spread, palms apart, and fingertips touching. You can steeple with your forearms resting on the desk, conference table, or chair arm. Be careful not to hold your hands so high that they interfere with eye contact. Just don't flex your fingers nervously back and forth, changing your steeple to what consultants term the "spider on a mirror."

Always remember that when body language and words disagree, body language is the more believable. One executive told about an interview in which the candidate spoke at length about his steely nerve and ability to deal effectively with stressful negotiating situations. As he spoke, he distractedly tore the Styrofoam cup he was holding into pea-size particles. "He might as well have worn a banner that said 'I'm a nervous wreck'," the executive recalled.

Personal Space

Each of us carries around a "bubble" of personal space. We expand that bubble when we are on our own turf and tend to contract it when we feel uncomfortable or threatened. We appear ill at ease or even frightened when we draw our arms, our legs, and our belongings into a tightly confined space. Spread out a little, claim some space, and you will look—and feel— more at home in your surroundings.

Simultaneously, be sure to respect the personal space of others. Using both arms of the seat on a crowded airplane isn't confident—it's inconsiderate. Spreading the contents of your portfolio across someone else's desk risks offending that person. A person's individual space also extends to personal possessions. Avoid picking up someone else's pen, phone, calendar, or any other object without asking permission.

The typical business definition of personal space is somewhere between three and five feet (arm's length). Others feel uneasy when their personal space is invaded, so keep your distance. Of course, we cross that invisible barrier for handshakes, passing things, and other obvious situations. The size of the personal-space bubble fluctuates according to the circumstances. Positioning that feels absolutely appropriate at a crowded cocktail party would be extremely uncomfortable in a conference room. Stay attuned to the reactions of your companions; if you invade their personal space, they will immediately signal you by moving away.

Positioning

A seemingly trivial issue like "who sits where" can influence the personal interaction. Even the decision to sit or stand sends a message. If an associate drops into your office when you are too busy to talk at length, stand to greet him, and simply remain standing. You can bet the interaction will be brief.

Talking with someone across the barrier of a desk can create psychological distance and a slightly adversarial or intimidating feeling. Many offices today have small conference tables or comfortable seating areas where two people can converse in a more congenial setting. In your own office, direct a guest to the seating area that fits your agenda for the conversation. As a guest in someone else's office, you can often suggest the seating that works to your best advantage.

At a small conference table, sitting beside the host rather than directly across from him or her sets a more collegial, less confrontational tone. In a seating area, select a firm chair rather than a soft, plush sofa that might envelop you so comfortably that your drive and energy diminish.

Sometimes moving out of your host's office entirely can strengthen your position. Surrounded by the other person's paraphernalia, ringing telephones, and other distractions, it can be very challenging to make your points clearly. We know one stellar salesperson who always brings along a slide presentation or short videotape because it offers the perfect excuse to meet in a private conference room.

In meetings, the power seat is immediately to the right of the chairperson. Other seats near the chairperson are also high-visibility choices. In a large meeting, the seats along the wall, removed from the table, are the lowest in status. Arrive early enough to select a strong location, but be careful not to usurp the seat of someone who outranks you. On someone else's turf, let that person select his or her seat before choosing your own.

If you are expecting a confrontation with someone else at the meeting, avoid sitting directly across the table from that individual. Choosing a seat on the same side, several seats apart, makes it easier for both of you to direct your comments to the chairperson and the group rather than erupting into a direct conflict.

At a business lunch, taking adjacent chairs leads to more cordial interaction than sitting directly across from each other. If a third party is present, the host should take the seat between that colleague and the guest, sparing the guest from both the middle seat and the awkwardness of maintaining eye contact to both her right and left sides.

Mirroring/Matching

The old axiom states, "People like people like themselves." You'll find it much easier to "connect" with others when you match your style and energy level to theirs. Vicki Sullivan, a successful booking agent for professional speakers, adapts her style instantly to the client's, even over the phone.

"If the person answers the phone with a cordial 'Good morning, XYZ Company, this is Jane Doe speaking,' I assume a relaxed, friendly demeanor. If, instead, the person answers with a clipped 'Jane Doe,' I take the cue to get right down to business," Sullivan explains.

"As we become more and more like the people we're mirroring, we build more rapport. Business relationships, like political and personal relationships, are functions of rapport—the more of it one can generate, the greater the chances of positive outcomes."

Michael Brooks, author of *Instant Rapport*

Matching is even easier in person. Adopt a similar posture, vocal volume, and rate of speech as the other person's. If someone is calm, slow down, stay controlled, and use smoother, less emphatic gestures. Show high spirit and enthusiasm when the other person demonstrates it. Once you have matched his or her style, you can move gradually toward your target style—a higher level of energy, perhaps, or a quicker pace to the conversation—and the phenomenon of mirroring and matching will usually cause the person to move right along with you.

Though it is our responsibility to be somewhat of a chameleon in business, don't carry matching to the extreme. It is important to keep within the integrity of your personal style as well. Copying a client's every movement could quickly degenerate to a game of "Monkey See, Monkey Do." Instead, aim for a similar level of energy, intensity, and enthusiasm.

Global Perspective

A direct approach, continuous eye contact, initiating handshakes, and confident posture are expected forms of effective nonverbal communication when doing business in the United States, but the global marketplace demands that we are respectful of differences in nonverbal communication when working with individuals of another culture. Roger Axtell, author of *Gestures: The Do's and Taboos of Body Language Around the World,* writes, "You will quickly recognize a gesture and know its meaning according to *your* society, *your* geography, and *your* ethnic influences. . . . Knowledge of these varied interpretations might some day save you from a stern look, a strained relationship, or possibly even a smashed nose."

"Many Japanese proverbs proclaim the virtues of silence, a common one being, 'Those who know, do not speak—those who speak, do not know.'"

Diana Rowland, author of *Japanese Business Etiquette*

Appropriate nonverbal communication is an expression of respect. Although most of us were taught that a firm handshake and direct eye contact is the only approach in business, individuals in the Middle East, Japan, and Korea are instructed that in their country a firm grip and direct eye contact are aggressive, intimidating, and disrespectful.

"When it comes to selling either your personal charms or professional abilities, body language talks loudest of all."

David Lewis, author of *The Secret Language of Success*

We forget the unleashed power of our unspoken word. Every phase of our communication can become stronger if we project presence through nonverbal language. Actions become congruent with the phrases we speak. Messages are not only heard, but they have impact because we choose to support what we say with the emphasis of posture, gesture, voice inflection, and the mastery of physical space.

chapter thirteen

business etiquette

> Always do right; you will please some people, and astonish the rest.
>
> Mark Twain

in an earlier time and a different style of living, etiquette was a "pinkies up" discipline for the social elite. But in today's business world, practical and gracious ways of dealing with people make interactions easier and more comfortable for everyone. In fact, as common courtesy becomes less and less common, the nuances of etiquette are an essential component of career success.

More than one manager has engaged our services because key members of the staff were unfamiliar with the basics of good manners. Practices that were part of every youngster's home and school training in an earlier generation have often gotten lost as our society has become more fragmented and mobile.

The general manager of a television station recently requested business etiquette training for the news staff. "These people have celebrity status in our community," she explained. "They attend prestigious functions where they are highly visible representatives of the station. Frankly, many of them are awkward. They don't know which fork to use or how to make a proper introduction. It's an embarrassment to the station."

Happily, business etiquette isn't a series of trivial dictates to be tediously memorized. Instead, it is the art of appearing poised and gracious while you make others feel comfortable.

Introductions

Opportunities to introduce yourself and others occur repeatedly in business life. Many of us mumble, fumble, or simply fail to make introductions for fear of making a mistake. The rule is incredibly simple:

Say first the name of the person to whom you want to show greatest respect or honor.

With that beginning, the introduction can go nowhere but the right direction: "Mr. Big, I'd like for you to meet my assistant, Rick Shaw. Rick, this is Mr. Big."

"Joe, may I introduce our sales manager, Ralph Half. Ralph, this is Joe Customer. His store in Cedar Rapids sells our Widgets very well."

How do you decide who deserves the greater honor?

- In business, old social rules about age or gender do not apply; instead, honor flows toward the respect of rank or authority.
- Within your own organization, simply envision the organizational chart. The higher-ranking individual is honored.
- Customers always receive greater respect than anyone within the organization, even the CEO.
- Visiting dignitaries receive honored status.
- When introducing people of equal rank, honor the person from outside your own organization.

The best introductions include a bit of clarifying information about each party, so the two have some basis for developing a conversation. When you need to introduce yourself, simply extend your hand, smile, make friendly eye contact, and say, "I'm Linda Curtin with the Antler Dance Corporation." The other person should always respond with his or her own name and a question or comment to initiate conversation.

Reintroduce yourself to a casual acquaintance who may not remember your name. Add a quick explanation to help them clarify your connection.

"I'm Tom Todd with Ace Insurance; we met at the Chamber meeting" usually elicits a response such as "Sure I remember you, Tom. I'm Fred Marks."

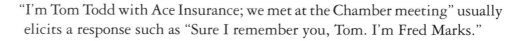

"One should plan a self-introduction. The best self-introductions are energetic and pithy—no more than ten seconds long. They include your name and a tag line that tells other people who you are and gives them a way to remember you. The self-introduction has two purposes: 1) to tell people who you are, and 2) to give them a pleasant experience of you."

Susan RoAne, author of *How to Work a Room*

The stickiest introductions occur when another person joins your conversation group and you can't remember his or her name. Rather than appearing thoughtless by making no introduction, apologize and admit your lapse. "I know we met at the conference in June, but I'm sorry I can't recall your name. I'm Sammy Smooth and this is Hal Honcho."

When you are introduced to someone who is approximately the same age and rank, it is usually appropriate to use first names. However, if you have any doubt at all, call a new acquaintance by his or her last name until invited to do otherwise.

Remembering Names

Dale Carnegie wrote that a person's name is to that person "the sweetest sound in any language." Remembering and using that name tells your acquaintance that you value him or her personally and professionally. It also says that you are a sharp individual. Now if only remembering names were easy!

Develop your memory for names by first admitting that it's hard work. It takes discipline and concentration, but few investments of your energy can yield a higher return in positive relationships.

Begin by refusing to think, "I'm not good at remembering names." Like many other negative messages, that can become a self-fulfilling prophecy. Faced with yet another introduction, you can be so busy thinking, "I'm not good at remembering names" that you never even hear the name when it is spoken. Instead, tell yourself that with effort you will improve your ability.

Be sure you hear the name correctly in the first place. When you are introduced to "Ms. Mumble-mumble," stop immediately and ask for clarification or even spelling. The person will be flattered that you care enough to get the name right.

Most of us process visual information better than auditory information (sounds). We remember faces but have difficulty recalling names. So as quickly as possible, develop a mental picture related to the name. Actually "see" the picture in your mind. It takes only a moment to envision:

- Julie wearing tons of jewelry
- Sandy on the beach
- Rich with money sticking out of his pockets
- Bill wearing a cap with an oversized bill
- Jim wearing his gym clothes
- Christopher standing arm in arm with your cousin of the same name

Use the name naturally throughout the conversation, but not so often that you sound like the stereotype of a used-car salesperson. Use it again when you depart; the mind-picture technique helps you feel confident that you will recall the name correctly. Exchange business cards if appropriate, so you can lock in the name visually and have a permanent record for later review.

Set realistic goals. Expecting to remember names of twenty people you meet at one gathering is setting yourself up for failure. Committing to remember five new names makes success more likely and can build your confidence for higher goals in future attempts.

Conversational Cues

"Small talk" in business or networking settings can have an impact that's anything but small. Conversation is a potent means to build cordial and productive relationships, yet many people avoid business/social situations because they fear they have nothing to say.

In truth, developing a witty repartee is less important than learning to draw out the other person. A great "Herman" cartoon shows an elderly man and woman sitting on a park bench. The caption reads, "I would let you talk more, but you're not as interesting as me." Each of us secretly believes something close to that, so artful questioning and active listening are the tools of a good conversationalist.

Questions that invite discussion, opinion, or background are more effective conversation-starters than simple yes/no or short-answer questions. "Where do you live?" usually has a one-word answer. "How did you happen to settle in that area?" or "How do you feel about the school bond issue there?" invites discussion.

Some topics have almost universal appeal and acceptance:

- Your conversational partner's company and industry
- Career background
- Achievements and future goals
- Hobbies and leisure activities
- Community involvement
- Entertainment—favorite movies, books
- Current events

Sports is a popular topic in business and social circles. Even if you are not an avid statistics-quoting fan, stay informed about the personality side of your local sports scene—player trades, management controversy, the new stadium, and so on.

Even controversial political topics can make for stimulating conversation if you have the discipline to express your own thoughts discreetly or remain neutral. If you disagree with an opinion being expressed, try the Barbara Walters approach. The famous interviewer frequently phrases her most controversial questions as someone else's opinion. "There are those who feel instead that . . . " or "Some people might take the opposite view and say . . . " are sure to stimulate lively discussion without giving offense.

A few topics are generally inappropriate:

- Personal purchases and their cost
- Private matters such as weight or health problems
- Gossip that's scandalous or damaging
- Negative comments about competitors
- Confidential company information

Consider vulgar language, gender-based comments, and racial or ethnic humor off-limits in any business conversation. The potential to offend far exceeds any possible entertainment value.

In the course of the conversation, your partner is almost certain to return a few questions to you. Answer them, of course, or your chat may take on the feel of an interrogation. But as a rule, try to talk about yourself and your own interests only when asked.

In group conversation, a poised businessperson subtly assumes the host role and draws each person equally into the discussion with direct questions and eye contact. No witty phrases are required. "What do you think about that, Mary?" should work to share the spotlight.

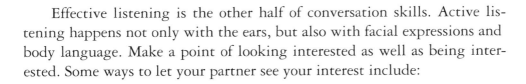

"Our extraordinary language is rich in subtext and innuendo. Those proficient in this subtle skill can open doors that are closed to their less eloquent (or glib) fellow Americans. Expert communication is becoming an enormous challenge. It's not just asking the right questions. It's asking them using the right words—and avoiding the wrong ones."

Leil Lowndes, author of *How to Talk to Anyone*

Effective listening is the other half of conversation skills. Active listening happens not only with the ears, but also with facial expressions and body language. Make a point of looking interested as well as being interested. Some ways to let your partner see your interest include:

- Leaning toward the speaker
- Making frequent eye contact
- Asking follow-up questions
- Rephrasing the speaker's comments
- Nodding in agreement
- Vocalizing appropriately (Uh-huh, hmm, aha)
- Showing reaction through facial expression

Deference

Deference means showing special respect for someone because of his or her status. In social situations, deference is based on age and/or gender. In business, deference is based on rank. Defer to those above you in the organization structure, to customers, and to honored guests. Deferential behaviors include:

- Standing when the person enters the room or the conversation group
- Opening or holding doors
- Offering help with unwieldy packages
- Allowing them the conversational spotlight for as long as they want it
- Handling unpleasant situations such as a room mix-up or standing in a long line

It is perfectly okay to show those same courtesies to someone of lower rank, especially if the help is needed. But it can be a big mistake to neglect deference when rank requires it.

Dining

The power breakfast . . . the business lunch . . . dinner with a client. Each provides opportunities to develop a more personal relationship with a colleague or customer. Each meal has its own code of behavior, and many general dining guidelines apply to all three.

Breakfast is the least expensive and time-consuming alternative, fitting easily into many busy schedules. The early hour can imply devotion to business, so keep breakfast meetings relatively short and to the point. A hotel coffee shop or dining room is a good meeting place with ample parking, smaller crowds, and relatively elegant surroundings.

Lunch is the most popular business meal, so avoid the crunch by meeting your guest at either 11:30 or after 1:00. Keep the conversation light until the meal is ordered to avoid interruptions. Save particularly weighty business discussions for coffee and dessert. When a client is visiting your offices from out of town, a catered lunch may be more time-efficient than a restaurant meal. The three-martini lunch is history in today's leaner and sharper business climate. Wine or beer should be the "hardest" liquors at noonday. Most businesspeople choose to drink only at dinner, and then only moderately.

Dinner with a client is generally a gracious, leisurely occasion with more social than business overtones. Dinner occasions do have three potential pitfalls:

- Lack of a defined ending time—make reference to your guest's rigorous schedule and promise an early evening.

- The presence of alcohol—arrive at the restaurant just slightly ahead of your reservation time to avoid a lengthy wait in the bar. Dining away from the client's hotel encourages more responsible drinking because of the drive home.
- The atmosphere similar to a date—when your companion is of the opposite sex, select a restaurant with no romantic ambiance, or invite spouses or a business colleague to accompany you.

"Your behavior, whatever type of entertainment setting is chosen—breakfast, lunch, dinner, party, holiday bash—is always under scrutiny. Business entertaining may stimulate the interpersonal relationships that help business grow, but it is still primarily business, not a social interaction."

Jan Yager, author of *Business Protocol*

Hosting

When you are the host, select a familiar restaurant that accepts reservations. There is an inherent elegance in knowing the menu offerings, the best table, and the maitre d'. Private business clubs are a terrific option if you or your firm has a membership.

Assume responsibility for everyone's comfort. Recommend favorite menu items, ask the server for beverage refills, check that everyone's food is to their liking, and handle any deficiencies. If a guest orders an appetizer or a drink, order one yourself so the guest isn't drinking or eating alone. Handle the check discreetly. Sign the check away from the guest's line of vision, and place it face-down. Generally, in private clubs, the check is signed up-front, so whoever pays is "off the table" right away.

Guests

Order only the basics (salad, entrée, beverage), unless your host specifically suggests an appetizer or dessert. Ask for suggestions about what to order, rather than going straight for the most expensive item on the menu. Let the host take the lead on when to order, whether to include cocktails, and when to turn the conversation to business issues.

Dining Protocol

As soon as everyone is seated, place your napkin in your lap. Smaller napkins are unfolded entirely. Larger ones remain folded in a triangle, giving you one half to wipe the corners of your mouth while the other half remains clean and unused in your lap. Avoid tucking the napkin into your belt or waistband. We've seen more than one diner leave the table with this loincloth effect still in place. If you leave the table temporarily, place your napkin on the chair to signal your server that you intend to return. When you leave at the end of the meal, place it loosely to the left of your plate.

Identify your place setting. The rule is solids to the left, liquids to the right (use the mnemonic device "slurp" to remember, SLLRP: solid on the left, liquid on the right, please). The bread plate to the left and the glasses to the right belong to you.

If you are seated nearest the bread or rolls, pick up the basket and pass it to the person on your right. The logic is that they grasp the basket with the left hand, serve themselves with the right hand, and then pass the basket along in the same counterclockwise direction. Ideally you wait to serve yourself until the basket has made its way around the table. Don't forget to follow with the butter in the same direction.

Eat bread by breaking off a single bite and buttering it. This leisurely pace implies that you are more interested in the company than in wolfing down the food. The most gracious diner will wait until the first course has arrived before eating any bread.

Make a relatively quick decision about what to order; you don't want to appear indecisive, even in small things. Order something that can be eaten neatly. Save barbecued ribs, corn on the cob, and oversized sandwiches for informal dining with family or close friends. Consider lasagna or cannelloni instead of tough-to-twirl spaghetti or linguini, crab-stuffed fillet instead of cumbersome crab legs. Of course if you're dining in Maine and your host insists on lobster, tie on a bib and go with the flow.

If the meal includes soup, remember to spoon away from yourself. Don't tip the bowl away from you to get the last drops; you'll appear famished.

It is fine to leave your spoon in a very shallow soup bowl, especially if it is served without a liner. Deeper soup bowls demand a plate liner, where you properly place your spoon.

Salad is supposed to be torn into pieces small enough to eat easily. If you find you can't, however, it is appropriate to cut large chunks with your knife and fork. When you have finished eating, place the knife and fork side by side on the plate in the four o'clock position to signal that you are done. In finer restaurants the server will replace your utensils with clean ones or the table will be preset to include a knife and fork for your salad and a set for your entrée. In more casual restaurants, the waitperson is responsible for removing your knife and fork from the plate and placing them on the table.

Formal table settings need not be confusing. The rule is to use the utensils in order from the outside in. Silverware placed horizontally at the top of your plate is for dessert. Between bites, place your utensils well onto the plate to avoid accidents. When you pause, but are not finished, leave your knife and fork in an open position (four o'clock and eight o'clock). This is the "code" telling the server not to remove your plate. Placing your knife and fork together at the four o'clock position signals that you are finished.

Recognize the two styles of dining—American and Continental. To eat American style, hold a piece of food with the fork in your left hand and cut with the knife in your right hand. Put the knife across the top of the plate, transfer the fork to your right hand and lift the bite to your mouth. (This method is reversed if you are left-handed.) To eat in the Continental style, begin in the same way but keep the fork in the left hand to lift the bite to your mouth.

If during the course of the meal you need to remove an inedible morsel from your mouth—fish bone, olive pit, or the like—discreetly remove it the same way it went in. Finger foods are correctly removed with your fingers; fork foods are removed to your fork and placed on the side of your plate. In the case of a minor emergency, use your napkin.

And a few miscellaneous reminders:

- The most easily recognized way to demonstrate fine table manners is to take small bites and chew with your mouth closed.
- Don't share food from another's plate in a business setting.
- If you drop a utensil on the floor, ask for a replacement rather than retrieving it.

- Don't use a toothpick, lipstick, or a comb at the table.
- Be polite and friendly, but don't joke or converse at length with your server.
- Don't make a fuss about anything; if a problem needs to be corrected, handle it quietly and discreetly with the manager or maitre d' if necessary.

Smoking

Smoking in business settings has become unacceptable. Most states have passed laws about smoking in restaurants and other public places. The safest rule today is to avoid smoking around others, even if they are smoking.

- Never smoke in someone else's car.
- Don't smoke in a restaurant even if everyone at your table is smoking.
- Don't even smoke in your own car on the way to an important appointment; the smell will linger in your clothes and on your breath.
- After an evening in a smoky environment, be sure to air your suit for twenty-four hours, shower, and shampoo your hair to remove the odor, even if you were not smoking.

Phone Issues

When You Are the Caller
- Always be pleasant and cordial to receptionists and secretaries. Many assistants are the key to accessing the boss. Match your telephone presence to the receptionist's. If it is warm and friendly, take time to establish rapport. If crisp and efficient, get to the point quickly.
- Identify yourself by first and last name and company, both to the receptionist and to the person you are calling. In an established relationship, first and last names are sufficient.
- Skip "How are you today?" Get quickly to the point.
- Ask "Is this a good time to talk?" only if you know the person and the topic is fairly lengthy. It is never a good time for a busy executive to talk to a stranger.

- Before calling, ensure an organized conversation by noting briefly the topics you need to cover on an index card. A study at the University of Michigan revealed that businesspeople forget something in 13 percent of phone calls, thus wasting an average of two hours each week repeating calls and filling in omitted information.
- Because it is more difficult to get agreement for your ideas by phone, use the call to arrange a brief future meeting where you can present your proposal in person.
- If you want to put someone on the speakerphone, ask her permission first, and let her know who else is present. Introduce everyone who will be a part of the phone call.
- If your topic is complex and/or the person you called seems busy, make an appointment for a detailed telephone conversation later. Being on someone's calendar for a specific day and time gives your call more weight and importance.
- Don't allow a conversation you initiated to be interrupted by someone dropping into your office or by another call.
- If the person you are calling is not available, leave a brief message. When requesting a return call, leave your number (even if you think the person knows it) and the times you can be reached most easily.
- Don't request a return call if the person doesn't know you.
- If you have to call repeatedly, avoid leaving multiple messages.
- If possible, ask the secretary what time is the best to call.
- If the call is accidentally cut off, the caller is responsible for calling back regardless of the cause of the problem.

As the Recipient of a Call
- Answer with your company name and your own first and last name.
- If you are busy, let the caller know immediately: "I am so sorry, I only have a minute."
- When the call requires you to find some specific information, ask the caller if he would prefer to hold or to be called back.
- Keep "holds" brief—sixty seconds of silence or background music feels like eternity. Asking someone "May I put you on hold?" is smart business.
- Return to the caller with a sincere "Thank you for holding."

- When transferring a caller to someone else in the office, identify each party to the other, and brief the associate on the topic of the conversation.
- If you are interrupted by another incoming call, take a message quickly, and return to the original caller.
- If absolutely necessary, explain to the original caller that you must be interrupted—an overseas call, for example—and promise to call back promptly. Then do it.
- If your call is accidentally cut off, the person who initiated the call is responsible for calling back. If the caller is your customer or client, however, ignore the rule and redial immediately.

Everyone can create a more effective telephone presence by observing a few basic pointers.

- Smile when you talk on the phone. Your voice will sound immeasurably more pleasant.
- Never, never eat, chew gum, sip a soft drink or coffee, or smoke a cigarette while you talk on the phone.
- Use vocal responses—not dead silence—to let the caller know you are listening.
- Do not try to work on another project. The caller can sense your distraction and may be deeply offended.
- Even in a rush, say goodbye, and wait for a response before hanging up.

Be polite to every caller, regardless of the circumstances. The owner of a large privately held company tells about being interrupted at home during dinner by a solicitation call for the Cerebral Palsy Foundation. Although annoyed, he patiently answered the caller's questions, listened politely, and requested a pledge card. To his amazement, the caller revealed that, in addition to being a volunteer, she was an employee of his company. She went on to describe him as the most gracious person she had spoken with in her years as a fundraising volunteer. The cause was especially important to her, because her son suffered from cerebral palsy. And though she realized that the company president didn't know her personally, she was gratified to know that she worked for such a considerate and warm-hearted man!

Voice messaging services can be a wonderful convenience or a major annoyance. Use the technology sensibly and with consideration.

- Keep your answering message short, gimmick-free, and up-to-date. A message "I'll be back in the office on Tuesday" doesn't enhance your image much on Wednesday.
- Give callers an alternative for emergencies—your mobile number or secretary's extension.
- When leaving a message, make it complete but concise. Don't ramble on. A busy person with dozens of messages to hear is likely to fast-forward through a lengthy discourse.
- Keep your information clear by using bullet points: "I need to discuss three issues. The first is . . . The second is . . . "
- Clearly articulate your name, company, and phone number.
- Don't leave a harsh or angry message. If you have a problem or complaint, simply say so, and request a return call to handle the issue.
- Check your messages frequently, and return every message in a timely manner, or have an associate follow up.
- Sometimes just leaving a message can complete the business. If you call very early, very late, or at lunchtime, you're more likely to get voice mail and avoid an extended conversation.

Using cell phones from a car or a remote location requires special guidelines. Consider the cell phone as a portable public phone: use it in private and with consideration for everyone.

- Just because you can make a call or answer a call, doesn't mean you should. If a call requires that you are sharp, highly focused, and professional, don't call or answer from a moving car or a public place. You will sound distracted and you won't be able to write down information. Instead, find a quiet place or pull your car over to the side of the road.
- Bad connections make bad impressions. If the connection is static-filled or it drops, wait until you have the confidence of knowing the line is secure and your conversation will not be garbled.
- Turn the ringer to vibrate to make sure you aren't disturbed during meetings.

- Business phones should have a professional ring, and not be too musical or too loud.
- Don't take personal calls during business meetings, unless you have let others know that you are expecting an important call.
- Maintain at least a ten-foot zone with no one around you when talking on a cell.
- Don't talk in elevators, places of worship, hospitals, or any other place where you will annoy others.
- If you need to answer in a noisy area, be sure to tell the caller where you are and apologize for the noise.
- Never have emotional or confidential conversations on cell phones!

Other Communication

The professional image you convey in a fax is just as important as any mailed correspondence. Remember to observe these guidelines:

- Remember that faxes seldom go directly to the recipient; don't fax anything that must remain confidential.
- Use an attractive, businesslike cover sheet with your name, company, fax and phone numbers, and always indicate the number of pages being sent. Artwork or a company logo creates an appealing presence, but avoid cartoon or joke cover sheets that can detract from a serious message.
- Try to type correspondence and use letterhead whenever possible.
- Call the recipient to confirm that the fax has been received; in large firms a fax can easily go astray.
- Avoid faxing more than a few consecutive pages unless specifically requested. Number each page of a longer fax to avoid confusion.
- Take the fax cover sheet along when you travel. Faxing from a remote location adds urgency and importance to your message.

E-Mail Etiquette
Because of its immediacy, e-mail is an excellent way to keep colleagues current, but with the heavy reliance on e-mail for communication even

between two people sharing the same office wall, there are some etiquette tips you should be aware of:

- Keep messages short and to the point.
- Save emotional messages for face-to-face meetings or phone calls. Avoid using "emoticons"—the punctuation smiley faces.
- Consider the confidentiality of the subject matter. E-mail is more secure than a fax, but privacy is not guaranteed.
- Respond to e-mail messages within twenty-four hours. If you can't do this, be sure to turn on an automated message to respond to your e-mails while you are away.
- Using all capital letters is considered shouting and is rude and annoying in the Internet community. Add an *asterisk* on each side of a word you want to emphasize.
- Advertising, commercial messages, get-rich-quick schemes, and chain letters should never be passed on to colleagues.
- Be sure the intent of your message is clear. Reread before committing it to cyberspace.
- Be sure to include a clear subject in the subject line of the message. Neglecting to do so could ensure your e-mail winds up being filtered out as junk.
- Never send an impersonal e-mail to convey a personal message of condolences, thank you, or otherwise.

"Some people seem to move with fluid grace whether they are entering an elevator, getting out of a cab, coming into someone's office, or using their eating utensils during lunch. They are at ease, and if you watch them closely, you'll find they move efficiently, quietly, inconspicuously. It takes practice, the skill of careful observation of others, but it also requires a certain amount of unselfishness. They know what to do, but their movements also show they are considerate of others."

Letitia Baldrige, author of
New Complete Guide to Executive Manners

chapter fourteen

savvy self-promotion

The expression goes: "It's not what you know, but who you know."

yet the real issue is who knows you—favorably. The most appropriate, attractive business look and the most assured presence have little value if they stay hidden in an office or cubicle. In fact, a *Wall Street Journal* survey of top executives revealed that those superstars attributed 60 percent of their success to exposure. Of course, they didn't mean exposure in the trench-coat-without-a-suit sense, but rather the exposure of putting themselves and keeping themselves in the minds of others.

According to the outplacement company Lee Hecht Harrison, 80 percent of job seekers find employment through networking and personal contact.

Create positive reminders of yourself and your abilities both within your own organization and in the larger business community. Use a variety of methods, such as correspondence, publication, public speaking, or membership in organizations and media coverage.

Correspondence

Each time you follow a meeting or phone conversation with a written restatement of the key points, you not only minimize potential misunderstandings, but you also showcase yourself as an organized individual with excellent follow-up skills. You can also bring yourself favorably to someone's attention with a thank-you letter for:

- A project well done
- A client referral
- A quick answer to a tough question
- Listening to your proposal
- Prompt delivery or extraordinary service

Tom Peters, author of several bestsellers, says, "We wildly underestimate the power of the tiniest personal touch. And of all personal touches, I find the short, handwritten 'nice job' note to have the highest impact."

Time-consuming? You bet. But the results are worth the effort. Tom Kaletta, director of conventions and special events for the Dale Carnegie training organization, is considered by associates to be the "king of written praise." He has dozens of stories that attest to the effectiveness of his countless notes. For example, Tom once noticed that the receptionist in a prospect's office did an especially gracious job of handling callers at the busy switchboard. Back at his desk, he wrote her a quick note complimenting her skills. She was so pleased by the gesture that she showed the letter to her boss, who called Tom back in and purchased more than forty course enrollments.

No one is too highly placed to appreciate acknowledgment. After viewing the movie *A River Runs Through It*, Tom wrote to tell the director about the audience's standing ovation in the theater. The reply hangs framed on his office wall: "Letters like yours are perhaps the ultimate reward. Sincerely, Robert Redford."

Whomever you write to, don't undercut your effective image with minor errors; double-check names, addresses, spelling, and other details carefully. Don't rely entirely on spell-check, which overlooks any misspelling that still forms an English word.

A computer okayed the following "Owed to a Spell Checker":

I have a spelling checker / It came with my pea sea; / It plainly marks four my revue / Mistakes I cannot sea. / Scents I ran this poem threw it, / I'm sure your please too no, / Its letter perfect in it's weigh, / My checker tolled me sew.

Avoid sounding stuffy or pretentious by keeping your written style simple. Follow Mark Twain's advice and avoid using a fifty-cent word when a nickel one will do.

Instead of this fifty-cent phrase	Write
For the reason that . . . / Due to the fact that	Because
Inasmuch as	Because/since
With regard to	About
Subsequent to	After
In the amount of	For
In the event that	If
For the purpose of	To
At the present time	Now

Keep sentences short—fifteen to twenty words on average—and limit most paragraphs to three or four sentences. A letter more than a page long is less likely to be read. Maintain a friendly, direct, businesslike tone rather than sounding overly chatty. Avoid unnecessary adjectives and adverbs such as *very, really,* and *exceedingly.* Don't use "weasel words" that weaken your message—*probably, try,* and *hopefully.*

Strive to use the active voice, where the subject of the sentence is doing the action rather than being acted upon.

- *Active:* Everyone had a good time. The guests ate cake and played games.
- *Passive:* A good time was had by all. Cake was eaten and games were played by the guests.

Business letters on letterhead should always be typed, and then hand-signed. For a more personal feeling, add a brief handwritten note.

Special correspondence should be handwritten on personalized stationary. Thank-you notes for personal courtesies or gifts and letters of condolence seem warmer and more sincere in your own writing. Don't let your self-consciousness keep you from writing such notes. It's far better to write something less than poetic than to fail to communicate your feelings at all.

Stay in touch with clients and associates easily by clipping and sending articles about their industry, their company, or their personal accomplishments. Add a quick note, and the job is finished.

Speakers' agent Vicki Sullivan uses customized postcards with her company address and logo to reinforce new relationships. On her flight home from an industry conference or trade show, she addresses and stamps the cards to potential customers she met. She adds a brief note saying that she enjoyed meeting the person, appreciated their advice, got some great ideas from their seminar, etc., and drops the cards into a mailbox when she lands.

Publication

Writing for publication is another way to increase your professional visibility. Book publishers and national magazines publish only professional material, but trade magazines, industry journals, and company newsletters welcome amateur submissions. Ask your colleagues or customers what publications they read, and then contact the editors of those you'd like to target. Find out about deadlines, topics of interest, and the preferred format. Some editors want to see a completed piece; others need only an outline to determine their level of interest.

The best articles are those that allow you to display your expertise on a hot industry issue. Avoid the temptation to write a blatant sales pitch for your products or services. An obvious "commercial" actually undermines your professional credibility instead of enhancing it.

If your ideas are worthwhile, but your journalistic skills lacking, enroll in a night school writing course to polish your prose. Consider coauthoring with a colleague or hiring a freelance writer who can turn your insightful ideas into perfect paragraphs. The credibility and "expert" status you gain from being published is worth the time and expense.

Send along a black-and-white photo and a two-sentence description of yourself and your company. Many publications will print both at the end of your article. Some will even include a phone number or e-mail address so interested readers can contact you. Have quality reprints of any published articles to mail to key clients. Include copies with handout materials when you give presentations.

Another option is to write and distribute your own quarterly newsletter. A one-page format with tips and industry or company updates would be interesting to your clients and prospects.

"To publish is to flourish," says Nancy Michaels, author of *How to Be a Big Fish in Any Pond*. Writing for publication boosts your credibility by presenting you as an authority in your field. Writing has the additional benefit of allowing you to reach a lot more people. When your article appears in print, you are essentially speaking directly to thousands of potential customers and clients. If you photocopy your article and distribute it with your marketing materials, your words can last for years.

Speak Up

It's a well-known fact that speaking in public is a legitimate fear for many businesspeople. As so few people like to make presentations, an executive who can deliver a message with impact is seen as a leader in the company and the community. Identify your target audience, and then find opportunities to address them:

- For internal exposure, volunteer to deliver the report on your team project to the board of directors.
- For industry visibility, speak about your company's new product at the national association meeting.
- To reach potential customers, deliver an educational presentation at a professional organization for their industry.

Some companies even host special events to showcase the technical expertise and speaking skills of their personnel. Deloitte sponsors an annual Accounting Update Day for clients and alumni of the firm. Presentations cover the newest rulings and procedures in the field.

"The information is extremely helpful for the audience," explains marketing director Teresa Martin, "and it also spotlights the abilities of our people. When a client hears a workshop on succession planning, for example, he is more likely to implement a program of that sort at his own company. And we're betting he'll come to Deloitte if he needs outside help."

Dress to match the mood you want your presentation to create. To make the most of your professionalism and prestige, select a high-contrast color combination in traditional business or boardroom styles. If you want to create a friendly, relaxed, let's-work-together mood, an ensemble in mainstream casual might work best.

Many business presentations are deadly dull, but the best are a careful blend of information and entertainment. Skip "the one about the traveling salesman," but use topical humor, real-life examples, and lively delivery to gain and hold the audience's attention.

A typical audience takes only sixty seconds to decide whether to listen eagerly to your message, so a strong opening sentence or two is a must. If you start with "I'm so pleased to be here at the Antler Dance Convention," your group may opt to plan their grocery list on the back of your handouts. Instead, choose an opening that is clever, catchy, or even controversial.

Organize the body of your presentation around just two or three key points. Unless your audience is very specialized, use everyday language instead of industry jargon or technical terminology. Use analogies to make sophisticated concepts comfortable for general audiences:

- Chemist Akbar Nayeem compares his company's molecule-matching software to a "crystal ball" for pharmaceutical chemists.
- Computer expert Tom Clark explains that his location management software helps companies "find that needle in the haystack."

Illustrate your main points with visuals. They make complex points easier for your audience to understand, and they can prompt you along the sequence of your presentation as well.

Computer technology makes presentations simple to create and easy to present with software programs like PowerPoint, the most widely used presentation software in business. Observe the "6 × 6 rule"—never more than six lines of copy, six words per line. Photography, large graphs, cartoons, and illustrations are better than words.

The last words of your presentation will have a lasting impact on your audience, so make them count. Whether you choose to summarize, to challenge your listeners to action, or to end with a relevant story or quote, close with energy in your voice and body language.

A polished delivery is an acquired skill. Four key points to develop include:

- *Posture*—Support and balance your weight on both feet. Do not sit on the edge of a table or maintain a death grip on the podium.
- *Eye contact*—A relaxed rapport with your audience is easier when you connect visually with one member of the group, then another.
- *Smile*—and let the smile go all the way to your eyes. Look like a person who is happy to be there, not like a deer caught in the headlights.
- *Talk conversationally*—Don't read or try to memorize your presentation. Have note cards outlining your main points, and then simply talk naturally about each item.

In presentation skills, as in other areas, practice makes perfect. Even highly paid professional speakers acknowledge dropping below peak form if they go more than a few weeks between speeches. Toastmasters International offers an amateur speaker the ongoing opportunity to gain that practice in a supportive environment, with constructive criticism from fellow members.

Organizations

Exposure also can come from participating in professional and civic organizations. Joining up isn't enough, though; you also need to join in. Because time can be a limiting factor, carefully select the best organizations, based on your objective.

- Groups in your industry—Society of Woman Accountants, Council of Realtors—help you develop contacts and visibility within your field. They provide an excellent chance to network with peers and learn about career opportunities, but little opportunity to meet prospective customers.
- Groups in your clients' field(s) let you rub elbows with others who may become customers. The American Society of Training and Development might be a good choice for the owner of a training company to meet corporate training directors.

- Community organizations such as Rotary, Kiwanis, and the local chamber of commerce put you in contact with area movers and shakers from a range of industries. Some may be potential customers or know people who could be. Others might tip you off to job opportunities.

Each organization has its own purpose and its own personality. Choose those that are compatible with your style and your personal priorities. Identify a number of likely groups, and then visit several meetings. Chat with the group's officers, and ask to receive a few issues of the newsletter. Your investigation should pinpoint two or three groups that best fit your needs.

As soon as you join, join in. Every organization seems to have a large roster of members who sit on the sidelines waiting for things to happen. By identifying yourself as a "doer" you can gain almost instant recognition. Take the president or membership chairperson out for coffee and learn about the inner workings of the group. Ask about the committees you might join, and pick one that offers visibility.

- Membership committee or greeting committee responsibilities move you immediately out of the "new member" mentality and into the role of a host—meeting, greeting, and making others feel welcome.
- Members of the newsletter committee are always in the know about group activities and meet both members and outside experts as they gather information for articles.
- As a member of the program committee, you have a unique opportunity to approach the most influential people in your field—or your most coveted prospects—and invite them to address your group. While you coordinate plans for their presentation, you have a chance to become better acquainted and impress them with your social skills and organizational abilities.

Introducing the speaker at each meeting gives you a minute in the spotlight yourself, creating instant name recognition and credibility. Building relationships with other members requires genuine effort on your part. Networking is just that—network.

Media Exposure

Coverage of your company, your product, or yourself by the media is publicity no money could ever buy. Whether you're interviewed by a newspaper or magazine or featured as an expert on radio or television, the impact and promotional potential are unlimited. Media coverage begets more media coverage. When one source finds you interesting, usually others will, too. If your company has a public relations department, it is best to inform them of your intentions. They may be able to help you secure an interview. However, if a public relations professional is not available, you can create opportunities for coverage, first by scrutinizing your local media:

- *Read the newspapers*—the city daily, weekly regional papers, and business journal. Pay close attention to the articles they print about companies or products similar to yours. Notice the reporter who covers those stories and the editor in whose section they run. Also watch for new articles about staff and policy changes at area TV and radio stations.
- *Watch local television programming,* including odd time slots such as Sunday and early-morning news programs. On each station, identify programs with subject matter similar to yours, and then carefully watch the credits for the name of the producer.
- *Listen to talk-radio programs.* Do they conduct interviews or discuss topics for which you could be a logical guest? What topics and approaches do they seem to favor?

When your investigation is complete, generate a group of ideas for possible media features. Call the target publication or station and talk with the program director, section editor, or reporter about your idea. Plan your timing carefully. Don't phone right before or during a local broadcast. Always ask a print journalist if she is on deadline or has time to talk with you briefly. If she expresses interest in your proposal, follow up with written material by mail. Media insiders tell us that proposals mailed without prior phone contact seldom, if ever, generate coverage.

Be scrupulously careful to get exact names, titles, and addresses. Reporters tend to feel that if you don't get those basics correct, they shouldn't trust your accuracy in other areas either. Phyllis Brasch-Librach, a reporter for the *St. Louis Post-Dispatch*, actually keeps a collection of the creative misspellings of her name. "Phillip Brasch-Librach" and "Phyllis Brashley-Brock" generated chuckles in the office, but she acknowledges that she isn't too likely to interview the careless correspondents.

Don't be discouraged when every idea isn't embraced with enthusiasm. Try another medium for that idea, and later approach the original medium with a new angle or related topic. Don't take rejection personally. They may have just covered a similar topic, or it may be a heavy news day in other subject areas. Keep trying.

Look for dozens of smaller ways to get your name into the media, too. Most newspapers have a weekly or daily section to announce promotions, new hires, and the like. Another column lists meetings of professional organizations and their scheduled speakers. A group that invites you to speak may publicize your appearance in their newsletter or industry magazine. One consultant's presentation for the Women's Board of Realtors had an audience of about fifty, but the group's newsletter, featuring her biography and photo, was circulated to more than 7,000 real estate agents.

Once you establish a relationship with a journalist or two, make sure you stay in contact. Drop a note, sharing some of the positive comments you've had about their story. Send a Christmas card. Put them on the mailing list for your newsletter. Invite them to your workshops or seminars. When they need to quote an expert in your field, they will immediately think of you.

Freelance writers are another group worth cultivating. These independent journalists make their living by writing articles, often on topics they suggest, for local and national media. If you can suggest a timely topic—featuring you, of course—they have a vested interest in selling the concept to one of the editors they work with. Locate these writers by watching for their bylines in your local paper.

Interview Tips

There are few more terrifying words than the first time your hear "Three, two, one—camera!" After the hard work of generating a media interview, you are likely to toss and turn the entire night before the big event. Here are some tips to ensure that things go smoothly:

- Narrow the focus of your interview. Decide beforehand what is the most interesting part of your story, and then focus your remarks around that.

- Restate your main points rather than being drawn into less important topics during taped TV interviews.

- Be prepared to supply visuals, especially for television. Bring a CD-ROM with photos or actual demonstration items. Try to provide an action photo for a newspaper reporter. And always have a professional-quality 3" x 5" black-and-white "head shot" of yourself available.

- Plan your clothing well. Blue photographs especially well, whereas red "bleeds" on film. Solids look fine, but small stripes, plaids, or checks can create distracting wavy patterns onscreen. Test your outfit seated in front of a full-length mirror if you are to appear on a live talk show. If the station has no makeup artist, hire one yourself. Even men can benefit from a foundation to even skin tones.

- Clearly ask interviewers not to distort your views. In an edited interview or printed article, you have no control over what will be used and how it will make you sound. If the topic is controversial, make friends with the reporter and express your concerns. But don't expect her to make time to send the article to you for approval before publication.

- Be frank, candid, and interesting, but always remember that nothing you say to a journalist is guaranteed to stay "off the record." Don't say anything that could embarrass you later.

- Keep copies of articles about yourself, and tapes of TV and radio appearances. Add a list of media credits to your biography, and include it with your written proposals for additional media exposure. The fact that you handled one radio or TV interview well helps make you "safe" for the next producer to use.

Savvy self-promotion demands awareness of and attention to opportunity. In his book *The Achievement Factors*, Gene Greissman writes, "High achievers are very aware of their environment and what is more important; they use the environment purposefully. They are able to see what is happening. They process what they see in creative ways and they exploit their environment for their own purposes." How you present yourself, in every facet of your business life—visually, verbally, and nonverbally—directly affects the impact and influence you have over the perceptions of others.

resources to get you there

chapter fifteen

traveling for business

Wrinkle-resistant, bulletproof, versatile, and strikingly good looking . . . this is my meditation when I pack.

Lisa Dugan, corporate image consultant,
The Professional Image, Inc.

many businesspeople find their calendars filled with business travel occasions that create some special wardrobe considerations. No one wants to be burdened with excess luggage, yet the schedule of events and weather is often unpredictable.

The best travel wardrobe is built around a single color scheme, so all outfits work with the same basic accessories. This carefully edited wardrobe should fit into a carryon bag, eliminating the risk of lost or delayed luggage.

For a man, the selection is easy, even for a relatively lengthy trip. You can rotate two suits (or sportcoats) for days if you pack a supply of shirts and ties. But even for a short trip, don't invite disaster by counting on getting your travel suit back from the hotel valet in time for an early-morning meeting.

For a woman, the coordination requires some additional planning. Select one solid-color dark suit—perhaps with matching pants—in a wrinkle-resistant fabric. Microfibers are virtually wrinkle-proof, and firm, fine-gauge knits are a close second. Woven silk suits and wool gabardine wrinkle when packed, but the wrinkles fall out fairly quickly when the garments are hung in your hotel room or steamed in the bathroom. Stay away from linen. After it is packed in a travel bag, you will have a hard time getting rid of wrinkles.

> "If I had to single out the one most outstanding contribution made to the world of fashion by Mesdames Chanel and Schiaparelli, it would certainly be their exceptional services in making knitwear elegant. At the time these two creators launched knitwear as high fashion, it was entirely made by hand and was therefore very expensive. But now machines have acquired the same—or almost the same—skill as the artisans, and this has contributed immensely to the fantastic development of knitted fashions in every price range."
>
> Geneviève Antoine Dariaux, former directrice of
> Nina Ricci in Paris and author of *Elegance*

Add an alternate skirt to wear with the solid jacket and an alternate jacket to wear with the solid bottoms. Several bright blouses (and perhaps scarves) change the basic looks. Include a fine-gauge silk sweater as a blouse alternative.

Be sure one of the looks can be softened for a dressy dinner or for other evening activity:

- Pair the matched suit with a charmeuse camisole and bolder earrings.
- Wear the lightweight dark pants with a dressy blouse or sweater and a distinctive belt.

Accessories can also work day-to-evening:

- Tuck a trim clutch purse into your briefcase during the day. It can stand alone for evening occasions.
- Take a belt with a decorative buckle for dinner.
- Don't risk having fine jewelry pieces lost or stolen. Take only those items you will wear continuously (such as a wedding ring or watch), and substitute quality imitations for the rest.

Sweat pants and a comfortable top can fill a variety of roles in a travel wardrobe:

- Loungewear in your room (substitute terry socks for bedroom slippers)
- Hotel wear—at least for a run to the ice machine
- Exercise gear if the hotel offers such facilities
- Swimsuit cover-up when you head for a relaxing soak in the whirlpool
- Comfortable pajamas

Packing

Whenever possible, travel with only carryon luggage—a size that will fit under your seat or in the overhead compartment and weighs no more than forty pounds. A garment bag will work nicely. Both styles are available with wheels and pull handles.

A fold-over garment bag lets you pack garments on hangers. Save space by hanging a cluster of garments on each hanger:

- Place pants on a flat surface and fold the top leg out of the way.
- Slip the hanger over the flat bottom leg about one-third of the way down. Fold the leg down over the hanger bar.
- Bring the second (top) leg up over the bar, enclosing the previously folded leg.
- The fabric layers will cling, keeping the pants securely on the hanger without pins.
- To pack a slim skirt, simply fold it in half over the bar.
- Button a shirt or blouse in place over the pants or skirt.
- Add a jacket layer, also buttoned.
- Cover the entire bundle with a long dry-cleaning bag.
- Knot the lower end of the bag loosely to retain the cushion of air, minimizing wrinkles.

When all your clothes are hung, place your overcoat (if applicable) around all the clusters, and place the entire bundle in the garment bag.

Fold up any excess garment length, and secure the center of the bundle with the garment strap. If the hangers are not custom-made for your bag, twist-tie the necks together to prevent one from falling during the trip and wrinkling the clothes.

You can fit shoes, hair appliances, and toiletries into the corners around the clothing. These are the areas that will be on the bottom when the bag is closed and folded double.

If you prefer a traditional suitcase, use the layering method to keep wrinkles to a minimum:

- Place the first pants or skirt, folded along its natural creases, in the bag with the waistline at one edge and the excess length hanging over the opposite edge.
- Add the second skirt or pants in the opposite direction, and continue for each additional bottom piece.
- Place the first blouse or shirt (buttoned) face-down on top of the pants and skirts, with its neckline at the suitcase edge and the extra length hanging over the opposite side. Fold the sleeves to the back of the shirt.
- Draping each garment with a plastic dry-cleaning bag also helps prevent wrinkles.
- Add the remaining shirts and jackets in the same position.
- Fill the center space with soft articles such as sweaters, pajamas, and underwear.
- Fold in the overhanging length of the bottoms and tops from alternating sides. Each garment is packed in a rounded shape, without unwanted creases.
- Add heavy shoes, toiletries, and the like along the bottom edge of the bag (nearest the wheels), or pack them is a separate zipper compartment of the bag.

Whatever type of bag you choose:

- Speed up packing chores by keeping a duplicate set of makeup and sample-size toiletries ready to go. Pack both in high-quality, secure, clear-plastic zippered bags for visibility and to ensure no leakage will occur.

- Slip each shoe into an old sock to prevent scratching or soiling other items.
- Neckties travel wrinkle-free if you roll them in a strip of tissue paper and tuck the roll into a sandwich bag.
- Bring disposable plastic bags for repacking a damp swimsuit or worn hosiery and underwear.
- Slip your curling iron barrel into a toilet paper tube in case you have to repack it while it is still hot.
- Leave your travel iron and hair dryer home—most hotels have them available for guests. Call ahead if you are uncertain about availability.

Don't leave home without your personalized version of the "top ten take-along" list. Here's ours:

1. Earplugs prevent lost sleep due to hotel noise. They also help you nap on a lengthy flight.
2. A CD or MP3 player lets you have your favorite music, fitness routine, or personal development program right in the room.
3. Letterhead, stamps, and fax cover sheets keep emergency correspondence looking professional.
4. A travel alarm avoids hotel wake-up call disasters.
5. A small foldaway umbrella, for the obvious reason.
6. A heating pad or hot-water bottle can be a lifesaver after a stressful day or a packed flight in coach section.
7. A customized first-aid kit—a metal bandage box filled with the remedies you use at home, such as pain relievers, cough drops, cold medicine, or sleeping pills.
8. A prescription bottle can hold needles, thread, safety pins, spot remover, and the like.
9. Manicure essentials travel in a zippered plastic bag to prevent spills.
10. An energy bar, granola bar, or candy helps on those late nights in hotel rooms.

Depending on your preferences and your destination, you might also include adapters and converters, a swimsuit (for the beach or the hotel spa), and an extra pair of glasses or contacts.

Travel in Style

Don't take chances when you take your business persona on the road. Wear a suit or executive casual coordinates on the plane. You'll receive finer service from airline personnel when you're well dressed and your seating companion may turn out to be a valuable new connection—someone to whom you'd rather not explain why you're wearing jeans or a jogging suit.

You also might share the experience of one client who booked a late-Sunday flight for an early-Monday presentation. Tired from a busy weekend, she chose to travel in jeans and sneakers. As luck would have it, she arrived in Minneapolis while her luggage went somewhere else. Since there are no twenty-four-hour clothing stores, her only option was to deliver the presentation in her travel clothes. The audience was outwardly sympathetic, but who knows how much credibility was lost. Certainly her confidence level was shaken.

Of course, sit-down wrinkles are a concern when you travel in business clothes. Here are two strategies for women to try:

- Wear your business blouse and jacket over coordinating soft trousers or quality knit pants. This gives you what TV anchors call "half an image." You look great from the waist up—fine while seated. Carry a slim skirt, neatly folded in a plastic bag, in your briefcase, and change in the airplane lavatory just before landing.
- Wear your entire business suit, but turn the skirt backward. Yes, backward! Just before landing, reverse the skirt. The real front will be flat and smooth from sitting, and the inevitable wrinkles will be in back, covered by your jacket.

Long airline flights can get you to your destination exhausted and uncomfortable. Reduce the discomfort with these tips:

- Restrict your intake of salt, caffeine, and alcohol, all of which can cause water retention and swelling.
- If you remove your shoes, put on a pair of short, warm socks to avoid both swelling and cold feet.
- Propping your feet up on your carryon bag helps maintain your blood circulation.

- Carry contact eye drops or cleaning solution, and bring your glasses just in case the dry air makes your eyes too uncomfortable.
- An airline pillow placed at the small of your back maintains a more comfortable posture and reduces neck and shoulder pain.
- If you want a pillow or blanket, request them as soon as you board the plane. The supply runs out fast on full flights.
- Drink lots of water.

Travel Safety

Make these simple plans part of your travel routine.

- Never put your home address on your luggage to announce to would-be thieves that you're not home.
- Be sure to arrive at the airport several hours early to accommodate the lengthy screening process.
- When going through metal detectors, put all your belongings together in the plastic containers that are provided by the airport. This will lessen the chance of theft as well as protect your personal property from the airport conveyer equipment that has damaged numerous purse and briefcase straps.
- A business card with a prestigious title is a tip-off that your luggage may contain valuables. List only your surname and business address or the address of your travel agent.
- Secure the strap of your carryon bag around the chair leg when seated at the airport. It will keep your bag from being spirited away while your attention is focused elsewhere.
- If the hotel clerk announces your room number aloud with others waiting in line, ask for a different one.
- Request a room near the elevator to avoid the necessity of walking through long, empty hallways or the chance of being followed.
- Ask ahead of time if the hotel has a safe for valuables. Be sure to lock your room whenever you leave, and try not to leave your laptop in your room if you go out.
- Keep the door double-locked when you are in your hotel room.

shopping and caring for a business wardrobe

Good taste shouldn't have to cost anything extra.

Mickey Drexler, former CEO, Gap

many of our clients acknowledge that, although they enjoy more opportunities to dress more casually, they always keep a power suit or jacket hanging on the back of the office door or in a garment bag in the back seat of their car, "just in case." When the day's schedule calls for presenting an important proposal, meeting with a client or prospect, or some other highly visible activity, only the most professional look will do.

For countless businesspeople, those important activities are the daily routine. Others, following time-honored advice, choose to dress for the position they aspire to rather than the one they already hold. In either case, a thorough understanding of the components of traditional business dressing is essential for any professional. Although the specific garment choices obviously differ by gender, the concepts of developing and maintaining a business wardrobe apply to everyone.

Shopping Ideas for Men and Women

Think of shopping for your business wardrobe as an investment in your professional future, not just a frivolous day at the mall. Keep a tracking system of your wardrobe, with a quick description of each garment and a snip of the fabric if possible (ask for the leftovers from your alterations).

Note the date purchased and price paid, so over the seasons you can track which items yield the best value. Your tracking system becomes a portable closet to help you match prospective new purchases to your current wardrobe.

Based on the items you already own, develop a "List of Five"—the five most important pieces you need to add. Each time you purchase an item from the list, add a new one in its place. Working from a list provides the discipline to resist "sale-o-mania," a high-pressure salesperson, or just impulse buying. A planned purchase at a sale price is a true bargain, but the biggest markdown on the rack is no value if you don't need it.

Shopping for business clothing should be a pleasurable experience. Upscale specialty stores and the better areas of department stores have sales consultants trained to help you find the items you need. Here are some tips to make your shopping trip hassle-free:

- Shop early in the season, when selection and size ranges are the most extensive.
- Shop when the stores are less crowded. Most other shoppers stay home weekday mornings and at dinnertime.
- Wear good undergarments, and bring shoes appropriate to the clothes you'll be trying on.
- Wear comfortable shoes and easy-off clothing, but don't dress sloppily. Style your hair and apply makeup. Salespeople—like everyone else—tend to judge people by their appearance.
- Bring along any current garments you would like to coordinate with new purchases.
- When you find an especially helpful salesperson, cultivate the relationship. Know his or her name, and make appointments to shop when he or she is working. Over time, that salesperson will learn your taste and can call you about new arrivals and impending sales.

Many businesspeople are so busy with career responsibilities that issues of shopping and wardrobe development never make it to the top of their to-do lists. For such men and women, professional wardrobe services are a lifesaver.

Wardrobe Consultants

An independent wardrobe consultant provides in-home service, evaluating current wardrobe pieces, recommending items to discard and to add, and suggesting updates for marginal pieces. The ideal consultant is honest and encouraging and has a strong list of referrals. This consultant should have a thorough knowledge of fabric quality, garment construction, and fit.

He or she usually begins the consultation by developing an understanding of the client's job responsibilities and position, as well as personal issues, such as coloring and body type. Independent consultants charge an hourly fee for services and typically offer personal shopping as well. Because he or she is not affiliated with any retail outlet, selection will be from a wider range of merchandise with an eye to the best pricing. Items are often brought to the client's home or held at the store until both the client and the consultant can return together.

In-Store Personal Shoppers

In-store personal shoppers are employees of the retail store and specialize in helping customers with wardrobe planning. Knowing your size, style, and budget, he or she assembles coordinated merchandise from various departments before you visit the store. In as little as an hour, you can try on the consultant's recommendations and make final selections. The service is usually complimentary, and, because the store wants your long-term business, you won't be pressured into questionable purchases. The consultant maintains a season-to-season record of your purchases, which helps with continued wardrobe development and makes reordering basics just as simple as a phone call. The best-known store offering this service is Nordstrom, although many Saks, Federated, and Allied stores also offer quality in-store consulting.

Custom Clothing

National custom or made-to-measure clothing companies carry this service a step further—actually bringing the "store" right to the client's office. A trained wardrobe consultant visits the customer's workplace with sketches and swatches representing a vast assortment of suits, jackets, skirts, trousers, shirts, blouses, ties, accessories, and sportswear. He or she helps with selections, coordination, and sizing. The clothing is ordered, fitted, altered, and delivered, usually requiring only an hour of the client's time each season. The best known is Tom James, although there are other companies with solid reputations and excellent quality.

Trunk Shows

Trunk showings generally target women. Several fine companies make upscale women's apparel that is not sold through retail channels. Instead, these companies market exclusively through trained wardrobe consultants, who work with sample lines at trunk shows or company-owned studios. The lines feature classic styling, often exquisite fabrics, and extensive color coordination. The consultant evaluates a new client's wardrobe, figure, and coloring, then recommends the most flattering and versatile additions. The client tries on garments from the sample collection, and then orders the item in her choice of style, color, and size. The consultant maintains a file with sketches and swatches of the client's purchases, spotting new items each season to fully coordinate an ongoing wardrobe. Such companies include Carlisle and Doncaster.

Custom Sewing

Custom sewing provides additional options. A skilled dressmaker or tailor can customize the fit of a ready-made garment or update the styling of an older item by shortening hems or sleeves, replacing buttons, or other small adjustments. He or she can even make a garment in a style, color, or size that isn't available in the stores. The best sewing professionals can offer style advice and help with fabric selection as well as quality construction. The Professional Association of Custom Clothiers (PACC) is a national dressmakers' organization with demanding membership requirements.

"One of the many advantages of having made-to-order clothing is that through the selection of proper styles, fabrics, and colors, many figure flaws and imperfections can be cleverly camouflaged."

Joseph Plata, Joseph Plata Designs

Here are some tips for locating and cultivating a real sewing pro:

- Ask to see samples of the individual's work. A good dressmaker, designer, or tailor won't be offended. Generally, he or she will have samples of work available.
- Ask if fees are hourly or per project. Per-project pricing lets you know exactly what you'll spend.
- Request rush service only in a genuine emergency. Generally expect to wait several weeks and sometimes up to a month. If a garment is being constructed, anticipate at least two fittings.
- Tipping isn't expected, but remember to compliment a job well done.

Clothing Care

A professional wardrobe for either gender represents a considerable investment and deserves the appropriate care. Minimize wear and tear by dry-cleaning suits infrequently and providing interim care yourself:

- Brush a garment lightly with a special clothing brush after each wearing to remove fiber-damaging dust particles.
- Hang skirts and trousers from clip-style hangers. Protect delicate fabrics by placing a scrap of fabric between the garment and the clip.
- Hang jackets from contoured, wooden, or padded hangers to prevent shoulder creases.
- Allow enough closet space to avoid crowding garments.
- After wearing, hang a garment outside the closet overnight to allow for the item to recover its shape and release odors and perspiration.
- Remove any stubborn wrinkles with a hand-held steamer.
- Avoid putting a hot iron directly on fine fabric. A pressing cloth will prevent the fabric from scorching.
- Have any small damage to a garment repaired before the next wearing. Many dry cleaners offer minor repair services.
- If a garment is stained, have it cleaned immediately; the longer it sits, the harder it will be to remove. And never press over a stain. The heat can set it permanently.

Dry-clean your suits only when absolutely necessary, because dry-cleaning solutions sap the life out of fine fabrics. When dry-cleaning is required, keep in mind these tips:

- Clean all matching pieces (jacket, skirt, pants) together to avoid showing uneven wear.
- Point out any stains, and let the cleaner know the cause.
- Cover delicate buttons with aluminum foil, or ask the cleaner to remove and replace them.
- Request light pressing. Excessive steam, pressure, and heat can make a garment look old and tired before its time.
- If the suit needs to be freshened, but isn't actually soiled, request a pressing only.

Do whatever research is necessary to identify a top-quality dry cleaner. Solicit recommendations from colleagues, clothing retailers, or dress-makers/tailors. If possible, use a cleaner that hand-cleans. This process will take longer and be a little more expensive, but the benefit is the prolonged life of your fine clothing. Some cleaning establishments will pick up and deliver to your home or office.

Few clothing woes are more frustrating than a food spot on an expensive silk necktie. Because of the silk fiber's affinity for soil, the bias grainline of the tie, and the multiple layers of interfacing, cleaning a tie is a very tricky undertaking. As the sports car commercials often say, "Don't try this at home." Rely on an experienced "spotter" at your dry cleaner's, improve your odds by explaining exactly what food caused the stain, and accept that the chances of success are fifty-fifty at best.

Store out-of-season garments in a cool, dry place away from direct sunlight. Plastic dry-cleaning bags hold heat and attract moisture. Exchange them for cloth covers before putting garments in the closet. Add cedar blocks or moth repellent for added protection.

Consider donating your business clothes and accessories to *www.Dress forSuccess.org* or other charitable organizations that help lower-income women transition into the work force. By recycling your slightly dated or gently worn items, you are contributing to the career development and future success of other businesspeople.

resource guide

Most of these companies offer catalogs and often telephone consultation. They can be a great timesaver for busy businesspeople.

Clothing Resources for Women:
Traditional Business and Business Casual

Bloomingdale's by Mail—Moderately priced suits and coordinates ranging from casual wear to business styles. (866) 593-2540. *www.bloomingdales.com*

Carlisle—Higher-priced, coordinated wardrobe groupings, in fine fabrics and exceptional styling. Sold by independent consultants. (212) 246-4275. *www.carlislecollection.com*

Doncaster—Higher-priced, coordinated wardrobe groupings of classic styles in especially fine fabrics. Sold by independent consultants. Sizes 2 to 18 and petites. (800) 669-3662. *www.doncaster.com*

French Rags—Business suits and casual wear. (800) 347-5270. *www.frenchrags.com*

JC Penney—Affordable business attire. (800) 222-6161. *www4.jcpenney.com*

J.Crew—Comfortable weekend wear. (800) 562-0258. *www.jcrew.com*

Jospeh Plata Collection—Custom executive wear and evening attire. (404) 351-4004. *www.josephplata.com*

Lands' End—Preppy styles of skirts, button-downs, and sweaters. (800) 963-4816. *www.landsend.com*

Lane Bryant—Affordable business suits and coordinates. *www.lanebryant.com*

L.L.Bean—A good source for rustic, outdoor wear. (800) 441-5713. *www.llbean.com*

Long Elegant Legs—Coordinates for the taller woman. (800) 344-2225. *www.longelegantlegs.com*

Mark Shale—Upscale, updated traditional attire. (888) 333-6964. *www.markshale.com*

Nordstrom—Spans from business casual to elegant. Prices range from moderate to expensive. (800) 282-6060. *www.nordstrom.com*

Petite Sophisticate—Casual wear and business attire with sophisticated styling. (800) 662-8042. *www.petitesophisticate.com*

Saks Fifth Avenue—These clothes range from resort wear to formal wear. (877) 551-7257. *www.saksfifthavenue.com*

Silhouettes—Plus-size clothing ranging from 14 to 38. They offer business attire, active and casual wear, and shoes. (888) 651-8337. *www.silhouettes.com*

Spiegel—A wide range of reasonably priced items for business or casual. Some famous brand items available. (800) 345-4500. *www.spiegel.com*

Talbots—Classical, tailored fashion for business and every day. (800) 992-9010. *www.talbots.com*

Tall Classics—For women with long arms and legs. Most styles add 2" to 4". (866) 825-5382. *www.tallclassics.com*

Tom James—Complete line of custom and ready-made executive attire, in home or office. (800) 625-2228, ext. 2407. *www.tomjames.com*

Weekenders—Versatile, comfortable, mix-and-match cotton-knit separates sold through in-home presentations. *www.weekenders.com*

Mail-Order Hosiery

One Hanes Place—Discount, mail-order hosiery, undergarments, and active wear. Brands include Wonderbra, Bali, Hanes, L'eggs, and Champion. (800) 671-1674. *www.onehanesplace.com*

No Nonsense—Sheer hosiery and support pantyhose, socks and trouser socks. Petite and plus-sizes available. Free shipping. (800) 575-3497. *www.nononsense.com*

Clothing Resources for Men: Traditional Business and Business Casual

Custom Shop Clothiers—Elegant, top-quality custom-made shirts and accessories. (888) 744-7897. *www.myshirtmaker.com*

Eddie Bauer—Good business casual options, plus a great selection of dress shirts in hard-to-find sizes. (800) 625-7935. *www.eddiebauer.com*

Edward Baumann Clothiers—Full line of men's clothing, will come to home or office. (972) 490-9797. *www.Edwardbaumann.com*

JC Penney—Affordable suits and casual wear. (800) 222-6161. *www.jcpenney.com*

J.Crew—A good resource for casual, everyday clothing. (800) 562-0258. *www.jcrew.com*

KingSize—Both business and casual attire for the larger-size man. (800) 806-4152. *www.kingsizedirect.com*

Lands' End—A good choice for business casual and outdoor wear. (800) 963-4816. *www.landsend.com*

L.L.Bean—Great business casual and outdoor wear. (800) 441-5713. *www.llbean.com*

Mark Shale—Upscale, updated traditional attire. (888) 333-6964. *www.markshale.com*

Men's Wearhouse—Affordable suits in a wide range of colors, fabrics, and sizes. (877) 986-9669. *www.menswearhouse.com*

Spiegel—There are some suits, but they offer more casual, everyday wear. Blazers, jeans, and denim shirts. (800) 345-4500. *www.spiegel.com*

Talbots—Classical, preppy-style clothes. (800) 992-9010. *www.talbots.com*

Tom James—Higher-end, custom-made business attire in quality fabrics, in home or office. (800) 625-2228, ext. 2407. *www.tomjames.com*

Color Analysis

Beauty for All Seasons—Color, makeup, and wardrobe consultants in most U.S. cities and many other countries. (800) 942-4336. *www.bfas.com*

Color Me Beautiful—Individual color analysis. (800) 265-6763. *www.colormebeautiful.com*

Associations

AICI—A worldwide nonprofit association of image consultants who teach appearance, and verbal and nonverbal communication to individuals as well as corporations. 972-755-1503 *www.aici.org*

Professional Association of Custom Clothiers—6491 Summer Cloud Way, Columbia, MD 21045. (877) 755-0303. *www.paccprofessionals.org*

index

about the authors

susan bixler is a widely recognized author, speaker, executive coach, and frequently quoted expert in the area of corporate and leadership image development. As president and CEO of The Professional Image, Inc., she and her company were the first to focus on the image and communication needs of corporations and businesses. Established in 1980, her company is one of the best-known communication and leadership consulting firms in the country.

Her client list of 1,500 includes many of the *Fortune* 500 companies: The Ritz-Carlton Hotel Company, American Express, Turner Entertainment, Deloitte, Avon, Hilton Hotels, Merck & Co. Inc., General Motors, General Electric, IBM, The Coca-Cola Company, AT&T, Bristol Myers, UPS, Walt Disney World, the Marriott Hotels, and Estée Lauder. She is a member of TEC international, a worldwide organization of CEOs.

Ms. Bixler has been referenced by the national media as the leading expert in her area. Her advice has been quoted in *Time, Newsweek, USA Today, People Magazine, The Wall Street Journal, The New York Times, Glamour Magazine, Vogue, Mademoiselle,* and more than seventy other national publications.

Ms. Bixler has been interviewed by Diane Sawyer, Oprah Winfrey, Maria Shriver, *Good Morning America, PM Magazine,* and *The Wall Street Journal Report.*

She won the distinguished 1992 IMMIE Award presented by the Image Industry Council for her contributions to the image industry. She was honored in 1996 as the first woman inducted into the Louisville Hall of Fame for her professional achievements.

Ms. Bixler has written and appeared in two of the bestselling corporate videotapes from American/Provant, Inc., *The Professional Image* and *Professional Presence.* Both videos won numerous awards including the prestigious Telly Award.

As an author, Ms. Bixler has sold over 300,000 copies of her bestselling books, *The Professional Image* and *Professional Presence,* published by G. P. Putnam and Berkeley. *Professional Presence* has been translated into eight languages. Other books published include *Take Action: 18 Proven Strategies for Advancing in Today's Changing Business World, The New Professional Image: From Business Casual to the Ultimate Power Look,* and *5 Steps to Professional Presence: How to Project Confidence, Competence, and Credibility.*

A graduate of Baldwin-Wallace College in Cleveland, Ohio, Ms. Bixler has a B.A. in English and education.

nancy nix-rice is an internationally known image consultant, speaker, and trainer with extensive background in fashion retail and corporate and personal development training. As a retailer, she has earned awards for improving store performance and has been a member of the advisory councils for both industry-buying services. As an instructor for the prestigious Dale Carnegie Institute, she has repeatedly been honored for outstanding classroom results.

In 1988 she founded her own company, First Impressions, to provide image development services to individuals, associations, and corporations. Ms. Nix-Rice has held training sessions in forty-eight of the fifty states. Her clients include Southwestern Bell, Ralston Purina, Monsanto, Deloitte & Touche, Malinckrodt Medical, Hyatt and Marriott Hotels, Jenny Craig Weight Loss Centers, Professional Secretaries International, the Association for Family and Consumer Sciences, and the U.S. Postal Service.

Ms. Nix-Rice's first book, *Looking Good*, is a comprehensive guide to wardrobe planning for women. The book is winning praise from both consumers and industry peers. Other image consultants have called it "the best available on how to dress with total confidence" and "a comprehensive resource for getting maximum value from each clothing dollar."

She has consistently earned accolades as a top consultant with Beauty For All Seasons, an international image firm. She has produced nine training videos in the fashion home-sewing field.

Her business has been featured on the cover of the *St. Louis Business Plus* and in *Income Opportunities* magazine. Ms. Nix-Rice has been quoted in numerous print articles and television features about business casual dressing.

Ms. Nix-Rice holds an undergraduate degree in accounting with a minor in fashion merchandising and a master's degree in corporate communications.

Also by Susan Bixler

5 Steps to Professional Presence
How to Project Confidence, Competence, and Credibility at Work
Adams Media, 2001

TAKE ACTION!
18 Proven Strategies for Advancing in Today's Changing Business World
Ballantine Books, 1997

Professional Presence
The Total Program from Gaining That Extra Edge in Business
Putnam Publishing, 1991

The Professional Image
The Total Program for Marketing Yourself Visually
Putnam Publishing, 1984